UNFINISHED BUSINESS

The true story of a career with the Russians

Published in the UK in 2024 by Albion Press

Copyright © David Cant 2024

David Cant has asserted their right under
the Copyright, Designs and Patents Act, 1988,
to be identified as the author of this work.

All rights reserved. No part of this book may be reproduced, stored in a retrieved system or transmitted, in any form or by any means, electronic, mechanical, scanning, photocopying, recording or otherwise, without the prior permission of the author and publisher.

Paperback ISBN: 978-1-0687750-0-0
eBook ISBN: 978-1-0687750-1-7

Cover design and typeset by Spiffing Publishing

UNFINISHED BUSINESS

The true story of a career with the Russians

David Cant

CONTENTS

7.	Prologue
8.	1984: Beware, the student canteen...
11.	1985: Interrogation and the first trip to Moscow
14.	1986
24.	My career with UB40
29.	1990: The day I died
33.	1987: Back to student days
38.	Soviet public transport
41.	International Post Office
45.	1988/1989: Time to join the real world
51.	Relocation to Russia
55.	1990
65.	Soviet phone calls
67.	Life's a bitch with puppies
71.	1991: Russian traffic police
77.	High-pressure environment
89.	The coup
93.	New Russia life
100.	1992
101.	Travel
110.	Time to leave Russia
111.	1993
114.	The man from the ministry
116.	A nod to MI6
118.	1994
120.	1995
122.	1996: Time to meet the Windsors
125.	1997
128.	1998-2002
139.	A brief chat
173.	2002-2004: Albion
183.	2005-2006
185.	2007-2012

195.	2013-2014
200.	2014
210.	2015-2018
233.	2019
239.	2020: Covid thunderclouds
243.	The phone calls that changed my life
245.	Lockdown Scotland
250.	The loss of the family standard
252.	Circling over Europe
253.	My personal Russian lockdown
256.	2021
260.	Luke's departure
262.	Digging out the cancer
264.	October 2021. The Marriott Grand, central Moscow.
267.	2022
268.	Invasion
271.	Resurgence
273.	25-year company anniversary
279.	A conversation with the Atlantic
285.	Interrogation and the last trip to Moscow
288.	Epiphany
290.	Epilogue
295.	Acknowledgements

PROLOGUE

This is a story of a career with Russia, a love story in a way, perhaps unwise, but genuine. Not everybody is going to like it. Ironically, they probably helped to create it.

Politicians, ambassadors, royalty, Westminster and Holyrood, millionaires, MI6 and the Kremlin do not escape scrutiny on these pages, all based on direct experience.

There is laughter and tears, along with death, fraud and divorce, theft, murder, beatings, bankruptcy and betrayal. Love, hypocrisy, joy, agony, deceit and bravery are part of it too.

Behind the "Russian story" is another, in some ways darker, more threatening.

The career taught me so much. I probably would not change it, but I would change, in a heartbeat, what came next. If only I could.

Conflict creates energy, and true light can only be found in the darkness.

Some names have been changed to protect people. But this story is true.

1984: BEWARE, THE STUDENT CANTEEN…

What a year. I am doing a three-point turn in a Volvo after a three-minute drive. Seated beside me is my mother. We have 350 miles to go, and I have already gone the wrong way.

What a start to a journey! And I'm not talking about the Volvo.

Some hours later, not enough hours according to my mother, we arrive in Bristol.

My sister had gone to St Andrews and Manchester universities, in fact on a special medical enrolment, which led to her commencing her medical degree when she was, I think, just sixteen years of age! My brother had gone to university in London and had a great time. Why I chose Bristol, I am not sure, but it was definitely something to do with being far enough away from home that I would be totally independent. Like my siblings, I think I wanted to experience life outside my home town or comfort zone.

Here, my journey starts. This is real life. I can go to the pub without being expelled. I can meet girls. I can even smoke…

And so, starts my single honours degree in German at Bristol University.

But no, that would have been too straightforward.

Day one, I meet Nicky. That meeting over a sandwich changed my life. She has just started learning Russian as a complete novice. I think about it, for a second. How much more interesting would learning Russian be than German! A lifetime of driving up an autobahn selling vacuum cleaners? In short, vacuum cleaners suck. (Thank you!)

I am captivated by the idea of doing something unusual and nobody else seems to be learning Russian. The truth is if Nicky had said she was studying Swahili or Cantonese, I'd have probably gone to that department instead, but Russian it was. So off I go to see Professor Peace (no kidding) of the Russian department.

He asks me why I want to learn Russian, for which I have no ready answer. I am not confident that I can even point to Russia on a map. It's big, that's all I know. I can't say that I just met Nicky in the canteen and she's doing Russian. So, I lie:

"I just always found Russia to be fascinating. The history, the culture, the music and the literature," I blag.

Had I been questioned on Russia's history, culture, music or literature, I would have been marched off the premises forthwith.

Professor Peace offers me a place on the course. My tutor is Dorinda; weirdly, she will also be my daughter's tutor some 34 years later. Dorinda had such enthusiasm for her subject and knew how to communicate to her students; without her, I'm not sure I would have stayed the course.

Lesson one, Dorinda tells us beginners, about half a dozen of us, that the Russian alphabet can be learnt in an hour. That's my kind of language learning. However, it turned out, that's not enough to say you can speak Russian. Many years later, we would have a client who was lost on the Moscow metro. He had learnt the alphabet but had not understood that it is a language, not a code, and had no idea how to get out and back to his hotel.

I was to discover the joys of vocabulary, verbs, tenses, declensions, conjugations and, worst of all, numbers. Here's an example. Take the number 365. So far so good. Now add a word in front of it. Let's say, "with". The three changes its ending. And the six, and yes, you've got it, so does the five. Now put "under" in front of it. Same thing happens, but this time, different endings.

"Through."

"After."

"Out of."

Then do that for every number you can think of. Dorinda does not mention this in the early lessons.

I am now doing German and Russian, two languages; Lord knows how many declensions or what have you. Two sets of literature.

Russian literature has Tolstoy, Dostoevsky, Pushkin and many more. Soviet literature has *Cement* and *How the Steel was Tempered*. How Ivan met Natasha in a factory, stirred up the work force, produced the tractors needed, and, then, (no actually that's it, nothing else happened).

But I learned that university is not only about study. I got stuck into the social life, joining societies, going to pubs, learning how girls think, joining a band and doing lots of acting. All of which were great, with the possible exception of learning how girls think, which remains a mystery.

1985: INTERROGATION AND THE FIRST TRIP TO MOSCOW

Dorinda is keen to show us the Soviet Union by experiencing it at first hand, so a trip to Moscow and Saint Petersburg is duly organised for us "ab initio" students. The advice for the forthcoming trip is to take something that represents our national dress. Pam takes her sari. I pack my kilt.

In 1980s' Russia, every item of luggage for arriving and departing passengers is searched. This system has its flaws of course. Upon departure, a lot of caviar will make its way back home after customs check the bags, but before the passenger checks in. In the "no man's land" between bag search and bag drop, you suddenly feel hot, pop your coat with bulging pockets into the case before you check it in. Obviously, I never did this.

I reach the head of the queue. My first ever visit to Moscow, so I know nothing and have more or less no language apart from "hello". Even that is questionable. My suitcase is opened and the immigration officer finds and considers my black kilt jacket with silver buttons. His face darkens at the leather brogues, the wool socks, the sporran, the grouse claw, and finally, the kilt. I am relieved I have not packed the sgian-dubh. He looks me up and down:

"Scotch?"

I could do with one; I am now terrified. I have seen the movie *Midnight Express*. Is that a crime, being Scottish? Should I have said something different? To my surprise, instead of escorting me to an interrogation room on account of my ethnicity, he starts flapping his arms, like a chicken unable to take off, repeating the word "volynka"!

It's all highly amusing to the lengthening queue behind me, but I am confused until Dorinda appears and explains that "volynka" is Russian for bagpipes. He just wants to know what that is in English.

Built for the 1980 Olympics, the Hotel Cosmos is big. That's it. Not luxurious, big – but not the biggest. That's the Rossiya, which was at one time the biggest hotel in Europe, and now has gone. But big is not the same as good. Once we are all checked in, Dorinda arranges for us to visit a restaurant on the top floor of a tall building in central Moscow, the "Lights of Moscow" on account of the view of the night-time city. In hindsight, I cannot imagine the lights would have been that impressive a sight. One of the whole points of Soviet Russia was the lack of bright lights. Anyway, I wouldn't know because I don't get to the top floor of the building. None of us do.

We make it to the building. We make it to the lift.

The Soviet Union ensured that there was zero unemployment under communism by creating all manner of unnecessary jobs, including having an attendant in a glass box at the bottom of every escalator on the metro, and an attendant inside every lift. What did these people do? They maintained the Soviet employment record of 100%. That's it.

We wait for the lift up to the restaurant and, after a while, the doors open and we are subjected to the attendant's beady eye. Dorinda explains in Russian who we are and what we want to do. The attendant appears sceptical; being unaccustomed to seeing foreigners, in her view, Dorinda, speaking fluent Russian, is an impostor. A very polite argument takes place, and being so convinced that Dorinda is a local, the lift attendant invites Dorinda to continue the conversation in English, to prove we are really from the UK. Now, this is odd, because if she had not focussed upon Dorinda and had stopped for a moment to look at the ragtag mob of students behind her, she would have had no doubt that we were not locals. For a start, we are talking to each other in English. Anyway, Dorinda and the lift attendant carry on chatting in English (I wonder how many British lift operators, if such a thing still exists, are multilingual), but it is not to be. The lift attendant concludes that if we are British, she is "a cosmonaut", and with those words, so angry is she that she has met an actual English person, and been proven wrong, that the lift doors close, and she shoots upwards alone, to the restaurant that I will never see.

Overall, this first trip was really good, a real privilege. I recall buying souvenirs to take back to family, because going to the Soviet Union in the 1980s was not common. I bought horrible cigarettes called "Golden Fleece", though I did not know that at the time. I bought sickly, yellow lemon vodka, which I gave to my brother-in-law and found some ten years later still unopened, and I can't blame him. And I met my first prostitute on the Nevsky Prospekt in Leningrad. Well, I say prostitute. I don't think they really had them, and those that claimed to be were all of a certain age, and bigger than me, and of course, working for the KGB. She sidles up to me, and asks me where I am from, as I walk along the street, admiring the beauty that is the city. I was so pleased to understand what she was saying that, when she asked if I would like to go to the cinema, I actually asked what they were showing. I quickly realised that was an error. It was not the time to practise language and vocabulary.

So much for early experiences, the trip was fine, and I knew a little more about the country and the language. I returned to Bristol for my second year, where I had a wonderful time; too good, by all accounts. I mentioned that I was doing a lot of social stuff and student drama. At one point, I was lead singer in a band, directing a play, acting in a stage production of *Cabaret*, involved in various societies and making the most of being a student. My tutor and my German professor wrote to me, reminding me that I was there to study, and not to just have fun. The fun is what formed my student memories, not so much the seminars about Brecht and Dostoevsky. I was lucky in that I seemed to be ok with exams, despite leaving the study to the bitter end.

1986

I passed my second-year exams, and everybody was happy. Then along came third year. The year that we actually live in the countries whose language we are studying.

Theoretically, it would be six months in Germany, six in Russia, but there was an opportunity to do things differently. I opt for two stints of one month each in Germany, to "bookend" a ten-month stay in Russia. Between these three trips, I go home to see family and get my washing done!

At this point, I genuinely do not know much about Russia, have no interest in politics and no real belief that I will ever be back in Russia. I want an experience, and I do not regret that one bit. I did my month in Germany, and met some great people, in the lovely town of Regensburg.

As always with travel, getting to Regensburg turned out to be quite eventful in itself. It starts off well enough. I sleep on my brother's sofa in New Cross, wake up to my alarm, but I am dismayed to find the station closed because it is Sunday. I take a bus back to Lewisham and await my train to London. It comes in. Unfortunately, not to the platform I am on.

Finally, I get to Charing Cross and descend into the Underground. This is in the days before any express train to the airport. I am now late. An American gentleman asks me how long to the airport.

"About an hour," I respond.

"Oh, I'm sure it's less than that! I think it's about 15 minutes!"

"I hope you're right."

Sadly, he is not right, but this train wheezes and chugs its way towards Heathrow, and does not make it beyond Osterley. No sooner has it broken down, than I am running up the stairs, with my massive Delsey suitcase, to find that every phone box on the wall has been vandalised, every single one, and this is long before mobiles. Delsey and I clatter down the stairs as another train pulls in, I dive on and head straight into the wrong terminal. I am already almost certain I will not make my flight; it leaves in 20 minutes. I run up to the desk, which is where I learn I am in the wrong terminal, and the lady asks if I have luggage.

"Yes," I pant.

"Then forget it," she smiles.

However, I could not help giving it one final attempt. I run at breakneck speed to the correct terminal, Delsey swinging precariously behind me on its little wheels. I get to the right terminal and the right gate, and to my immense relief, I see that the aircraft is still there and, in fact, there are even passengers still not boarded.

I hand my passport to the lady at check-in and she glances up at me.

"Sir, you look terrible. Do you want to go and get some water?"

It is true, I do look terrible, though perhaps I could have done without her telling me. I have blood in my mouth, I am perspiring and I am the colour of a beetroot.

"I won't have time! The flight's leaving any minute now!" She seems unperturbed.

"Oh, don't worry about that sir," she smiles. "Your flight is two hours late."

Regensburg was fun, lots of nationalities, lots of parties and even some language learning!

Now it is time to prepare for Russia, an altogether different experience. I have a girlfriend. We have been travelling together in Europe, a lovely few weeks together in Athens and Corfu, Venice, Rome, Bari, Brindisi, all over the place. Then the time comes. She comes with me to Heathrow and we say our goodbyes. She was one of the first girls I loved. She and one other. Not counting Jill, the neighbour, whom I planned to marry, but I was only five. I had to end that relationship when Jill told Mrs Todd. You can't trust a four-year-old fiancée with a secret.

September 1986, and I am ready to spend nearly a whole year in the Soviet Union. We shall be in the city of Voronezh, and our accommodation will not be particularly good, but this is going to be an experience. I am not overly concerned about accommodation. I pack all sorts of food items, because they will definitely not be available in that town. Shortly before I leave, I am told by telephone that I am to stay in Moscow. The teabags may not be so critical.

So, I say farewell to my girlfriend and I go down into the airport meeting room to meet lots of students whom I do not know, but some of whom will become lifelong friends.

On arrival into Moscow, we are taken to a hotel. It's not a luxury hotel, but not a hostel, which is what we have been promised. Most of us have shared rooms, and it is pot luck who we share with. I get a guy who is heavily into Russian vocabulary, almost certainly knows how to say "under 365" in Russian, hates Russians and loves milk. I have to say, such was this individual's apparent dislike of Russia, Russians and all things related to Russia, I thought what a pity he did not relinquish his place to somebody who actually wanted to be there, because these 10-month slots were sought after, few and far between.

One of many statues in the beautiful Moscow Metro underground system

But apart from the milk and the carpentry programmes on TV and my room-mate's desire to learn "electro-submersible pump" in Russian, this seems like it's going to be OK. It was, more than. I'm going to meet many friends.

One such friend is Richard, whom I meet shortly after arriving at our student accommodation, on the first morning, in fact. Despite the fact that he is sporting white socks, pressed jeans and a centre parting, we hit it off immediately. We enter the restaurant for breakfast (sounds posh, but sadly not), and I become stuck on the first word I see on entering the room. It is only three letters, for goodness' sake, but it is well beyond my range. Richard describes in detail that "sok" is the product of a process where the Soviets extract liquid from fruit. He goes into some detail. What they do is, they extract the liquid and discard the pulp and rind. The liquid is separated into a container, and retained, because this is what is going to make the "sok". Until it dawns upon me what he is describing.

"You mean juice? So, "sok" means juice in Russian, right?"

He stands in front of the buffet table and thinks for a moment.

"Oh. Yes. Juice…"

We remain friends to this day.

We are not all in quite the same boat. You see, yes, we are all in our third year at university, but most of the others studied Russian *at school*. My first ever exposure to the language was just two years before and starting from zero. I mean, not even being able to point to Russia on a map. So, we are in different language groups, basically, smart, good, average and then my group. Dorinda had been doing her best, but, let's face it, she had an uphill struggle from day one.

We tried, but we did not seem to be destined for linguistic greatness.

Moscow Winters

How bad were we at this language? Let me illustrate with an example of a lesson. The teacher is handing us back our translations and has a bemused look on his face as he returns to his desk and sits down.

"Look," he says (and this luckily for us was the nice teacher, not like Elena Alexandrovna).

"I know you've been cheating, but the problem is, I don't know who's been cheating off whom."

Turned out, we had all repeated the same mistake in our "translations". On the face of it, it was a small mistake, but one which was bound to be noticed. We had written about that famous novel by Fyodor Dostoevsky entitled *Punishment and Crime.*

Just days before this, the first day at the institute, that was to be our alma mater for nearly a year, had already confused me.

And the confusion started, not with the institute, the speeches or the registration, but with a student from our group, who unexpectedly addressed me in Russian, although she was from Surrey. Her amazing capability with the language was matched only by my incompetence. She only said one word. "Prisazhivaites'." I know this has something to do with sitting down.

And that was that.

We are welcomed by the dean and invited to take a seat. The dean speaks for 30 minutes, none of which I take in, as I am trying to figure out why the Russian for "take a seat" has been said in the way it was. Is it imperative? Is it about how often you do it? How you land on the seat? Such was the complexity of Russian, and I was stumped even before day one. More than 30 years later, I remember vividly trying to understand why she used that declension of the verb, or conjugation, or whatever it is.

I was to learn that a simple word in Russian like "to go" was not good enough. They would change the word completely depending upon, for example, if you "go" frequently or just once. If you "go" in a group or alone. If you "go" in a mode of transport or on foot. And if you arrive, that is a different type of "go". I was beginning to think the language might not be for me.

It did not end there. One subject was called "stranovedenie" and for the entire year, neither I nor my fellow students knew what it was. Years later, although now a fluent Russian speaker, I still don't have a clue. You can google it of course, and it will tell you it means "party leadership", but that is inaccurate. It is difficult to translate or indeed to teach because it is a nebulous collection of ideas on what makes a country tick.

How was I to know that if a Russian says "I feel unimportant", they are feeling unwell? Or if you ask them how they are, and they say "normal" that means "fine, thank you".

Moscow at this time is an austere affair. They do not have the same things as we have. In fact, it is a physically grey experience. So grey, that I recall to this day when I came back to the UK and took the London Underground to Green Park. I had seen London a hundred times before, I was used to it, but as I came up the steps onto Piccadilly, I remember stopping in my tracks. The explosion of sound and colour hit me like a physical force. I must have stood there for a couple of minutes, watching the buses and the neon, listening to the noise and bustle. This was to become a recurring theme; I particularly recall a couple of years later when a colleague, Valerii, who had spent all his life in Russia, was sent to Helsinki. He came back ashen white, and said, "We've been duped all this time." He was right, and the same has been happening ever since.

Soviet Life was generally grey

So, Russia is grey upon our arrival and will remain grey until roughly 1993. There is nothing in the centrally run shops. There is a shop called "Cheese", and in it is one type of hard cheese. In the shop called "Milk" there are empty shelves throughout, then a small pile of blue-and-white cartons of milk in a chiller that does not work. In the shop called "Fish", there is no fish, and in "Vegetables and Fruit", there is no fruit and there are no vegetables. It would take me a long time to work out how to go shopping.

There are no bars, no places to go. It is frankly an awful place to be in your early twenties, and I regret being there in some ways. I was going to miss an important part of what most of my friends were going to have back home.

Of course, with the grey, and the lack of nightlife, bars and restaurants, comes something else – a more intense level of human interaction.

But Soviet Moscow is where I am, and good friendships will emerge, Russian, British and others.

Evenings are spent with a few friends and a small stove in our room, somehow making an omelette fun! On one occasion, weeks later, I stand on a street corner on a Saturday evening in central Moscow and we ponder what to do. We have already exhausted our abilities to watch another opera or play. We have visited new friends time and time again. We have been for walks, and spent evenings watching the state broadcaster offering TV programmes about weaving in Turkmenistan. On this evening, we are flummoxed. We approach a van to buy ice cream wafers, because that is all they have. Saturday night in Moscow was not Saturday night in London or Bristol. My friends back home are going to clubs and pubs and generally doing the things you do when you are 22 years old. I am buying ice cream wafers.

One evening proves to be different though. This same friend and I are walking around, as we did, but this time a little further along the river from the city centre itself. We come across a massive building called the "World Trade Center". We wander around it and see that it contains apartments, a hotel and an office block. Just out of curiosity, we enter the hotel. Now, here's the thing: we do not really have any right to enter these hard currency hotels, and in any case, we have no money. But the elderly men in yellow hatbands seem a little unsure about what will happen if they stop a westerner from entering, so they generally let you in if you have a passport – not always, as you will read below, but generally.

In we go, bold as ever, and we have a good wander round. The first thing we see is a massive wooden column in the foyer, and perched on top, a huge wooden cockerel which crows every 15 minutes. Why a chicken was put in the foyer, I have no idea and still do not, but the chicken remains to this day. There are shops and bars, restaurants and cafés, even a little supermarket! Little did I know I would end up living here in two or three years, of course. Suddenly, we come across a bar, the Warsteiner Bierstube. We go in. An actual bar with tables, beer and glasses! With chatter and waiters and plates of food. Are we hallucinating? Why have we no money when all these business people are so loaded with cash? So many questions. We cannot stay because we shall need to save up some cash, but we return to our accommodation, like scouts, telling everybody about the bar in Moscow. We shall later discover that a very small number of hotels in Moscow, the Intourist, the Budapest, the Cosmos, all have a hard currency bar. We shall later drink beer at a few of these, but only very occasionally, because it is approximately one month's rent for a pint of warm, watery Heineken.

Twilight in Moscow

Who were the elderly men with yellow hatbands? Well, we do not really know. They have gone now. We know about the red armbands though. I mentioned earlier the women who sit in glass boxes at the bottom end of the platform in the metro. Their job is to watch the escalator. Other women wash telephone boxes. Others stand in lifts to push the buttons. Nobody really knows where they are from or their purpose, because not one of these jobs is actually necessary. Have you ever seen a phone box being sponged down? Ever stared at a moving staircase long enough so that it does something unexpected? I remember once a friend in the institute asking why it was illegal to be drunk in Moscow.

My teacher, the terrifying Elena Alexandrovna, glares at him and says proudly, "Well, it is obvious! A drunkard on the street could enter the metro, stand at the top of the escalator, fall forwards, pushing everybody forwards, then at the bottom, the person on the platform is pushed onto the platform and if a train is coming in, they roll off the platform and under the train! So drunken behaviour could lead to death!"

There are two things about that statement: it feels like, in some parallel universe, it could be true, so I had no response for Elena Alexandrovna. But in hindsight, she was wrong, because nobody can fall on a Soviet escalator. They have a woman in a glass box for that.

Being wrong would not bother Elena Alexandrovna too much. She was not a nice person. Very sarcastic, but let's face it, teaching foreigners was not what she had envisaged when she signed up to be an architect of the utopian socialist idyll. In fact, she managed to humiliate me already on day one of our lessons. Half a dozen of us are in the room, and she is asking us in Russian if we are "Filolog" or "Lingvist". I do not know either word, but I imagine the latter means studying languages, and that is what I do. So, when she glares at me and requires my response, I reply that I am studying languages, "Lingvist". Well, that was what I thought I was saying. What I was actually saying was that instead of studying language and literature, I was studying the science of how language is constructed, its derivations and systems, and its strengths and flaws. None of which I was studying, so that was a fun two minutes while she laughed at me. Nobody else in the room was laughing, of course.

Anyway, the red armbands are basically there for the same reason. They keep the unemployment figures at zero. Although, that is not quite true, because these were actually volunteers, wannabe architects of that socialist idyll. Quite creepy really, when you think about it. The red armbands were called Druzhiniki, which means friendly or something very similar, but of course, they were not. Let me explain.

It's 1986, and in Moscow, we see a poster for the tour of a band called UB40. Only a small number of bands are allowed to play in the Soviet Union, and we genuinely thought most of them had been dead for years, such as Nazareth. With the sole exception of Pink Floyd, whom I saw in

Moscow, and who were of course superb, most of the permitted bands were B-listers, or dead, but there was another group that was permitted, and that was the bands with similar politics to the Soviet Union. So left-wing, socialist bands would probably be OK, and what could be more socialist than a band named after a document to claim unemployment benefits?

So UB40 is coming to town. We hustle, we beg, we ask around, and – as you did for everything including an egg – we queued.

The Russians loved queuing in those days. Not now. Now, they love to form an orderly crowd, but in those days, you could join a queue without knowing what it was for. See a queue? Join it fast because, whatever it is, it must be worth it. All Russians carried a plastic bag in case they spotted a queue. And, by the way, queuing was an art form. I recall when I arrived in London with my Russian wife, years later, we went to Clapham Junction train station and we joined the queue to buy a ticket. But not her. Oh, no, she joined three queues. She left me in one, then joined another, then prodded the guy in front in the back, and said, "If anyone asks, I'm here, OK?" Then she stood in another queue. I could not because I am British and we do not do that kind of thing. However, here we were in Moscow, queuing, as we did a lot.

MY CAREER WITH UB40

We are at the Luzhniki Stadium, standing in a queue for tickets for UB40's forthcoming appearance in Moscow. We're not fans as such, but we all know them. Not the guy behind us in the queue, though. Here's the conversation:
"Are you waiting for the UB40 tickets?"
"Yes, we are. Do you know them?"
"No. Who are they playing against?"
"Pardon?"
"What football team are they playing against? Dinamo? Spartak?"
"Well, they're not. They're not a football team. They're a band…"
"Oh. OK."
Silence ensues. Then a moment later:
"Heavy metal or new wave?"
"Well, no, they're a mixture of reggae and ska."
"Pardon?"
"Reggae. It's a form of music, where you use the bass… Oh, never mind! New wave."

So, we get our tickets to the gig, and the day finally arrives. But we have a problem, which is that our seats are miles away, up on a balcony. The stage is the size of a postage stamp from up here. This will not do.

But… the red armbands are everywhere. Their purpose is to scrutinise us to ensure we are in the correct seats, to ensure we don't make noise above permitted levels, and to ensure we have not brought anything in that we should not have. So, we have a problem.

We're not staying here. Well, Daren is. He's brought his Russian girlfriend and she is not prepared to get into trouble, which is fair enough. But Richard in particular is determined. He's not staying here. I tag along, knowing that my Russian is only sufficient to get me into trouble, but not out. We stand up, and move towards the end of the row, leaving poor Daren staring into the middle distance, unable to move.

We get to the end of the row, and a red armband stops us. "Why are you leaving your seat?"

"We're just going to pop down there for a moment to see our friends, but we will absolutely return to our seats. Look, we even left our friend there as proof."

"OK, return quickly or you will be in trouble!"

Much of my memory of living in the Soviet Union was following people who knew what they were doing more than I did, and who could explain themselves, who could understand what was happening, and so on. I follow Richard down several flights of stairs to the main hall and forwards, all the time being stopped and questioned by red armbands, until finally we reach the mixing desk.

Young readers probably won't know what a mixing desk is. It's what they had before the laptops came along.

Here's the interesting bit. We stay by the mixing desk, as if we have reached the corral; it's going to be OK now we have reached this point. The lights go down, the music starts, and the red armbands have absolutely no idea where we are. We had a great evening. UB40 did not have the same fun as we did. Everything they said into the mic was interpreted by a Soviet interpreter. Not translated, interpreted. For example, Ali Campbell is exasperated by the fact that the only people in the entire stadium dancing are two guys by the mixing desk. This is what happened with the interpretation:

Ali Campbell, lead singer of UB40, in exasperation: "Guys, you can dance! This is dance music; enjoy it!"

Interpreter: "You may move quietly to the rhythm of the music, whilst remaining seated!"

The only person who enjoyed that concert less than the band was Daren, four miles away on a balcony. Two people by the mixing desk were happy.

One little postscript to this concert, as the embassies sometimes had parties, but the British embassy was not very good at them, the band rolled up to the American embassy for a party. This embassy was next to a derelict, brand-new building which was to be for the US embassy's use. They however trusted Russian contractors to build it, and unsurprisingly, found that it was full of bugs and listening devices, so they refused to move in. We follow UB40 to the American embassy party, and the US marines on the gate were informed that we were part of the band.

So briefly, very briefly, I seem to have been in UB40. And yes, of course I gave a demo tape of my band that evening to the trumpet player, who was known as "Buttons", though I never heard from him again!

But I digress, the yellow hatbands.

You see, Russians were very resilient. They had to be. They had so much to tolerate. I often have said, if I have to go into the jungle, I would rather go in with a Russian, because they are pragmatic, resourceful and funny. And so it was with Soviet life. I return in the middle of the night when it is -18 degrees C (which never stopped the trains or planes in Russia) and I was given a pizza! How? Because our driver had kept the engine running and the pizza in its box sat on the carburettor. These are the Russians, whom I came to love and respect.

The system was full of strange things, so, oh yes, the yellow hatbands. Like the women looking at escalators or washing telephone boxes, these people had two purposes:

Stare at people as they enter the hotel, and ensure they have a hotel card.

Maintain zero unemployment.

Where we were staying as students was actually a hotel, and whilst it was not luxury, it was pretty good. We had brought teabags and washing powder, because we assumed we would be staying in hostel dormitories and certainly not in the capital. Indeed, many students were placed in hostel dormitories, with the infestations and the noise. We met some students and we saw their accommodation. It was horrible. We asked, and the institute explained to us that the infested accommodation was only for Americans. The Americans took it all in good humour, and we would have happily moved there, but we were not allowed to do so.

We had a pretty good arrangement. Ian was so convinced that we would be moved into a hostel that he didn't even unpack for two weeks!

The yellow hatbands stood vigilantly by the hotel doors, scrutinising us, but we came to understand that there was a nuance to this scrutiny.

They couldn't see that well, and they had absolutely no memory.

So, we took advice from some Russian friends, and they explained how we could even throw a party, despite the doormen. It was so simple and we repeated it many times during our stay in Russia.

Enter the building, present your card. Go to room.

Put card in sock with a spoon, tie the sock and throw down to Misha.

Misha enters building and comes to room. Gives card to student.
Repeat 2, but throw to Svetlana.
Now throw to Andrei.
Anna.
Natasha.
Repeat as required up to 30 times.

One problem remained. Watching us on every level of the hotel was a woman behind a desk. She was called a dezhurnaya. It does not really translate that well, something to do with shift working, but she could usually be won over with a smile and some chocolate. She actually didn't really care, because we were truly not fomenting revolution. We were drinking beer and listening to music. The dezhurnaya was our ally. Kind of. I mean, not really on our side, but willing to be silent. If we stayed out all night somewhere, we still had to ruffle the bed sheets before we left, to pretend we had slept in our rooms. She was an ally who would betray us if somebody brought her a bigger box of chocolates…

Red Square Guard

A moment ago, I mentioned the Russians' attitude towards the Americans. They really had a problem with them. Although the hostel issue I mentioned was not in itself that much of an issue, and it absolutely did not bother the Americans, there was a genuine political issue. It was never personal. The Russians and the Americans are all people and we all get along just fine. No, it was definitely politics. I found this out the hard way. Let me briefly take you forwards a few years to illustrate this.

1990: THE DAY I DIED

Russian style speed restriction

I'm in the office, a few years later, now a businessman. I feel cold, but hey, we're in Russia. No, I actually feel really cold, so I tell my colleague that I need to go home, and she graciously suggests I take the rental car that we took for the duration of the exhibition. No offence to the Lada manufacturers, but this technology was old even when Fiat sold it to the USSR. As I climb into the loosely assembled hairdryer on wheels, I could not have felt worse, so I clatter and lurch this "car" to apartment 1223. I go to bed fully clothed. I put on a jumper. I put on another, then a dressing gown. I am now what I can only describe as violently cold. I am becoming anxious because I know that the apartment is not cold. I can't stand up. I roll off the bed and crawl towards the phone in the lounge. As I am halfway across the floor, the door opens and my colleague Mark walks in. Thank God. He sees me wearing a suit, two jumpers and a dressing gown, crawling on the carpet.

"What are you doing?" he asks.

I explain, and he immediately stops being the chisel-jawed girl magnet that he of course was and makes a call. The hotel paramedics arrive.

Then it gets weird.

They prod me and ask me things, but cannot agree. One says it's appendicitis. The other shakes his head.

I say, ironically (totally forgetting that the Russians don't do apologies, thanks or irony), "Guys, there's beer in the fridge, grab a cold one and have a cigarette; let's chat this diagnosis through!" Remember: every word in this book is true.

One of them looks at his watch, and says, "Thanks, but I don't think we have time."

Mark is torn. On the one hand, he is beside himself with laughter. On the other, this Limey is poorly, so he takes control. They put me on a hotel chair, and take me to the lift, or as Mark insists on calling it, the "elevator". It arrives on the twelfth floor. Doors open. It's 18:00. Moscow rush hour leaves the lift, every single one of them taking a good look at the weird scene of the chair, the patient, the two paramedics and the American, chisel-jawed girl magnet… and they go to their apartments. We get to an ambulance. It's called an RAF, but it's basically a van with a stretcher. Beside it is a wheelchair, which my two guys clearly have forgotten about, or they hadn't thought this was going to be serious. The other interesting thing about this RAF was that the rear door does not close. So here I am, on a stretcher, which slopes down towards the door, and the paramedic slams the door several times, but it does not shut. He gives up and jumps in the van, and off we go. I clutch the handle on the ceiling because if that door fails, I am going to bounce on the tarmac at speed. Mark jumps into the company car, a blue Volvo 240, but all is not well. Not only because this car is really on its last legs and is in fact about to be scrapped, so it is not equipped for a high-speed ambulance chase, but also because his exit is impeded, so he can't even make a quick getaway. You know, sometimes, you need to have somebody have your back? Well, that was Mark, that day. He moves the car to the ambulance but is hindered by a driver behind, who cannot wait and clearly does not understand what is going on. What does Mark do? I am unaware, because I am going in and out of consciousness. Mark is not abandoning me. He rams his vehicle into the obstructing car behind, and sets off behind the ambulance. He stays with me.

He follows the ambulance at high speed. We arrive at the Botkin Hospital. It's grim. They take blood, using a lancet from a cup on a table. After they take blood, the lancet goes back in the cup – used on patients before me, and now waiting for the next.

Nobody has invented mobile phones yet. Mark has had the good sense to make contact previously with my other colleague, and she goes to the British embassy to get syringes. The British doctor refuses to speak to her, so she converses via his secretary. She says he cannot give syringes but he can sell them, for dollars… in the British embassy.

These guys are moving fast, but by the time Mark makes it back to the Botkin Hospital, I am already being operated on. I later wrote to the then PM, Margaret Thatcher, that is how angry I was. They were prepared to look into it, but the case was dropped at the request of my colleague, who did not wish her name to be involved, and that is why I have not named her here.

Perhaps more interestingly, I met that same embassy doctor at a London event some 20 years later. He was selling a book about his years overseas. I told him that I would expose him if I saw any publicity for his forthcoming book, because it is my opinion that his prevarication and delay could have cost me very dearly.

So, whilst this is going on, I am being shaved, and they are wondering if I should be airlifted to Helsinki.

"There is no time," says the doctor. That was quite chilling. My appendix needs to be removed without delay.

They wheel me up to theatre, and the last thing I see is a bulb blowing as they pull the lights over the table.

And then I wake up. I am in a lovely room, with flowers, furniture – a private room – but I don't really understand where I am.

I spend a few days in the Botkin Hospital and have the best care in the world. The medical treatment is first-rate, the nurses are kind and, from time to time, people visit me, including my boss, Michael. And Mark, and

Mark's girlfriend, who brings me soup. One of his girlfriends, I suspect. Anyway, this one gave me soup.

Each day, the surgeon walks in, reads my notes, tuts a lot and tells me I cannot leave. He also told me I was dead.

It was briefly, a couple of days ago, on the operating table.

And it is true. I don't remember being dead, and that is not something you would think would slip your mind. I recall darkness and faces looking down at me, muttering. That's all. I think that was when they had revived me. It was all to do with the anaesthetic, apparently. Mark later spoke to the surgeon, who explained that I had needed urgent assistance… but they got me back… or I would not be writing this.

But I did not know then, and still do not know, what they used that had such an effect upon me. A normal person would have probably taken the trouble to find out the name of the medication that killed me. I have had a few operations since that one, and there is always a little frisson of not knowing if I will wake up again!

After several days of being told I could not leave, I ask a visitor to the hospital to contact my colleague to bring the car to the back of the hospital. I leave via the fire escape. The red Volvo, the replacement for the one Mark drove on the way over, arrives like an angel and transports me, despite my still unhealed wound, through the Moscow streets to apartment 1223. I feel, with excruciating pain, every bump in the road on the way to the apartment, as the stitches pull and threaten to tear, but I cannot stay in the hospital any longer. It's full of ill people.

There I stay in the apartment to recuperate.

Then I feel bad, because they have treated me well at the Botkin. Russian medics are known across the world, and I was privileged to be a patient in Russia. So, I return. I returned to the hospital with chocolates and flowers and full of praise. They were absolutely lovely.

The hospital director calls me in. It's a brief conversation, then we discuss payment and he requests my passport.

Finally, he returns my passport and apologises, "I am so terribly sorry. We thought you were American. We do not require payment from you."

Yes, the Russians have a real problem politically with the Americans, and it is based upon a genuine assumption that America's aim is to end Russia's existence. This explains much of their behaviour politically.

1987: BACK TO STUDENT DAYS

I am misleading slightly when I say there was no nightlife. I do remember being in one club for young people. It felt like regimented fun. Several of the girls are wearing the same design of dress because all shops are state-owned with virtually no choice of what to buy. All the guys wear the same thick, dark jeans, and the music is quite literally reel to reel. We go there once and not for long.

We have to be a little careful about the Russian friends who approach us. One in particular, with an American drawl, very clearly was KGB. He had no interest in us as people, but oh, he tried to obtain details. Probably living somewhere totally different now, so much time has passed.

Walking by the Kremlin one day, apparently looking like foreigners, we hear a voice shuffling up to us: "Jeans?"

Our first encounter with a street hawker comes early on; he wants to buy our jeans, and we chat to him awhile. He introduces us later to his circle of mates, including Misha, who will become a very close friend as the years go by. For now, he just wants to buy our jeans and change money. We are poor and the rate is six times better than the official rate, and we quite like the intrigue of it all, ducking down an alleyway furtively glancing to the side and behind, but obviously, we do not do this. We also do not shimmy up a wall with a penknife and remove a Soviet hammer and sickle flag (of which there were hundreds during national holidays).

Soviet items were very retro even then. They used to sell badges, and I recall selling them again at the Edinburgh Festival a year or two later. I too have somehow obtained a Soviet hammer and sickle flag, which I lay on the pavement festooned with the little glittering red-and-gold badges. They are popular. However, it wasn't the selling of retro that was interesting, it was the procurement.

We have our eyes on Soviet military greatcoats. With their tapered waist and wide lapels, they are and were iconic, and there is no shortage of ex-soldiers who will let us have one for a few roubles. We meet in the metro, on the station platform, "last carriage" as the Russians always said, and a swap takes place of a big bundle, wrapped in brown paper and string, which we take home and gaze at admiringly, whilst no doubt our ex-soldier enjoys the winnings. I eventually, years later, realise I have too much Soviet memorabilia, greatcoats, badges, submarine clocks, model cars, posters, all sorts of things, which I later auction and give to charity.

As we come to know our new friends, we realise how similar we are, apart from a taste in music. I reflect on how many Ozzy Osbourne records I will have to buy just because that was the only thing they knew. Still, it could have been Modern Talking.

There is one other curious feature about being here at this time. This is still very much the Soviet Union, with all the good, the bad and the ugly that involves. But at its head is one Mikhail Sergeevich Gorbachev (now passed away).

"Gorby" was no democrat and will later bitterly regret losing hold of the USSR; indeed, he is now largely vilified for it by many Russians (and none more so than Putin), because in their eyes he cost them the empire. It is often assumed that he was a democrat, whereas in reality he was a pragmatist. He looked at the country's balance sheet and realised that far too much of the USSR's GDP was being spent on arms. Put simply, they could not afford to keep up in the arms race, so he commenced a careful structural change, where certain enterprise was allowed, and with that had to come limited freedoms, including on things like speech and travel. The chances are it just became too difficult to put the genie back into the bottle and the rest, as they say, is history.

Up in the frozen north, and even in the capital, conditions can be pretty tough. Not only can winter be harsh, but careers tend to be tedious, and with no possibility to travel, there is not that much to do, but a lot of scope for drinking or getting divorced, two of Soviet man's favourite pastimes.

Gorbachev tackled this by introducing the "dry laws", making it more difficult to purchase alcohol, also, more expensive and from fewer outlets. Of course, our stay in Russia had to coincide with this new alcohol law. Therefore, if you want a drink, you stand outside one of the few shops which sell alcohol, and only at the exact time they have some stock. There are two problems with this, more specifically, one with a direct consequence.

The queue-waiting time can be four hours in whatever weather Russia chooses to throw at you. When you finally get in the door, the chances are that all that is left is Tokai or cherry brandy (so sweet that you need a spoon).

What do we do as students? We queue four hours for a bottle of Tokai, which we affectionately rename "Dr Krapalot".

The queue for Dr Krapalot

One option remains for those who want some kind of social life involving a drink – and no, it is not a good option – the beer hall.

These cavernous spaces are few and far between, and hence, yes, there are long queues. I recall being in one queue so long, with my Russian friend, Misha, that I lost all feeling in my left foot. He removed my boot and rubbed snow onto my bare foot till the feeling was restored.

Worse than that, the beer is not really beer. It is foul-tasting fizz dispensed from machines. What do we students do in this situation? We queue hours and drink foul-tasting fizz from machines.

One night, we are all sitting at a table, which has taken us hours to secure. We are chatting, laughing, smoking. Our waiter is a man by the name of Pokryshkin and the beer hall is the Zolotoi Fazan, or "Golden Pheasant", behind Kyiv station. Glamorous, this is not. Finally, the time comes to leave, but Pokryshkin is nowhere to be seen.

Nor, for that matter, is any waiter. We try, genuinely try, to be noticed. We go and look, but no staff seem to be around.

This lack of staff is not uncommon in Soviet Russia. They have no reason to be there; they will be paid regardless so long as they are somewhere and have clocked on. I was later told by Michael, my soon-to-be boss, and later, friend, how he was hosting a dinner in the Belgrade Hotel and became so fed up "waiting for the waiter" to return that he wandered into the kitchen and eventually found him playing chess. When he remonstrated, another waiter told him to be quiet because his waiter was pondering his move! In fact, I recall also going into a hotel kitchen and opening cupboards and oven doors, trying to find our dinner. Nobody gave us so much as a glance.

Anyway, back to the Golden Pheasant. We cannot see Pokryshkin or any waiters, so, we leave, not in an attempt not to pay, but because somebody will finally see that we are leaving and will come to get payment. Suddenly, we are heading back along the road towards the station and chatting again, and we have forgotten all about it. We are not in a rush, and Daren decides he should have gone for a pee. The only thing nearby is the wheel of a disused lorry in some bushes, so Daren selects this place to relieve himself discreetly, unseen thanks to some bushes. The rest of us, on the other hand, are visible… to the police Lada that clatters up to us and stops, and to the waiter in the passenger seat of the police car…

Misha explains to the waiter and the police officer that we tried to pay, that nobody appeared, so we left the payment under a plate on the table. He accompanies them to the table, where the money under the plate has of course vanished. We graciously pay again, while Daren remains aloof from proceedings and still telling jokes.

Going out was not always simple. It seems strange to see how young Russians take for granted the bars, restaurants and clubs that stay open all day and all night, because in our Russia, Soviet Russia, they were just not there. I recall, with a few friends, visiting some café on Kutuzovsky Avenue. No mean feat in itself, as it involves waiting over an hour on the street, and all for a warm beer mixed with the previous diner's remnants.

We have been sitting there a while when we hear a noise, in the rafters above, and notice a white rat. That in itself is not unusual, but we bring this to the attention of the waitress.

Misha says, "There is a white rat just above us in the roof space."

She confirms it is a rat, and walks off. After a while, the noise above us stops, Misha stands up, jabs it with a fork and confirms it has passed away… Nobody seems surprised; nobody thinks it unusual in any way.

We would go to the theatre. Of course, buying a ticket is not possible unless you are a hotel guest and pay ridiculous amounts of hard currency. The locals are not that stupid. The Soviet elite could buy tickets, the tourists paying hard currency could buy tickets, but not ordinary people. There were kiosks where they had no tickets and, of course, the internet did not exist except to a few scientists. So we would go to the theatre and stand outside waiting to find somebody who could offer us a ticket. It was pretty grim. Seats were overpriced and were never together. Daren was a true theatre lover. He would not only stand and wait for tickets, he became friends with the actors, he visited their homes and truly loved Russian art, great as it always was.

Even the simplest thing, like making a call home, was a challenge. To make that call, you had to book it over a local payphone a couple of days in advance, also advising how long you wished to speak for. Your entire conversation would then be monitored by a phone operator, who, just as you were chatting to your parents back home, would interrupt bluntly with the words "Time up" and cut everybody off.

There was not a lot of trust in this country; a bit like now.

My brother visited me whilst I was out there and asked me to translate for him as he went to various apartments in town, offering Bibles. In hindsight, this innocent activity was very naïve on his part and although I helped him, I remember wishing I had not been asked to do so. This was the USSR, not London, and this was not OK.

Winter in early 1987 was hard, even by Russian standards and even in the capital. It reached -25 degrees C some days, and that makes your eyeballs crackle.

SOVIET PUBLIC TRANSPORT

We are coming out of winter; it is already March, but still bitterly cold. The buses are operating but look like ice cubes on wheels. There is no chance of seeing out of the window. The buses are definitely worth a mention; 1950s' technology, which is probably good given the weather. The trucks were the same, totally rugged. In the winter, you would often see a truck driver warming himself at a fire he had lit under the truck to warm the oil in the sump. They just knew things, like driving on frozen lakes, so much more savvy than us. The buses seemed unbreakable. These buses are not pretty. They are squat, little yellow things that wheeze along at 20 mph, but they get the job done. At the back of the bus is a little machine called a "komposter". Upon entering the bus, a paper ticket is passed toward the back from one passenger to another and the person by the komposter imprints the ticket, which then makes its way back to the original passenger. It is all done on trust, and no talking is required. The reason this system exists in the 1980s is because there are so many people on board that it is difficult even to have both feet still on the floor. Breathing has to be done in turns and only if truly necessary. There is one major issue with buses this busy, and to a lesser extent, it is the same even now on the metro, though the space down there is so much greater. Crammed in as we are, clutching a plastic bag, which may be suspended above someone else's head, you have to plan your exit in advance. This is not easy in the winter when you cannot see out of the window. This is a logistical exercise. As the bus pulls away, fingers prod backs all over the bus as passengers check, "Are you getting out now?"

At the beginning, I had no idea what was happening. I thought, frankly, I don't know you and it is none of your business if I am getting out or not, but I worked it out eventually. This was a necessary part of bus travel. Additionally, if you were innocently but by chance standing anywhere near the exit, then prepare for this: those doors will open. Those passengers will be pushing to get out, so you had better be ready because you will be catapulted out whether this is your intended stop or not. It's game over if you are by the door. Just make sure you get back on before it wheezes off again. I have to say, despite their looks, the whole transport system in Russia was better than anything we have in the UK decades later. It wasn't pretty but it was always on schedule, despite truly tough weather. Of course, perhaps sadly, those little, clunky yellow buses have all been replaced by modern, more grown-up buses!

The Russians have two words for train, at least two that I am aware of. One is train, and that is the one that goes long distances, and the other is the electric, and that is basically a suburban train. They all run on time. I loved train travel, but not so much the electric. A train ride to the city of Ekaterinburg took days. Seated in a compartment with people you would know well by the time you arrived, often with a bottle of vodka and dried fish or something else that would ensure the place smelled more strongly of that than the Soviet cigarettes we were all smoking. Actually, it sounds horrendous now, thinking about it, but at the time it was just normal.

Definitely worth a mention is the Moscow metro. I have not been in a system more organised, clean and punctual than this. Sorry to the Russia haters amongst you, but it is true. The most beautiful stations are on the ring or circle line.

It wasn't just that they looked good, they were spacious, and a timer above the track never in all my years rose above two minutes, the time since the last train left. Imagine that on the Northern Line in London.

My only complaint about the whole thing is that, for reasons that even the Russians don't seem to understand entirely, they give different names to what is essentially the same station, depending on the lines that connect there. For example, the station "Lenin Library" will also be called "Alexander Gardens". It also boasts the name "Vorobitskaya" and, just for good measure, a fourth name, "Arbat". But come out of each of these stations, and you are effectively in the same place. OK, you may be the other end of the square, or the other side of an intersection, but the same place nevertheless. I have had Russians coming up to me asking how to get from Alexander Gardens to Vorobitskaya. Simple, just follow a few staircases and escalators, or go outside and cross the road!

The Circle line is probably the most stunning on the transport system

Of course, there is a reason people use the metro in Moscow. In fact, I can think of at least two. It works very efficiently and gets you where you need to be on time and, up on street level, there is absolute gridlock.

INTERNATIONAL POST OFFICE

Back to late March and our winter boredom. There was one chap in the group, whom I shall not name, but he was absolutely the nicest guy you could hope to meet. From time to time, things would somehow happen to him, and he always took it in good humour. Well, mostly.

In Moscow in the 1980s, if somebody back home sent a parcel, we would receive a postal notification to collect it from the International Post Office on Varshavskoye Shosse. To get there, you walk to the bus, which takes you to "Universitet" metro station, take the metro into town, change stations and get from where we are to another part of town altogether. Once at the correct metro stop, it's a long ride on a trolleybus to a place reasonably walkable from the International Post Office. All in all, it takes two hours to get there, and two hours to get back.

That is what we have to do whenever a parcel arrives, so when it happens, you want it to be worth it. Or at the very least, on this bitterly cold day on April 1st, you want there to be a parcel, and not a little note where the parcel should be, saying "April Fool". What a cruel thing to do to a nice bloke…! I, of course, wash my hands of this incident, because I don't have a sufficiently cruel mind! Anyway, it was the only time I saw him mildly irritated.

Spring and summer brought some respite. By now, we had really made some good Russian friends, and we knew which ones were the spooks. We could go on picnics in the park, and occasionally I was taken incognito on a bus (told not to say a word), and we would go to visit an underground gig somewhere. Those were fun if slightly scary outings.

We would from time to time go to various embassies for some event or other. Not so much the British embassy, because I do not recall there being much going on there, or our being very welcome anyway. They had a British supermarket in the embassy run by the diplomats' wives. We were allowed in "so long as we behaved ourselves". I recall being there one afternoon looking for things I could not buy in the Soviet Union, Marmite, Worcester Sauce, that kind of thing, and I overheard one of the wives at the till talking to another about "the students". They did not like us. They did not know us of course, but they decided they did not like us. The British embassy was not our port of call on the very few occasions that we were involved with embassies. I remember the American, German and particularly the Canadian embassies as having the best parties. I am sure I won a limbo-dancing competition at one party or other.

Once on this circuit, we learnt about the Hash House Harriers, and, despite it involving running, there was the promise of beer at the end, so I reluctantly agreed. The Hash House Harriers, as many will know, is a tradition, which seems to be mainly for diplomats and expats, where they take part in an organised run, and at the end meet for a few beers. It was alright, I suppose. Apart from the running, of course.

I would have chewed off my right arm just to go to the pub even once…

But apart from the runs, the occasional parties, and of course the embassy shop, we really did not have any contact with the expat community. What we saw of it was not particularly attractive, and we had good friends in the group and amongst the Russians.

There was one aspect of Soviet infrastructure that was always a mystery to me – an enigma, hypocrisy and a slur on the socialist idyll – and this was the "Beryozka". Literal meaning "birch tree", which in Russia has Stalinist connotations. The Beryozka was a chain of hard currency shops; the closest to where we lived as students was a couple of metro stops away. They could be found in hotels in the city centre. In these places were rows of tins of caviar, sturgeon and salmon, black and red, along with beer, vodka, Russian dolls and balalaikas, plus clothing, souvenirs, all sorts of things. None of this was really available outside in the real world. Ostensibly, these shops were for tourists and, inevitably, there would be a stop on any tour to help relieve tourists of their cash. That may sound very logical, a win for socialism, a distribution. Of course, it was not that simple. Russians were not allowed in, and although a bus driver was paid more than a doctor in Soviet Russia, even a bus driver's salary would not have given much spending power in a Beryozka.

But hey, what a surprise in this corrupt, non-socialist regime, the Soviet elite were allowed in!

In fact, they were given cards to allow them to shop there. The whole structure was rotten to the core, and Gorbachev knew it. Ironically, we have come full circle and Russia is rotting with bureaucracy and corruption. As students, we were on a limited budget though. Our monthly stipend was some 250 roubles per month at the time, when the exchange rate was 1:1 to sterling. This was roughly the same as a Russian doctor's salary. Really, it was not much. We were in these places only rarely. They were expensive, but occasionally we would buy a few beers and often would buy things for our Russian friends, who of course did not ask us to buy them anything.

There were other ways to entertain ourselves. We would visit new friends in their homes, a real privilege, because at this time it was not usual to fraternise with the few foreigners that were in the country. Let's face it, we were aware of being followed from time to time, of the need to be discreet at all times, of the restrictions. It wasn't like now. I recall one of my tutors in the UK recounting how he was tailed in Moscow by some spook, so he lost him in the metro finally, by jumping up and out of the carriage just as the doors were closing.

To spend some time in somebody's apartment was a real big deal. No politics though. Perhaps, with the television on full volume, and after a lot of alcohol, and with people whom you could really trust, possibly, you might touch upon politics, but not really. It was more about beer and bands and girls and jokes, not much more.

I also learnt how to skate in Moscow at this time, and the lovely thing about those evenings was that we would just go to a park and step straight onto the ice, nobody around, no need to book, no time limit, just the frozen lake, the trees and the stars, and the occasional whump as I fell over again.

We were largely unable to travel, except on official tours. I recall being taken on a coach to the town of Klin, some fifty miles outside the capital, which is where Tchaikovsky spent his last days and wrote his final symphony, and is also home to a factory manufacturing thermometers. These were not great excursions, and memorable for all the wrong reasons.

Having spent a great year in Russia making new friends, going to the theatre, opera, ballet, visiting underground gigs out of town and buying Soviet military greatcoats, it was time to go to Germany for a few weeks for the second half of my two-month course, then back to Bristol to commence my final year – and exams.

A few of us, before graduating, went back to Russia on a memorable trip, but this time we took a bus from Kings Cross, London, a ferry across the Channel, then the train to Moscow, via Berlin, which was then still partitioned. We had fun and it was an amazing experience. I mention this because it illustrates that behind the fun and the laughter and learning was a sinister, rather intimidating atmosphere. On the way back to the UK, somewhere near the Russian border, I realise I have a small number of roubles in my pocket. As I wait for the train, I crumple the money up in my pocket and throw it away. That is how much I did not want to be found by customs officers, even with this laughably small amount of money accidentally left in my pocket. That is how strict the regime was.

Final year was very different to all that had gone before. I found the library finally, and stopped going to so many parties. Now I had to focus. I did, and I graduated, and left the safety of being a student, part of an institution.

1988/1989: TIME TO JOIN THE REAL WORLD

Now the prospect looms of having to find employment. With little idea of what I want to do next, I complete a journalism course in Cardiff and receive my Diploma in Journalism, learning shorthand at the same time. Cardiff was fun in a way, great students and great lecturers. It was only a five-month course, and again, because most study periods were at least a year, this was quite a difficult course to enrol on, so I was going to make the most of it.

The then love of my life I had lost whilst I was in Russia on my year abroad. It was probably just as well. She was a lot smarter than me and I suspect she would have demanded an upgrade anyway at some point. The relationship was doomed to failure, because she was studying languages, and was in the year below. No sooner would I have returned from my third year in Germany and Russia, than she would be off to do her third year in Germany and France. But I had been truly smitten by this girl, and remained full of regret. Oddly enough, the way the relationship ended made it somehow worse. I received a letter and read it in the café in Moscow. I was surrounded by noise and chatter, but as I read it, I knew that I was being dumped. Worse, she was seeing the lead singer in a rival band, a sort of me. I know that probably now sounds comical, but it wasn't at the time.

Music was important to me. My band was important. We had won Battle of the Bands, and we had done lots of recording studio work. Were we groundbreaking? No, but we did get a demo tape to Andy Warhol, who died soon after he said he liked it. To be honest, I am glad we did not pursue this as a career, not only because there are many bands far better than we were, but also because the recording studio was a source of immense boredom to me. What fired me up was to be live on stage. I absolutely loved it, getting a crowd singing along, quietening suddenly for the drum solo, coming back for an encore. There is no feeling in the world like being on stage, and nothing better than being on stage creating music and getting the crowd involved – but not the recording studio…

Whilst living in Cardiff, I could sometimes be seen in my brother's little Triumph Herald, driving across the Severn Bridge to see her. Alasdair had given me the use of this car, which I was grateful for. He had the patience of an angel, because I had at one point managed to crash it, and I remember being humbled by his lack of anger, which would have been deserved. He always had empathy, my brother. I remember on a trip to see our grandparents, whilst children, I forgot my pocket money, and without hesitation, he reached into his pocket and gave me half of his.

In hindsight, this girl was incredibly gracious with me. She knew I was hurting and she was kind. The relationship had been over a long time, but she still agreed to see me. She was just not a cruel person, this young lady of just 22 years. Early twenties is a tough time.

During the course, we are often assigned local stories to find and write. So, many is the drizzly Tuesday afternoon in Cardiff when I will be wandering around petrol stations trying to find something to cover. The institute also organised a brief internship, mine being with the London Newspaper Group.

I commence writing stories about skateboarding ducks and lost dogs. This is not what I had envisaged. I wanted immediately to be Reuters' chief in Moscow, but it does not quite work like that. It seems there will be a lot of this before I get to that stage.

There was another element that turned me off journalism. I am at the door of the flat of an elderly woman, with a cameraman behind my shoulder. This lady is to lose her home because the Housing Association have chosen to dispose of the asset. And whilst in our heads we are trying to portray her side of the story, I also have a mic thrust in front of her and am blocking her front door with my foot. I suddenly feel that the cameraman and I have just become a part of the problem. I withdrew my foot from the door, finished my course, and left journalism for good. This was not for me.

By and large, Cardiff was fun. Not as much as Bristol, but that's because I was there only five months, with no chance of immersing myself as I had before. But I emerge with my diploma.

Still unsure what I am doing next, I hedge my bets and write to some companies with a view to getting some business interviews.

I send a total of 69 handwritten letters (the word processor not being readily available at the time) and I receive very few replies. Those which I receive are mostly "Dear John" letters. This is early 1989, and I remember now some of the names of the companies I wrote to. Those heavily involved in business with the USSR would in some cases cease to exist soon after this. Such was the rate of change, with the economy changing, the law, the system struggling.

I also place an advertisement in the bulletin of the then British Soviet Chamber of Commerce, which helped UK companies to do business in the Soviet Union. This produces two responses, where my letters have been largely failing.

One letter is from an Indian company, whose typewriter only has red ink, and is missing the "O" key, which is instead replaced by a neat hole in the paper. They suggest I sell fly spray on a commission-only basis. I will have to pay for my own travel and accommodation. Despite their broken typewriter, and their clearly ridiculous offer, I might actually have taken it, but for the only really positive letter I was to receive.

An American company invites me to an interview at their Surrey office. This is with a forceful American lady, who is also utterly charming. My second interview is with the president (who has flown in from the US) and vice president, based in the UK. The interview is conducted almost entirely in French, German and Russian, with both American executives flitting between languages, almost in the same sentence. It's a gruelling two hours, spent in my grandfather's three-piece suit, which seems today to be tighter and hotter than I remember it being before.

At this time, before my next move is really clear, I am still in south Wales. Following these interviews, I spend a couple of days in my bedsit on the Newport Road, trying to figure out a way to cheat the next part of the application process, a detailed, lengthy "psychometric test" which this American company has asked me to complete.

You cannot cheat these tests; it is uncanny. Oh, I try. One question will be, "What do you enjoy, going to the pub or writing poetry?". Easy! Going to the pub!

Then, and several pages later, "What do you enjoy doing, drinking with friends or kayaking?".

Never having been on a kayak, I could not say that with a clear conscience, but to say drinking again probably looks bad.

Kayaking.

Next page: "If you enjoy kayaking, describe your most interesting kayak experience". Er…

I send off my form, with a forlorn sense of the inevitable.

Imagine my surprise when I receive a letter, asking me for my phone number because they want to discuss the possibility of a job offer. Now I have a problem. Mobile phones do not exist, and my bedsit barely has floors let alone a telephone. I give them a day and time and the number of a red telephone box not far away from the bedsit. Bizarrely, this works, the phone ringing at 16:30 on this dark Tuesday afternoon.

My future boss has a deep American voice, quite authoritative, and he seems to be grilling me again, but he offers me a job at £8,000 per annum. I go silent. Uncharacteristically, he offers several reasons why they cannot offer more to somebody with no experience, no contacts, no training, and whose Russian still needs improvement. Had he known the actual reason for my silence, he could probably have saved a bit of cash, because in that cold phone box that afternoon this student was thinking, *Eight… Thousand… Pounds*. I had never heard of such an enormous sum of money.

They offered me my first proper job, initially in the UK and then based in Russia. They also gave me a small amount of cash to buy a new suit, so that I did not have to wear my grandfather's any longer.

Based in Woking, with its head office near Washington DC, Argus chose to train me in the UK for my coming role, based in their Moscow office. I was to replace somebody who had had an unfortunate brush with Soviet customs, an incident evidently created to order, by means of a briefcase and documents placed inside (whilst the owner of the case was making coffee for what he thought was a regular business meeting). He was pulled to one side as he headed home on a flight later that day, and his visa was annulled.

I knew nothing about this at the time of course, learning about it much later. Nevertheless, it is the Russian way, it was then and it is now. If there is no evidence, make it up seems to be the thinking.

Even as I write, an American man is in a Russian prison right now after a memory stick was suddenly "found" in his jacket. It is astonishing how the Russian authorities can find things so easily.

This company had various offices, in the USA, UK, France and of course, Russia. They had carved a niche for themselves in exporting to the Soviet Union, mainly Russia, and they were one of only a few companies doing this. There was no particular reason for this except that most companies did not really consider the USSR as a market. Argus would visit the various state buying houses and establish their needs, for example, oil and gas equipment, mining and so on, and they would then source suppliers in the West. They had a very useful role because not only were there relatively few Western companies operating in the USSR, there were virtually no private or small enterprises in Moscow that could even travel to the West, let alone visit suppliers and arrange export, installation, support and so on. Argus was something of a pioneer in this business.

The office in Woking is modern, functional, with everybody seated in their own room behind a desk. Except me. I am in the corridor outside the boss's office. That's fine, because I am only to be here a couple of months. Occasionally, the boss has to bring his children into the office, and his little boy stations himself by my desk and stares at me. It is very odd, but of course, Boris finds it hilarious and encourages his little boy to annoy the new guy!

This company is ahead of its time. Even as I write, this seems strange, but in those days, people are still mainly using the fax for fast communication. Telex is still in widespread use also. It will all change very quickly of course, but email is unheard of right now, and certainly not widespread. Mobile phones still stubbornly refuse to be invented.

I actually remember a ski holiday in France with my girlfriend, where I was chatting to a guy in a bar about this new email "phenomenon", and how my girlfriend laughed afterwards, teasing me for talking about this new thing. It seems like a million years ago now.

Yet this company is already on email, albeit a very clunky and cumbersome version compared to today. Between their offices in the UK, Russia and head office in the USA, they communicate via email, each office sending a list of project questions, comments, instructions, once or twice per day. Each item has initials next to it, so you know who is to deal with it.

Sure enough, *"Day One: Project ABCD /End-user 1234-DC."* The last two letters are chilling, so this item is for me:

"Please call company XYZ and ask when they plan to open the L/C."

That's it, and a phone number. I am eager to please, particularly in my new suit and on my first day. I race in to my only task. The phone rings, and a secretary picks up. I deliver my message.

"What's an L/C?" the secretary responds. I have absolutely no idea.

"I shall call back later," is the best I can come up with, and off I go to find out what an L/C is. Perhaps she did the same.

Letter of credit, by the way…

I learn the ropes.

Around this time, my brother marries, and one of the final family events before I left for Moscow was to attend their wedding, which was a truly joyous occasion. Meantime, my sister is pregnant with her first child, our parents' first grandchild. This was a time of change for all of us.

With some excitement and trepidation, I fly to Moscow in June, 1989.

Some months later, my father is diagnosed with pancreatic cancer and given just 12 weeks to live. I return to the UK and the entire family, including my new and first niece, Katy, accompany him to the hospital for his surgery. He was remarkably upbeat, considering, and I remember he unusually told us all we were going to the pub before he was due to go in for surgery.

I mention this not to be morose (he made a full but unusual recovery, living many more years) but because this feels suddenly very real, not the fun of childhood or student life.

RELOCATION TO RUSSIA

My pass to apartment 1223, which curiously gives my middle name as "USA"

My Moscow home is to be suite 1223 in a large building, walking distance from the town centre, with a lounge, a double bedroom, tiny kitchen and bathroom, with a great view of the city and the river. The same building that my friend and I had found by accident when we chanced upon what we believed to be the only bar in the Soviet Union! Plus, there is the use of a car, a big, red estate Volvo, for my sole use except when we have colleagues in town. I still remember that little apartment as if it was yesterday. It was a little oasis of calm, high above the town, a sanctuary, away from the fumes and the queues. There was still not much to do in Moscow in those days, and I missed my friends back home, but this was my chance.

They give me an Amex card to be used for all expenses, including travel and food. This is not only a forward-thinking company in terms of technology, but also ahead of its time in the way it treats its staff. This is all because of one man, Michael.

Michael is one of a few people who really influenced my life. A polyglot with English, Russian, German, French and a little Farsi to his name, he is a superb businessman, and yet at the same time, very kind, empathetic, and incredibly knowledgeable. He is a walking encyclopaedia in fact. He could be pretty cutting when needed, and he taught me how to ask for my first pay rise a year or two into the job, but his criticism was always constructive. I learnt a lot from him.

It takes me a while to pluck up the courage to use the car to get to the office, because I am more used to the metro and the trolleybus, but after a few Sunday practice runs, you could often see a red Volvo, with UK plates, driving along the river, past the Russian federal government building, through town to the office, Pereulok Sadovskikh.

I will go on to meet some very interesting people here in our company, also clients and our host corporation. The secretaries are all employed by a "government agency", let's call it that, so you had to be careful about what you said.

Like many offices at that time, this one has its own kitchen, presided over proudly and elegantly by a lady with an infectious laugh, known as little bird, "Ptichka". When I picture her, I mainly remember a woman with a smile and a razor-sharp wit.

I even have a secretary! Imagine, an actual secretary! Again, she is a really nice, bubbly young lady, Marina, for whom nothing is too much trouble. And when I make regular mistakes in those early days, she will be kind enough to pretend that's a perfectly acceptable way of doing it, but I could try this other way instead.

The gentleman running the host corporation does not seem to have very much to do, and frequently stands at the door of our tiny, smoke-filled office (yes, not great, in hindsight), and he chats. It seems impolite not to listen, but oh, he talks. Towards lunchtime, he retreats to his massive office with a preprandial or three and usually the chatting stops by about 3 o'clock. I will be very surprised if he is still with us.

The only person in this office whom I do not take to is his secretary, Liudmila Georgievna, who seems to consider herself to be more important than anyone else including her boss. Moreover, she makes an unkind comment to a colleague about my surname, not to me of course. From that day, I consider her to be ignorant and boorish.

You will notice how I referred to this woman. Russian names are worth a quick mention. The second part of the name is called "the patronymic". It is generated by the father's first name, so for example, Liudmila, daughter of Georgy would be Liudmila Georgievna. Her brother Ivan would be Ivan Georgevich and so on. But here is the curious thing: the more closely you get to know somebody, let's say Mikhail Ivanovich, the less you use this formal address. So, he becomes Mikhail. Then Misha, and then, when you really get to know him, the name gets longer again, "Mishochka", "Mishundy" or some other absurdity. I have had Russians crying with laughter when this is pointed out to them, but such is the language…

My arrival in Moscow was roughly the same time as a large event, arranged by the then Barry Martin Travel, which brought together UK exporters in the form of a month-long exhibition. It was a very successful event, and I recall one of my first roles was to man our exhibition stand and interpret for our clients and any possible visitors. One of the companies represented was a UK brand, which was established in many industries, but on this particular visit, they were focussing upon their gas bottle production. Jacky was the formidable lady who was representing this company. I found myself thrown in at the deep end, as a couple of men marched onto the stand in their badly pressed suits and thick state-produced spectacles. Immediately, I knew I was in trouble, as they addressed me in Russian and Jacky looked on, waiting for the English version. Well, she waited a while, because these two men were not stopping in their explanation of what they needed, their existing facility, its location and their customer base. I am not sure if that is a summary of what they were saying, it is more of a guess, because whilst they spoke and Jacky waited, I felt my collar becoming tighter, and my body temperature rising. As they droned on and on, I sensed their voices had become somehow disembodied, floating around above my confused head. Finally, the men stopped talking and silence ensued.

It was broken by Jacky, who looked directly at me and said, "Well?"

"I think they want to buy some gas bottles," was all I had.

I would need a while to get into this new role.

1990

These are happy times. I learn quickly, and the company promotes me from USSR representative to CIS director, that being the "Commonwealth of Independent States". Because of course, they are not only in Russia, they have business in Azerbaijan, Kazakhstan and elsewhere.

On a reasonably frequent basis, the American management from the UK or the USA travels in, and I attend meetings with them. Initially, my language lets me down a bit, but with time, it improves and of course so do my business skills.

I drive in early and am the first to put the coffee machine on, which annoys my French colleagues. In hindsight, the coffee I drank at that time was weak and tasteless. I bring in the overnight emails from the UK and the USA. This is my time. Even writing about it now brings it back. I knew what I was doing, preparing the staff meeting, printing out the questions, instructions, over a quiet coffee, tepid, weak, revolting as it was, before the day began.

Both bosses were American, both very different. The UK-based Boris was laconic, dry and sardonic. Great company, but he could be very cutting if he wanted to make a point. I remember being called into his office in Woking for an appraisal, whilst being briefly back in the UK. I hope I am getting a pay rise. I am wrong. Instead, he speaks about the need to have "fire in the belly". I have never forgotten that conversation, and that expression. I get more stuck in after that, less afraid to make mistakes, keen to learn on the job.

Then there was Michael, whom I mentioned a moment ago, polyglot, seasoned businessman and overall owner of the company. Erudite, well read and hands on, Michael didn't generally do anger. He did "disappointed", and that's worse.

Actually, I did hear him angry once. He tended to do his own translations, and he had been working on a document one evening in Moscow. We were all there, which was pretty common, despite it being about 8 o'clock, and after perhaps fifteen pages of doing his translation on a PC, without saving his work, there was a brief power cut, and it was gone. I remember being glad I was at the other end of the office. Still! I learned a new swear word. Every cloud…!

The early 1990s was a famously dangerous period in Russia. The Soviet economy was morphing from a command to a demand structure. Power grabs and bankruptcies were common, as was corruption – and murder. Nowhere was this more noticeable than the capital, where things were moving fast. The big corporations and embassies would be protected from all this because they had central offices, cars and drivers for staff, who would often live on compounds. We had no drivers, no compounds, not even our own office, just a room in someone else's office.

At the first opportunity, as "glasnost" and "perestroika" opened up opportunities, I moved out and stayed in an apartment. It was not particularly nice, but it was bigger than where I was and it was private. This came with drawbacks. There was little security. There suddenly was a big business in steel doors in the early nineties. Generally, a steel door would be installed to protect the small entrances to two apartments, certainly in the case of my future mother-in-law.

She lived in a standard building, each floor with a pair of apartments off each side of the stairs. Her small flat was in one of thousands of eight-storey apartment blocks built under the Soviet regime. They had two bedrooms, a lounge, small bathroom and tiny kitchen. They were functional, not grand, and I think they are now to be pulled down and replaced.

I am now well ensconced in my new Moscow life. I have grown used to it; I have a routine, friends, girlfriend and I have come to know my job pretty well.

Glasnost was the notion that people could start speaking more freely, and perestroika was the idea that certain institutions and even assumptions needed to be rebuilt. It was an exciting time and a scary time.

I would quite often host client dinners when there were exhibitions, for example. The clients did not know at the time, but our trick was usually to speak to the waiter in Russian and ask him to be sure to present the bill to anybody but us at the end. This usually worked. Possibly I should not have shared that, but this was some 30 years ago!

I recall parking the car to take a client to a restaurant near Krasnopresnenskaya (we called it KP), and a young lad approaches the car.

"Hello, would you like your car washed whilst you are in the restaurant?"

"No, but thank you."

"Would you like me to protect it?"

"You're nine."

"But I could protect it."

"It's fine."

"What if it is not when you return?"

We drove off to find a restaurant that was not run by a nine-year-old mafioso wannabe.

This was a bad, bad time. Our mutual friend, Dima, was an interesting guy. We had met him whilst we were students, along with others. I recall him telling us how he avoided military conscription by registering mental health issues. That got him out of the commitment to shovel snow for a year or two, but it came with drawbacks as it turned out. He could not travel, nor could he get into any management positions in a company, so he started his own business.

Dima became pretty successful in his chosen field of videodiscs, but he was swiftly warned off by the mafia.

When the Russian mafia warn you off, you take it seriously. I knew of one colleague in the UK who had become quite successful in importing timber from Russia, and the Russian mafia warned him off. One day, he was in the north of England, and stopped at a service station on the M6 motorway. Two *local* men walked up to him and told him that he needed to take the warning more seriously. They made it clear that he would regret it if he ignored this second warning. He left that business, but what was chilling was that he was at the time driving a hire car. They had clearly full access to his private life and his movements.

The mafia warned Dima off. He did not take it seriously. He was taken to the forest and murdered, and according to the police reports at the time, it was done slowly.

A girl, whom I would later hear about from my girlfriend, Tatiana, was followed from the metro to the lift of her apartment, where a man produced a knife and suggested he remove her finger, or if she preferred, just the ring. His parting comment? "Wear gloves on the metro."

I would not speak English near our apartment and my car was never parked near where we lived. It was all pretty intense.

You may remember the yellow hatbands back when we were students. That was all innocent then, but this of course was different. What was the same was that, somehow, as foreigners, we stood out. Not only because we wore suits and drove foreign hire cars. Not only because we did not have Slavic features, but somehow, there was something in our demeanour that set us apart. We could speak Russian, but we would never be mistaken for a local, not by a Russian. On one occasion, I was asked if I was from the Baltics, which I was pleased about, but in all the years, nobody ever thought I was Russian.

We had to be particularly careful in these years in Russia.

So, Tatiana. I walk into the café "Glazur" with a client from the USA. He loves the menu, and that was not all he loved. The waitress comes to the table, and offers us drinks. She gives us the menu.

When she returns to the table, the client points to various items on the table and asks what they are in Russian. She patiently gives him the Russian words, though the one I remember was the one I did not know, dill, which turns out to be "ukrop" in Russian.

After four times and a dual-language summary of assorted vegetables and herbs, I ask my client to desist. He likes the sound of her voice.

I was struck by her patience, her laughter. People do not laugh in Russia, not publicly.

Some days later, I ask her out. Actually, that is not quite true, because my shyness makes it all a bit awkward. I give her a card, and say that it was lovely to eat in her restaurant, and that I would be delighted to hear from her if she would like to have a coffee some time. And she called me, so, technically, she asked me out! Then, if I cut a long story rather short, we married and had two lovely daughters of whom I am immensely proud, but that is not for now.

I am sitting in that café one afternoon, hanging around to see the waitress. The door bursts open and my colleague comes to my table, distraught. I follow her and we drive to the apartment of her Russian in-laws. My colleague is British, her husband, Russian, or more specifically, Tatar. The apartment has been burgled with the elderly parents of the husband inside. There is blood everywhere. We clean the entire place, because returning to that would have surely compounded the misery of two people whose only crime was to have a British daughter-in-law. Moscow in the nineties was a nasty place.

One minor point about this incident, but one which illustrates the Russian psyche, was with the neighbours outside her in-law's flat. They are congregated in the hallway outside the apartment, whose door is open, and they are discussing the incident. They do not offer help, nor do they ask if everybody is OK. They just gossip.

"How could it happen? Are we safe? I told them to put locks on the door. I always said foreigners are trouble" that kind of thing. My colleague is unimpressed, and tells them so in fluent Russian. The word "Soviet" in Russian literally means counsel, or, to put it another way, "advice". The Russians are famous for dispensing it, on any topic, and that is what they did that day. No help, just gossip and advice.

As an aside, the Russian language has no word for "privacy". (Don't believe anybody who tells you otherwise because all their words connected to "private" do not encompass the concept of privacy.) Why? Because they do not really have the concept. Many is the time I have been in an otherwise empty train carriage, when a local walks up to me and stands right beside me. Private space is not to be found in the biggest country in the world.

With the tendency to offer advice is an assumption that we somehow do not quite get it, that we are less informed, that they have a sort of soul, an angst, which we do not understand, and that their ways and beliefs are simply right, that they know what we do not. I see it even now.

Somewhere wrapped in this mixture of gossip and advice, of a grand assumption, there is a deep but real cruelty in this Russian soul, something that is hard to put a finger on, but it is there. You can see it in Russia's history. Even their national poet, Alexander Pushkin, was shot in a duel. The things that have happened there, and that they do to each other, are often hard to believe. I have seen a little of this myself.

When I lived in Russia, there was a TV programme called *600 Seconds*. It was a round-up of macabre goings on in Moscow, so far as I recall. They would show stabbings and murder scenes, road traffic accidents, and they would show it all in graphic detail. I remember being astonished when the cameraman entered a bathroom to show the viewer what an old woman looked like when she had died in the bathtub but not been found for two months. It was frankly grotesque. There was not a thought for the families or loved ones of the corpses mangled in a car crash, or lying on the floor with a knife in their chest.

Very recently, a Russian newsfeed, to which I no longer subscribe, sent a video, which I viewed before realising that it was showing a young man being eaten by a tiger shark in Egypt. Disturbingly, the Russian woman filming it, and not getting help, was providing commentary as the poor young man cried his final word, "Papa". Before deleting and unsubscribing, I heard her announce, "Now it's eating his remains".

This is normal, in Russia.

The French branch of the company would occasionally send colleagues to Moscow. They used to annoy the Russian staff and me, because they insisted on taking long lunches in the office kitchen, with a bottle of wine. Very civilised of course, but here we always were, waiting to be allowed in for a quick bite before our 14:00 meeting, but they were not to be moved.

I recall on one occasion, we have a French client in town, but our French colleagues are not in Moscow. It was down to Michael and me to drive out to the new Novotel, by the airport, and have dinner with this gentleman. Michael that evening spoke French, English and Russian. People think language just goes into the ear as English and comes out of the mouth as Russian, but it's not quite as simple as that. Some thinking is involved, some kind of neurocomputing. But this was something to behold, and I have only seen it with Michael. He did not use his German that evening because it was not needed. He converses in French with the Parisian, discussing details of business that were themselves complex. The waiter arrives and Michael checks the wine list, asking in Russian if the Merlot is available, whilst turning to me and enquiring in English if I would also like some mineral water, as I am driving.

This was not for show. Oh no, this was just how Michael conversed. I aspired to be like him.

Boris was rather different. He was also highly educated, of course, and a polyglot, plus a thoroughly nice man, very charismatic. A dinner with Boris ran thus:

We're at "The Taganka Café", Boris (the boss), myself, Sasha and Dimtry: four men celebrating a contract in Soviet Russia. We are obliged to pay in roubles for the food and, of course, for the vodka. The conversation flows. Boris orders another shot for each of us.

"I am sorry," responds the waitress. "You have reached the normative quantity of alcohol for local currency consumption as stipulated under the relevant Soviet legislation."

Game over. But no, Boris spots the latent message. "So, if we pay in dollars we can buy what we want, right?" he asks in Russian.

"Of course," she smiles sweetly.

"In that case, we'll take a bottle of Glenfiddich!" exclaims Boris.

Boris would not usually pay in a Russian restaurant for a bottle of Scottish malt whisky, because it is ludicrously priced. Whether he did it to test the system, or whether he had more vodka than he realised, he was committed now!

It duly arrives. We genuinely try to start on the 12-year-old malt but, you know, the Soviet legislation must be based on some kind of science, because we swiftly understand that this evening is over. We settle up and leave. Boris, in remarkably good spirits considering the amount we had just paid for a malt we did not drink, takes that bottle with him, quite rightly.

The rush of cold air on the street hits us like a train. Sasha nobly starts walking towards the metro, whilst Boris, Dimtry and I remain briefly outside the café. I say "walking"… Sasha goes left, bounces off the building and, in a genuine effort to go forwards, oversteers and lurches rapidly to the right, bouncing off a parked car. Undeterred, Sasha compensates once more and bang, hits the building! This is one final attempt to head north, which his body believes to be east. The car is undamaged. Boris takes matters in hand, telling Sasha to join us in a taxi.

In we climb, clutching our bottle of malt.

Now add the motion of the car to the fresh air and, oh yes, the Soviet norm for consumption of local currency vodka, a dram of malt whisky, the smell of stale tobacco and ten-year-old cloth upholstery, and I'm not feeling too good.

I am seated in the middle of the rear seat. To my right is Sasha in his ill-fitting suit, to my left, Boris. Dimtry is seated up front with the taxi driver. I am no expert, but I took the decision that throwing up on the boss would probably be unwise, so I decide it will be more prudent to throw up on Sasha. It's not a great suit, and I can replace it more easily than I can replace Boris' suit, which looks expensive. All this thinking takes place within seconds, but I have one last chance to save that cheap suit. I lunge at the door handle, trying to vomit out of the moving vehicle from the middle of the back seat without being noticed. Sasha is having none of it.

"What are you doing, opening the door, we are moving!" he exclaims.

The taxi driver receives the malt whisky as compensation for his upholstery. Sasha and Dimtry go to Dimtry's apartment, and my boss and I go to the two-room apartment rented by the company, suite 1223, my home, but very much company territory, where incidentally I was taught to cook by Boris some months earlier. I say "taught to cook"… What he actually said, in response to my comment that cooking was not my strong point, was:

"Can you read?"

"Yes," I replied.

"Then you can cook."

Another lifehack, which turned out to be true.

Thursday morning arrives. I open my eyes. To my dismay, I see that I am still wearing my suit from the previous day. I look at the clock, 09:15. That's it. I have been fired, of course, because I should be in the office at 08:00. I lie there pondering what my next move will be in life. What a stupid way to end a career…

"Argh *&)((%&*."

But wait, the voice from the main room can only come from my boss! My career is safe!

But not our heads. Off we go to the office to find Dimtry and Sasha. Dima is reasonably OK. The cook, Galya, has made him a cup of strong, sweet black tea. Sasha goes the other way, known as "the hair of the dog that bit me". Well, it bit him again, and by the time I arrive with Boris, he is physically grey in colour. He is sent home.

Interesting fellow, Sasha. He's a lovely man to work with, but possibly not the most effective. He always wore the same brown suit, one size too small (and vomiting on it did not improve it) a yellow shirt, which I like to think was yellow when he bought it, and crumpled shoes. For client-facing, it didn't really work. He used to sit at his phone, earnestly trying to do deals, which never once materialised, chewing on sunflower seeds as he spoke.

Until one day, he is on the phone and, just before he dials, he hears an extract of a conversation he had had some days before. You see, we always sort of knew we were being listened to. In fact, this became abundantly clear when a new secretary started and, within a few days, told us that she had been asked by the authorities to continue the good reporting work that her predecessor had been engaged in… Those were the rules. We were under scrutiny all the time, with all offices being formally registered with the authorities. Nothing was left to chance. Not that there can have been much to report on except the rather dull comings and goings of office life.

Such as the day the director hides under the desk in his office. Yes, that happened. I know, because I am that director. I had no choice.

I hear the voice of Pavel Ivanovich talking to Liudmila Georgievna at the front of the office, and without thinking, I dive under the desk. Pavel

Ivanovich was more philosopher than businessman. He thought he was a businessman, but rather like Sasha, nothing really ever seemed to get done. I recall strolling through a graveyard with him, chatting about Dostoevsky and the Russian soul. Walking through graveyards seems to be quite the thing with Russians. I think it helps them to think more existentially. So, with Pavel, walking along the pathways between the graves, interesting though the chat was, I couldn't help wondering if this is what my bosses were really paying me to do. There were so many discussions on topics ranging from Pushkin to euthanasia, but rarely about business.

I cannot afford Pavel the time, not today. I have calls to make!

There I am under the desk, in my sharp Kings Road suit, when Pavel's shoes appear, and Pavel is wearing them. He has marched into my office and right round to my desk. Now he is staring at me and wondering why I am under it.

I quickly grab a pencil, which thankfully I find by my head, jump out from my unsuccessful hiding place, saying, "There it is! I've been looking for that for days!"

I don't think my pencil ruse convinces Pavel. I have time to ponder that as we sit in the "aquarium" (just a meeting room with a glass wall) discussing Brecht. That and how many calls I have waiting for me after he leaves.

Of course, sometimes working in Moscow in those days could be dull, and the work itself was probably similar to anywhere else. Although, we did have a feeling that we were doing something a bit unusual, and there was something of a pioneering spirit to all who worked in the company.

Entertaining clients was part and parcel of the job, and we could not really leave them to sit alone in their hotel room all evening. Without the language, and without knowing where they were going, many would simply not venture out, which is why we would take them for lunch or dinner. We wanted them to have good memories of the place and of their experience with our company.

Not all the entertainment came from our table at these corporate dinners. I particularly recall one evening, we were seated in a restaurant, when we became aware of a Russo-Japanese dinner taking place not far from our table. Not unusually, the Russians were doing vodka toasts, and the Japanese were responding with their response toasts. It was really quite civilised when you think about it. There was one problem.

The young Japanese businessman doing the interpreting was doing a great job, translating the various toasts in and out of Russian and Japanese. There were smiles and appreciative nods from both parties around the table as they ate their food and listened to the translation. However, these toasts were coming too fast, and the poor interpreter was unable to eat, because every time he stopped interpreting, somebody on one or other side of the table would spring to their feet and launch into another toast. These were not "here's to our negotiations!", oh no, these toasts would involve somebody relating their childhood, the similarities between Japan and Russia, the importance of business in global understanding and the desire for peace above all else. They were long and involved. Well, eventually, the inevitable happened.

Right there at the table, with a belly full of vodka and absolutely no food whatsoever, the interpreter fell over, right over the table.

We witnessed a lovely demonstration of Russo-Japanese cooperation, as four men grabbed a limb each and carried the interpreter to his room.

Somehow, they managed to continue without him.

SOVIET PHONE CALLS

Making telephone calls may sound innocuous, but whole days could be lost in this way. Why? Because in the Soviet Union, nobody felt the need to work, which is why you could not simply go to a restaurant and have a meal. No, because there would be a sign on the door saying "full", behind which was a deserted room with dining tables and a couple of scruffy waiters having a cigarette. They saw no reason to open the restaurant because it was state-owned. They would be paid just for being there. Besides which, in the era of glasnost, there was no food in the restaurant except spring chicken, which they had just run out of. Oh no, to book a table at a restaurant, you had to go the previous day armed with flowers and a bottle of vodka, depending upon who you ended up speaking to. That was just the way it was, very frustrating, but not for changing.

Anyway, making calls was a problem. Nobody would ever be "there", and nor was there any information about when they might be back, or could they perhaps take a message. A conversation, nine times out of ten would go like this:

Phone rings. Someone answers (they always answered in case it was the boss).

"Allo?"

"Good afternoon, my name is David from a company called…"

But the phone has already gone dead. So, we receive training in how to make calls in Soviet Russia:

Phone rings. Someone answers:

"Allo?"

"Ivan Evgenivich, please!"

"He's not here." Then the phone goes dead.

The technique, as we were literally taught, is to get in the phrase "when will he be back" in the nanosecond before the phone is put down, because quite often this would surprise the recipient of the call into accidentally blurting out a response before hanging up.

Half the time this worked, and half of those times, the response was true. So there was only a 75% chance that the phone call would not be a success.

However, the system had a flaw, as my colleague discovered one Tuesday afternoon.

The telephone rings. Someone answers:

"Allo?"

"Vassily Ivanovich, please!"

"Died last Thursday."

"When will he be back?"

Awkward moment.

What was living in Soviet Russia like? I could say it was great, I could say it was awful, but I can definitely say it was memorable. Just perhaps not for the right reasons.

LIFE'S A BITCH WITH PUPPIES

In August, 1990, I was due a holiday and went with my friend Jon to Thailand.

What a trip that was! We went around the capital, and before heading south to the beaches of Koh Samet, we spent some time up in the jungle areas around Chiang Mai in the north. Whilst there, we took a trek in the mountains and the jungle. A trek so unexplored that the guides got lost on day one. Our entire group also became split up, and I recall at one stage only finding them by seeing some footprints in the dried up riverbed. We had to stay overnight in the jungle because we were all off our route. We built rafts out of bamboo and floated down the river, at one point all being thrown off when we literally went over a waterfall. This sounds more dramatic than it was, and we were laughing until we saw that we were all covered in leeches after falling into the water. (Quick lifehack: do not attempt to pull them off. Use salt or a lighter.)

From there, to conclude our trip, it was to head south to the beaches.

Unfortunately, we had flown to Thailand on Air Kuwait, the cheapest option. On our lovely holiday, two things happened at the same time:

I was bitten by a dog.

Iraq invaded Kuwait.

It may have been in a different order, but that is basically what happened, all within a week.

The problem with being bitten by a dog is that we are on an island, miles from anywhere, and it is night-time. Jon has just graduated as a doctor, and whilst it is good to have him there at this awkward moment, I think he would now be the first to admit that his knowledge on rabies was sketchy.

"It never usually comes up in exams, so I didn't revise it," he says, as I urgently ask him what he knows, blood dripping down my leg. "I do remember that, the closer to your head you are bitten, the quicker rabies sets in. Also, apart from that, you can get tetanus, which gives you lockjaw and is a horrible death."

When I ask how long I have if I have been bitten on the calf, he tells me he hasn't a clue.

Years?

Months?

Minutes?

"Nope. Don't know. Sorry."

We find a doctor, who kindly opens her door when she hears foreign voices. I explain the predicament. Again, this is the actual conversation that takes place when I tell her I have been bitten:

"What colour was the dog?"

"Black."

"Oh, that's OK then, she bit a Japanese businessman a couple of days ago and two children the day before that. That's just a bitch with puppies."

"Could it be a bitch with rabies?" I ventured.

Her face suddenly changes. "You'd better come in."

She cleans me up as best she can, and Jon later gets to practise using various things he's brought in his medical kit, but we are staying in a cheap mud hut on the beach, not really equipped for medical care. Next morning, we cannot immediately leave the island, so wait for a boat to connect to a bus to Bangkok. I recall lying on the beach as we waited, and thinking of this blood coursing through my veins, towards my brain, with absolutely no idea how this was going to end.

Well, here is how it ended. Bangkok, hospital, injections and eight ampoules of serum to be injected into my arm over the course of the next two weeks, with the danger of rabies reducing by 50% on each injection.

Jon would be able to take care of the jabs, but above all, says the doctor, "Keep these ampoules cool!"

Well, how a backpacker on a budget is meant to keep ampoules cool in Thailand is a mystery. I did my best, of course, in our hostel accommodation. We set about finding a route home, but this is where the Iraq Kuwait war comes in, which we had not really factored in.

The long story short is that, after many trips to the airport, to various airline offices, to the embassy and so on, we could not get an alternative for the Air Kuwait flights, which had been cancelled because of Iraq's invasion of Kuwait (a point often forgotten by the way, when people talk of Iraq).

While this chaos was going on, and I was taking medication for rabies, I sent a telex to the Woking office.

It basically said, *"Bitten by dog. Kuwait invaded. Flight cancelled. Non-endorsable. Please help"*.

I am paying by the letter. Brevity is key.

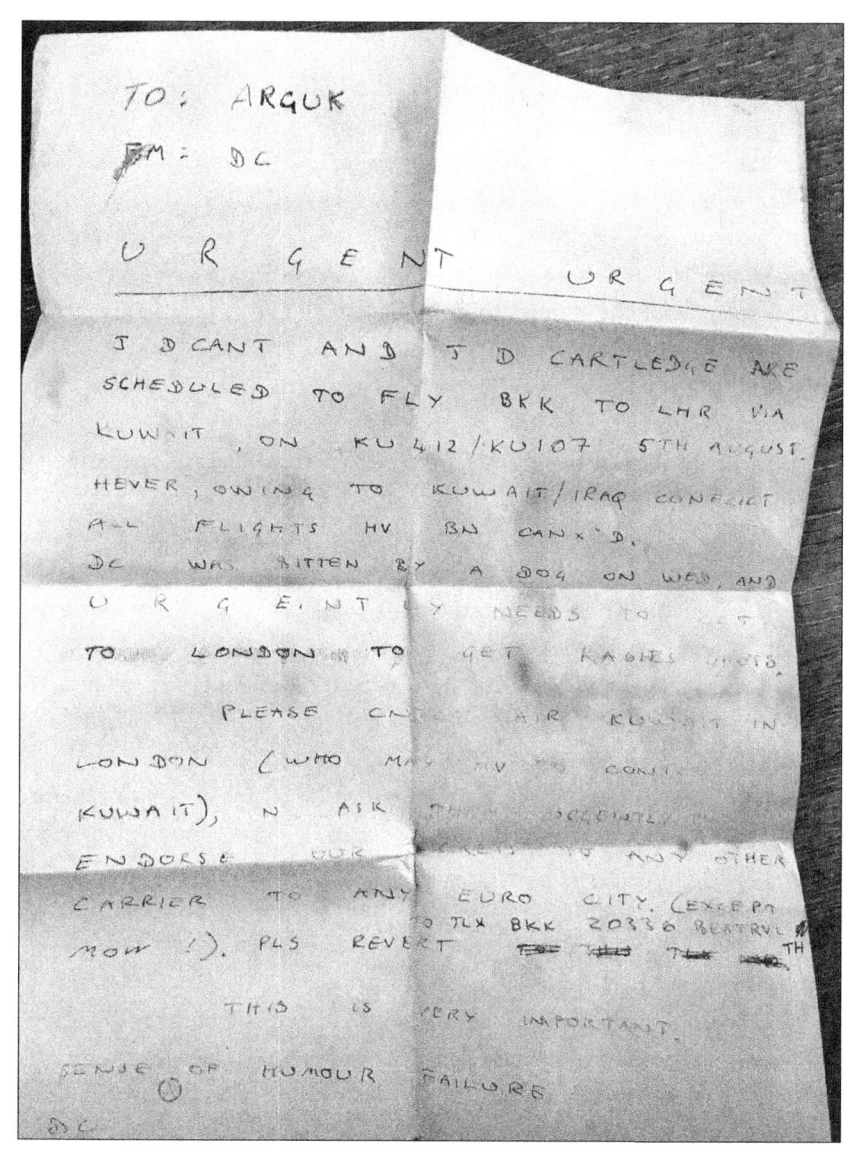

My fax to Judith

I spend a second day in the back of a Thai tuk-tuk (a tray on wheels) trying to sort it out. When I return to the telex office on the Khao San Road, I am relieved to see that Judith has responded. Her telex reads:

"*Ha, ha, ha.*"

Perhaps Judith was also paying by the letter. Anyway, that is the price I paid for always joking around.

A little postscript to this:

The only way we could get back to the UK was to buy a new flight. I did not even own a credit card, but Jon paid on his so I could pay him back. What was then the cheapest airline and route? Aeroflot via Moscow. I had actually only just left Moscow a couple of weeks earlier, but so be it.

By coincidence, my then girlfriend, Tatiana, was leaving that morning for Sri Lanka. It was just a few days, along with colleagues connected to her work: a treat from the restaurant. I called her briefly from the airport and wished her luck. I had not slept because we'd only had plastic and metal chairs all night, so I was relieved to arrive in London for a few days before returning to Moscow and work.

I recall getting into a minicab to go to the office in Woking, and chatting as I generally do. I told the driver about my encounter with a dog in Thailand. For some reason, it seemed that he thought he might catch rabies by speaking to me, so by the time we arrived the driver was actually driving whilst climbing halfway up his car door, with as little interaction with the interior of his vehicle as possible. He had shifted sideways to do this and was trying to keep as far away as possible. I explained to him that I was not planning to bite him and that talking was not a known form of spreading rabies, but he was having none of it. I did not tip.

At the Royal Hospital for Tropical Diseases, a young doctor listens to my tale as she looks at my rather damp remaining ampoules, hauled around the world over the last few days. As her foot presses the pedal bin, and my ampoules are despatched, to my dismay, into the bin, she tells me her friend Jon had just been in Thailand; they had studied together.

"Did you study rabies?" I ask.

"To be honest, it never comes up, so nobody bothers," she responds.

I leave with my new ampoules and it is much easier to keep ampoules cool in London than in Bangkok.

Bizarrely, upon arrival in Moscow, I discover that Tatiana has been bitten by a monkey on the beach. I did the decent thing and gave her my last ampoule. I think I can now safely say I avoided rabies and so did she.

1991: RUSSIAN TRAFFIC POLICE

A Tuesday night, early February, and I am in my car. I have been in the office and it is late. I am driving home by the most delightful part of central Moscow known as Patriarch's Ponds. So far, all is normal.

Such is the Russian penchant for controlling everything that their "passport" is actually not a passport at all. It is an identity card, which they call a passport. If you actually want to pass through a port, you need a "travel passport" (or what you and I would call a passport). This control applies at this time to pretty much everything.

Take for example, tourism. You can only change so much cash, and you cannot change it back. You must stay in their limited choice of official hotels and you do not know which hotel has been allocated to you until the transfer bus pulls up. It is the same with cars. Most cars have a standard black-and-white number plate, all registered of course. Again, this is perfectly normal; cars must be registered and drivers must possess a licence.

Of course, it is different for foreigners. Why would it not be in this nosey and corrupt world that was and may soon again be the Soviet Union?

The diplomats have red number plates; the business community and all rental cars have yellow plates. I suspect this allowed the traffic police to ignore the red plates, and to stop yellow plates if they needed quick cash for a holiday or a birthday present. I have a foreign car with yellow number plates, which attracts attention from the police. Not because I am doing anything wrong, but because, well, just because.

Anyway, the police have the power and the radios, and we have the powerful foreign cars, so it's fair. There is a temptation to buy your way out of a problem, but I didn't ever do that. No, really. It seemed degrading to me and to the police officer, even if it was what he wanted.

One summer, I am driving too fast from the countryside into town in our company "Volga", and I am pulled over by a young policeman. I am made to leave the vehicle and climb up into his kiosk overlooking the road, whereupon he issues me with a fine. This involves a lot of paperwork and a lot of time. During this process, his colleague, considerably older, considerably larger, waddles across the road and clambers laboriously up the steps to enquire about what was going on. The young officer explains that he is issuing the foreigner with a fine because he has been speeding.

"Idiot," responds the older man. "He's a foreigner. You should have taken a bribe!"

I really didn't get involved in bribes anyway. I always had a feeling that if I tried the old: "Maybe there's another way of resolving this, just between us?" conversation, I would immediately be against a wall, frisked, whilst a SWAT team of paratroopers descended on ropes from helicopters. No, not for me. I left that to people who knew how to bribe.

On that topic though, I did try to influence somebody once. We represented a big cosmetics company.

I have a potential buyer from Turkmenistan, a big chap, with a suit two sizes too small for him. He perspires a lot and wheezes, but he is from the Ministry of Trade in Ashgabat, and I need to impress him. I take him to the Night Flight club in the centre, which you may have heard of. If not, read on because it will come up again! He has a lovely time and the next morning, his driver arrives in the official car, also a Volga.

I still recall filling up this large gentleman's vehicle. As he sweats and gazes on approvingly, I load him up with lettuce face mask, cucumber rub, strawberry lip salve and aftershave balm with essence of Madagascar palms.

I shall get this guy to introduce us to the Turkmen market. We will be in meetings before you know it, and this is going to be big.

I watch in satisfaction, give myself a mental pat on the back as he heaves his large frame into the back seat, and the vehicle, weighed down by him and an absurd amount of jojoba oil, trundles off towards the airport.

I will never see him again.

I mention "company Volga", and this is because in some frustration at being constantly stopped by the police for driving a foreign car, I sent our driver, Kostya (yes, we have a company driver now, that's how posh we have become) to the town of Nizhny Novgorod, where those cars were made. With him was a bag, stuffed full of roubles. He returned with what he described as "the least bad vehicle at the factory". This car was at the lower end of the automotive food chain, with very limited technology.

That did have a plus side, because not much could go wrong. There was no onboard computer, no GPS, no airbags, no air con, no anything really. It just clunked along, popping its linkages from time to time. We named her Fifi. It doesn't matter here what the first two letters stood for, but the last two were "farm implement". Despite Fifi being a really bad car, there was one attempt to steal it. Such was the amount of theft in nineties Moscow, that we had got into the habit of putting a metal steering lock on the steering wheel at night. Seated in the "aquarium" for a meeting, I am interrupted by Kostya, who suggests I go check on Fifi.

Fifi has her side window smashed. On the passenger seat lies the metal steering lock, still fully intact. The would-be thieves instead had simply sawn off 10 cm of the steering wheel itself (that's how bad it was), and released the wheel. They failed to hot-wire the car for one simple reason. The car already had such problems starting that Kostya had taped a coin under the dashboard, which connected two wires, which otherwise were not long enough. This is fairly typical of Soviet manufacturing. New cars were not really going to work until the owner had fixed all the problems, such as wires being too short or missing components. As the thieves had fiddled around with the steering wheel, the coin had dropped to the floor, severing the connection, and the thieves gave up.

Fifi was saved by her own utter uselessness.

Tuesday night, and right now I am not in a Volga and I am not speeding. I am in a Mitsubishi, I have yellow number plates and yes, I stick out like a foreigner.

A police officer emerges as if from the ground. I lower my window. He salutes, as is the way. A brief conversation ensues, in Russian, during which he explains, routine check. I show my documents, we have a brief discussion about why I am in the Soviet Union, and he salutes and sends me on my way.

So that's good, right?

Wrong.

I broke my own rule. Never speak Russian to anybody wearing a uniform.

Thursday morning. I wake up later than I should have. The alarm has not gone off. I dress as quickly as I can and head down to the car. I have a thought. There is a road behind the "White House", as the locals call the Russian Federation parliament building. It would be a lot quicker. I would not look like an idiot when I arrive later than staff. I could never understand why the boss in Russia always arrived later than the staff. It seemed to me I should arrive early, to set an example, so that is what I did every morning. I always arrived so early that I could make the rancid, weak coffee for the French colleagues. Sorry, Michel.

It's Thursday morning. I am late, and the only problem with the road behind the White House is the sign that says "No entry". Still, it's a couple of minutes and what are the chances of being seen?

By the way, the Russian word for the "No entry" sign is "Kirpich", which literally means "brick". Imagine my confusion as I dropped a girl home and she explained that the fastest way back for me is to keep going straight at the lights and ignore the brick at the end of the road. I had no idea.

Anyway, Thursday morning.

I drive, and at the junction, I do not turn right, then left and left again, I go straight on. Not fast, that would attract attention, but slowly and respectfully. Within seconds, a traffic officer appears. Unbelievable. I lower the window, he salutes, requests my documents, as always. I have been in such a hurry to get to work that I forgot to bring my licence (never leave items like this in the car because there are frequent break-ins). He starts a conversation, and I naturally, even instinctively say, "I am so sorry, I do not speak Russian".

You know the rest. Why does the same officer work on the Thursday, and how can he possibly remember me? But he does. I am forced to hand him my passport as a "hostage" and return to my apartment to get my licence. I then go back to him to receive my passport, show my licence, and pick up a document to be used to pay the fine. I could not have arrived at the office later than I did!

One last traffic police story. I slightly turn left where it is slightly illegal. I slightly ignore the traffic policeman who emerges, goodness knows from where, as always. I drive on. My passenger is nervous. I am nervous, but I drive fast. However, I forgot that they have the radios.

"Red Mitsubishi, stop on the right" comes a voice from a police car (where do they all come from?). I stop and yes, I am caught yet again. At least this time, I did not personally know the police officer! I was, by now, quite well known in all the wrong circles.

My relationship with traffic police generally reached a new low when I drove my car down the steps of a park to take a shortcut. I did it carefully of course, so as not to wreck the suspension.

It's a bit of a long story, how it came to be that I did this, but at the time I'd just had enough of being stopped and being expected to "settle this somehow" when I had done nothing wrong. I had thought there was a gate at the end of the park and I could get out at the other end. I was mistaken. In fact, I was mistaken about cars using the road in the park at all. I just assumed that because I had seen other cars (in hindsight not very often), then it must be OK. Anyway, OK, I had done something wrong. I get to the locked gates, and notice in my mirror the headlights of an approaching vehicle. To my dismay, I then see that it has a light on the roof, and stripes, and a sign saying "Police". To my right, I see the municipal steps that lead down and out of the park. They are broad, and although they are long, they don't look too deep. I don't think about it for long because the car is closing in on me. I get to the top and don't stop, I just clunk down carefully, all the time looking in the mirror and seeing with relief that the headlights of the car behind remain at the top. Once at the bottom, I had to get back fast so that their colleagues could not find me, so I put my foot down.

OK, I did two things wrong.

Many is the time I walked past those steps years later and wondered, what if that hadn't worked? How could I possibly have explained that to the Russian police who had been behind me but did not venture down the steps?

Michael and Boris did not know about any of this, by the way. I like to think of them reading this for the first time, but they're miles away in America!

Only one traffic police officer was nice to me in all the years. Of course, they had no reason to be nice to me. I heard tales of people being stopped, paying up and then being given a blue light escort across town, but of course I did not pay those "fees." However, on one occasion, there was a spontaneous act of kindness from one of these people. I had a meeting with somebody in the evening, and despite it being -20 degrees outside, we had arranged to meet on the street near Paveletsky Station. I had forgotten to bring my fur hat, which was a serious error. After twenty minutes of waiting, I decided to return home. I do not recall whom I was meant to meet, but I walked back to the car and jumped in, lights on, engine, heating.

Within seconds of setting off, I was pulled over for crossing a white line whilst driving around the corner of the station. However, as I wound down my window (yes, remember winding down windows?), and the officer saluted me, all I could say to him was that my ears were burning. The pain was intense, as circulation returned and the cold ebbed away. It was severe. As if suddenly forgetting that he had planned to issue me with a fine, he beckoned me to leave the car, he took off his gloves and he massaged my ears until the circulation seemed to return to normal. They are nice guys deep down.

Business was something I had to learn, and of course, Michael and Boris were great teachers. They were patient. I was eager, especially since the "fire in the belly" comment.

The lessons were often difficult. I recall when we took a stand at a trade fair outside of Moscow, in a small town called Podolsk. It was a railway-themed event, and our client from the USA was promoting a technology which made a modular integrated unit, interchangeable from road to rail. It was ahead of its time, at least in Russia. In hindsight, it would have needed goodness knows how many licences and quality tests, but it was good technology. The problem was that you couldn't transport the product. A train carriage is too big to place on a small stand, so our client had a video, which he played on a loop.

For four days.

Then there was our client in pharmaceuticals. I shall call him John, though that is not his real name. John was important to our company or rather, his corporation was. They were a client and Michael and Boris had big ideas, but John was a bit complicated. I recall his first visit. He had an annoying voice and, frankly, an irritating face. From that first trip to Moscow, and in the 30 years since, he is the most irksome man I have ever met. Everything was apparently "the same as China". He had this worked out on the drive from the airport to his hotel. He became a regular visitor, unfortunately.

This client was from a division of the "mother ship", a massive chemicals company. There were several individuals, whom we dealt with: a tall Dutchman, a great guy with a name that reminded you of swashbuckling explorers, another, a hard-nosed New Yorker who constantly chewed gum, which he would leave stuck to a filing cabinet for later use, and "John" from the UK. As a fairly small part of our company, whilst I enjoyed company perks like apartment, car and Amex card, I also had to accept that with this came responsibility. This is why I spent more time waiting for clients at the airport than I care to remember. Oh, the smell of Soviet tobacco…

HIGH-PRESSURE ENVIRONMENT

One of the other parts of this was dealing with clients. That meant taking them to dinner. Yes, it could be fun, if they were nice people.

It also involved travelling with them. Again, that is OK if they are good people, but could be carpet chewingly awful if they were "John" from that particular client company.

Then there was the owner of the client company from the USA, whom we referred to as JF. He was an elderly gentleman, who came to Moscow with his wife on one occasion, which remains etched on my brain.

In addition to JF and his wife, both my immediate bosses were in town, Boris and Michael. That was how important this client was to our company.

You may recall that my company took pity on me at the interview, and in addition to a job, they gave me a small amount of cash to "stop wearing my grandfather's suit". Hence, two new suits followed. I would wear one of these two new suits to meetings in Moscow. I remember the light grey suit I was wearing that day, as Michael invited his most important client to dinner later at the "World Trade Center" (as it was called), just west of central Moscow. In this centre were the hotel, a business tower and a residential block. This was the block where I lived. Strung between these three large buildings were vast malls and corridors, with various shops and a couple of restaurants. Anyway, dinner was duly booked in one of these restaurants, and a rather formal occasion ensued.

I was seated to the right of JF's wife. Opposite JF was my ultimate boss, Michael, and to JF's left was Boris, my other boss.

A word on this light grey suit and please keep in mind, we are just coming out of the 1980s. In addition to its colour, it also had improbably wide lapels. There is a reason I remember this.

Small talk and aperitifs ensue. A waiter takes our order. Michael is not telling the waiter to give the bill to the guy opposite, as we so often did. This guy is too important. We shall foot the bill. The first course arrives. Talk turns to business. I am largely out of my depth, which is almost certainly why Michael and Boris have not seated me near JF. I chat to JF's wife. She is not great company, but she probably thinks the same about me. My principal aim here is not to say or do anything stupid. The pressure was intense. I could sense the piercing glare of my boss as he scrutinised me, trying to make sure I was not embarrassing the company, whilst at the same time talking to JF. My bosses had this knack of speaking different languages at the same time round a table, keeping an eye on me and chatting with the client.

The second course arrives, and I have ordered the chicken Kyiv. I have not ordered it since.

It was an error of judgement. I mentioned the intense pressure around the table, some of it imagined, some real, as we negotiated our way through the meal and (probably) some high-level discussion about next steps, to which I was not party because I was talking to JF's wife about brass rubbing in Winchester Cathedral.

However, the pressure was nothing, compared to what was upon my plate; hot chicken breast and inside, steaming hot, pungent garlic sauce. My fork descends towards the cutlet, knife poised. The conversation continues, brass rubbing, exclusive distributorship, Rioja, winter getaways, contract terms, medieval traditions, mineral water. My fork and knife simultaneously pierce the chicken.

The knife plunges into the high-pressure chicken.

Then it happens.

You may recall when we went for dinner, and I sensed, when we got in the taxi, that I was feeling sick. I had a choice: be sick to my left, where my boss was seated, or throw up on Sasha, to my right. This was similar.

As fork and knife pierce the outer, crumbed surface of the food, then into the hot, dark chamber created by the chef and full of hot sauce, and conversation murmurs in the background, excursions, confidentiality agreement, bread rolls… a funny thing happens.

The pressure inside the chicken is so intense, that no sooner has the cold metal pierced it, than a high-pressure jet of garlic sauce from within is released, and a stream of yellow and strong-smelling, sticky sauce shoots up and heads for us.

This is instantaneous, but when I remember it, it happens in slow motion. I actually see the stream of yellow sauce as it rises furiously from the plate. I see the faces and I can hear myself saying "noooooo".

Where is it going? This time, unlike in the taxi, I have no choice. Will it hit Michael opposite? Please no. Me? JF's wife, seated beside me? That would be awful. Even hitting Boris would be preferable to the client or the client's wife. This is where we would take a commercial break if this were television.

I am not going to do that, though. What I thought might be interesting would be to relate how, some years later, I would find myself working in the meat industry for a colleague and friend, and being driven around Poland in a fur-upholstered Cadillac by a local vegan, visiting abattoirs on business.

Or the time I was in a Russian helicopter with Sergei and the girl beside me felt sick.

However, all of this would merely waste time and, let's face it, we left JF and his wife in a potentially sticky situation.

The uncertainty.

The garlic sauce heading upwards.

The possibility of a career ended.

The notion that a man's career could be decided by the trajectory of garlic sauce.

But this is not television, and we must return to our hapless diners.

The landing spot of the garlic sauce?

JF?

Michael?

Boris?

JF's wife?

In my mind, the sauce is developing a personality and drive all of its own. It is planning something, and deliberately keeping its plan as secretive as possible whilst we can only gasp and stare.

OK.

It hits me.

More accurately, my 1980s' wide lapel grey turns to yellow. Murmur turns to silence, dry turns to wet and wool turns to garlic.

What do I feel? I know I am probably going to be fired (I was not, largely because JF seems oblivious), but I felt relief that I was the target of the vindictive, evil sauce.

I was lucky that I lived in that same building, otherwise I would have worn garlic sauce for the rest of the evening.

Nobody needs that pressure.

John, from the UK branch of this corporation, is here again in Moscow, and this time, we are scheduled to visit a factory in Ukraine, in the town of Ladyzhin.

The town is grey, the buildings are grey, the clothes, grey. Everything is grey. It was a three-day trip. One might expect that the three days will be spent touring the factory and discussing business, but this is Soviet Russia.

The three days are spent in a room on the third floor, with the insufferable John and some Soviet directors who have not enough to do. They also have no deodorant budget. In the middle of the table is a document called a "Protocol of Intent". How I came to despise that piece of paper.

We do not see the factory. We do not discuss business. We discuss the discussion. Three days, and all that time in one room, looking at one document. So intent were our Soviet hosts upon receiving this signed document, that we scrutinise every word, every piece of punctuation – endlessly. At the end of the day, they take us to our hostel, each room with its single bed, and each floor with a bathroom in the corridor. In the evenings, we try to negotiate the room that says "restaurant" on a door which is permanently locked.

On day three, we understand there will be no business here. We are in danger of missing our flight back to Moscow. We sign the document, which outlines what we should be discussing and who is responsible for what.

What was on the last line of this document?

"*This document is a Protocol of Intent only with no legal force.*"

I mentioned that Michael taught me how to negotiate a pay rise, after I had been in the job a year or so.

We are driving along, I broach the subject rather nervously and he asks me to elaborate. I explain that I have certain costs, obligations, that I would like to save up to buy an apartment and so on.

"Let me stop you there, David," Michael says, not unkindly. "I am not prepared to give you a pay rise because you want to buy a property. Ask for a pay rise because you are committed, you are a fast learner and an important part of the team. So yes, you should have a pay rise, just not because of the apartment."

I came to understand the nature of meetings in Soviet Russia. They include dusty afternoons in large buildings, talking contracts and payment terms. Vyacheslav Sergeevich lights a cigarette. Slowly, the smoke curls up towards the stained ceiling. Vyacheslav equally slowly, deliberately, places the lighter onto the centre of the table in front of us.

On the lighter, always, was the name of our competitor.

They were smart, these guys, but they were working in a strict regime. Everything was controlled, as is the way in Russia, even now – particularly now. I don't think they understood that we were smart also.

Author in Ladaland, Moscow 1990

Meetings could extend into days, even weeks, as we discussed specifications, delivery times, cost, installation, insurance, packaging, internationally agreed delivery "Incoterms" and spare parts. All this time, on both sides of the table, we knew exactly where we were heading, because it was the same every time. We were heading towards the final chat.

The chat was a tradition, a game, where both sides knew the result before the start of the match.

They would win.

We would win.

The final chat was always about discount. We had a remarkably simple system in this company. We were issued with "daytimers", diaries with inserts as you requested, calendars, schedules, notes pages, all sorts of useful pages customised to your style, but we all had one extra piece of paper, taped to the inside cover, and in full view of the guys across the table. Just 1 centimetre in height and 10 centimetres long with the letters A to J, and as an aide memoire, the numbers 1 to 10.

Every proposal we did had a code after the name. AE was 15. BG was 27. Per cent, it was the markup. In a dusty, smoke-filled room, we were armed and given full power to negotiate. This was a simple system, but curiously, the Russians never cracked it.

This was the lesson of life, a lesson about trust.

The discount chat starts.

The Russians pretend it is an offhand, almost unimportant additional request.

We pretend we are shocked at the sudden request for a discount.

The game has started. What ensues is not poetic but sequential, predictable, so long as both sides maintain the pretence.

The explanation, the threat, the plea, the compromise, the give and the take.

One smoky, Tuesday afternoon, we shake hands on 8% discount.

My daytimer says AE.

They won.

Moreover, so did I.

Drinking was an issue in those days. At every trade fair there was a bar, and each stand had another bar. At 10:00 in the morning, downtrodden men would walk in with their crumpled brown suits and their crumpled blue shoes to negotiate on behalf of their state employers, not because they would receive a bonus or even recognition, but because if they did not get the deal they would end up somewhere else counting trolleys or stacking shelves. This way, they got to speak to foreign businessmen, "negotiate" (ahem) and occasionally get free samples.

"Good morning, Viktor Borisovich," Michael would say, as the figure approached. "Ah, Ivan Gennadivich, how good to see you!" They never, ever worked alone. The entire system was based upon lack of trust. Much like today. We appear to have come full circle.

Michael remembered their names always. Lord knows how. He remembered their spouse's name, their kids' and even their pets' names. He had a memory that surely no human could possibly have.

On the other hand, did he have a special page in his daytimer?

Driving a foreign car in Moscow was a hazard because the traffic police regarded you as a meal ticket (which probably gave rise to a desire to drive down steps to get away from them), but also because you could get involved in an accident.

The first bump I was involved in was on the way to work. It was all rather odd.

A lorry moves away at the lights on the embankment. I am a couple of cars behind, but something happens. The car in front hits the truck, and I then hit the white car. No particular damage and nobody is hurt in this 4 mph crash. The lady in the white car and I agree the fault lies with the lorry driver, but the lady then talks to the lorry driver and drives off. Now I have a problem, a foreigner in central Moscow in a foreign car, trying to win an argument with a lorry driver and a police officer. The policeman arrives and says it's my fault because I am the driver behind.

I counter: "That's absurd." The lorry stopped for no reason and the woman in the white car agrees it's his fault!

"What woman? What white car?"

I suspect the police officer thought this might have had an outcome that would keep him happier, but that was not going to happen, not only because I don't do bribes, but because at this very moment, Valerii appears, our office landlord's driver. He sorts everything, and is *very specific* as he tells the lorry driver to sign a piece of paper.

"No objections."

Before we leave the scene, Valerii ensures he has a document to stop subsequent problems. It is a good lesson. Every man for himself, avoid responsibility and assume they will try to have a go at you a second time. Then you'll be OK.

On another occasion again, in the centre of Moscow, I was driving along when a car appeared out of a side street onto my main road. I went straight into it.

Here we are, the male driver and female passenger of the other car, and myself, both cars slightly damaged, nobody hurt. Suddenly, a whole bunch of Georgians appear, goodness knows from where, to offer their opinions.

Their opinion, every one of them, is that it is the Russian guy's fault, which it clearly was, because he hadn't stopped at a stop sign, but his passenger becomes animated.

"Just hold on one second," she remonstrates. "Look how long it took for the foreign bloke to stop! He was going too fast!"

She had no evidence, no tyre tracks, no witnesses, nothing, but oh, she was confident. The guy admits responsibility, I get a piece of paper saying "no objections" and we go on our way, including the Georgians.

Another lesson learned. Never mess with a Russian woman!

After working a couple of years for the company, I receive a bonus. This is new to me. Salaries are not high, but expenses are included, and there is now this bonus of ten thousand dollars. It's not far off what I earned in my first year.

I do not really "need" this amount of cash. I already purchased a flat in London, which I am renting out. What I need, or rather, what my family need, is a "dacha".

A dacha is a small dwelling outside of town. Most Russians lived at that time in small apartments. My mother-in-law's kitchen was nine square metres, and a balcony used for storage. In the winter, they would store the summer clothes in a roof space above the flat (yes, Russian apartments have lofts) and vice versa in the summer. They were cramped.

To counter this, many have a smallholding in the countryside, a dacha, where they have more space and a plot to grow vegetables. I ask if the bonus can come in the form of a dacha for my mother-in-law. This proves tricky, not because there is a problem from Michael or Boris, but because we cannot find a dacha in our price range, unless they are dilapidated. We kiss a lot of frogs on that search in every town outside of Moscow, as far as Zagorsk.

We finally find one, half brick and half timber, perfect for our needs. It needs work, and the location is not ideal, but it is very pleasant. Two rooms below, and upstairs, a large room with two little eaves rooms to the side. No toilet, that was outside. No, the only problem was to pay for it without losing the money. This is the nineties. I do not trust the vendor and he does not trust the purchaser. We pull it off by going through a third party, and become proud owners of a smallholding of five hundred square metres of land.

This was one of the best decisions we could have ever made. It gave Rita a place to go, to relax and even to spend the summers. It gave our children a place to learn to be children, to pet the goats and have lazy summer afternoons.

I was not there often, but enjoyed my stays. Apart from the visits to the outdoor toilet, which still give me nightmares. We did a lot of work to it, and made it a real home from home. It is one of the things that I am proud of. Our family were happy there.

Another thing that changes is that we can finally leave the previous office and find something bigger, more suited to the relatively free conditions and opportunities. We settle upon a rather tired-looking place north of Belorussky, reasonably central, and with parking. It needs full refurbishment. It has 14 rooms, plus a larger room, which we will use as a kitchen, an entrance hallway, and a room with a glass wall, which I have mentioned, the "aquarium", to be used for meetings.

Most intriguingly, it has 14 toilets and 14 showers, because this has been a hotel wing for the students of the "Higher Party School", basically budding communists. I often wondered what it must have been like to arrive there from some faraway Russian region, to study communism and then return to some town, later to become a party boss. Where did these people go when it all ended?

The refurbishment was fraught. Tom, originally from California, working out of the Rockville office, kindly agrees to fly over to oversee everything. He is thorough. He finds contractors, and ensures that they will not paint over the sockets, but remove them before painting, all the things that will make a difference. The contractor to build and fit the kitchen came over from the UK, a nice guy by the name of Dave. It must have been an interesting gig for him, working in Moscow with two Russian assistants, whom he could not understand! But it worked, and finally, we had a refurbished office suite with meeting rooms and two bedrooms, a brand-new kitchen with UK sockets throughout. One curious nuance was that Dave ran out of silver carpet strips for the doorways, so mine had a gold one. The locals assumed this was because I was director. It was not. It was because Dave could not count.

We really could work from this place. We could take on staff, and spread out, we could host our colleagues from the UK and USA, and we could conduct several meetings at the same time in separate rooms. It was a whole new experience compared to the smoky, little room we had in the previous place.

I was a very hard worker; I wanted to make an impact. Despite being only in my twenties, I would often be found in the office late evening, or weekends. To be perfectly honest, Moscow then was not what it would later become. There was not that much to do at that time!

One evening, I am standing in the office kitchen, making a cup of tea, whilst finishing up some work. From outside, there is a loud crash in the dark. I recall, quite vividly, thinking, *That wouldn't be my rented Audi of course?*

I part the curtain, and four floors below, see my Audi. In its back seat is a little red Lada. I run downstairs before the perpetrator could vanish. I need not have bothered. When I arrive, the Lada driver is staring in front of him, still holding the steering wheel, and I have a feeling he may have thought he was still driving. He is conscious, just bleary, and the windows are steamed up.

From nowhere, the obligatory crowd of Georgians appear to dispense views on what has happened and what should happen next. It is all pretty obvious.

It turns out that he is an off-duty fire officer, has been celebrating something or other, and perhaps unwisely, borrowed his friend's Lada to drive back to the fire station, just a minute's walk from our office. He almost made it. Whether he planned to sleep it off, pick up his own car, or report for a shift, I have no idea, but he ended up with his car firmly planted into the rear end of mine. The police arrive and take him away, and later they remove the Lada from my car's rear seat. Additionally, the Georgians vanished!

Two days later, Sunday, I am again in the office when the doorbell rings. I open it and standing in front of me is a bald man.

"Do you have a white Audi?" he asks.

"Most of one, yes," I reply, thinking I am hilarious, but my attempt at humour was misplaced. This man is upset. I change my tone. I have no intention of making him feel bad. I recognise the fireman from the red Lada, but when I last saw him, he was not bald.

"I crashed into your car on Friday. Of all the cars to crash into, it had to be an 'inomarka'." (This is the term the Russians then used for a foreign marque.) "I have lost my job and my wife has had enough. I spent Friday night in a cell and they shaved and showered me. I am facing court. I need to know what you are going to do to me."

I am stunned. I don't know what to say. This is not an act. He is trembling; he is scared. I tell him that I am not going to do anything to him at all, that it is covered by insurance, and he could take that worry off his list. Just to go and look after himself. The gratitude upon his face as he left made me feel awful. Yes, stupid, but I was not going to add to his misery. The worst thing you can do when somebody is feeling bad is to judge them or tell them they need help. Just be kind. It's so easy to be kind.

The Audi 100 was repaired and it came back. To this day, I would love to own one. This of course was rented, as were all company cars, since we dumped the blue Volvo in the forest outside Moscow some years previously. We had a red Volvo with UK plates, and we rented cars when required. I like to think the blue Volvo is still there, a kind of Harry Potter ending, but a Volvo instead of a Ford Anglia. Far more practical for the Russian winters.

Yes, the rented Audi attracted a little attention, but it was not ostentatious. Russians just like cars. They assumed that the guy behind the wheel was a foreigner, and therefore an idiot who spoke no Russian, but I was not; I was a foreigner, and an idiot who spoke bad Russian! I drove as I would drive anywhere else, by the rules, and if somebody cut me up badly or undertook me, they would get the same blast of the horn as any driver would give.

One incident stands out, because in nineties' Moscow, I did a really stupid thing that could have got me killed.

I turn right from Revolution Square onto Gorky Street, now called Tverskaya. There are three lanes north, three south. I am driving north, away from the Kremlin. To my slight but not complete surprise, a car is approaching me on the northbound *side*, but heading *south*, basically using the oncoming fast lane to get past slow traffic. It was a very stupid idea. A bit like when I watched a man using a cigarette lighter in the winter to thaw out his car's petrol cap…

It's a Volga taxi, yellow in colour. My job in his view, as a foreigner, in a foreign car in his country, is to let him merge back into the southbound flow, where some other poor soul will also have to yield to allow him to do so, but that does not happen. Here's the stupid thing that I did.

Nobody lets him in, and I do not change lanes or reduce speed. I head straight for him. He is forced to stop, as am I. I am irritated by this man, and I am in no hurry. He wants to keep driving in the wrong lane and in the wrong direction, but I am not in the mood.

It's a stand-off. In 1990s' Moscow, this was unwise. There were guns and many stories about people who got in a taxi and were never seen again. Nevertheless, here we are, with the Moscow traffic slowing down to look and in some surprise seeing that there has been no bump; the vehicles are half a metre apart.

The taxi driver lights a cigarette.

I light a cigarette.

He smokes it and throws it out of the window.

I do the same.

Several minutes more pass. The traffic continues to edge past, the other drivers continue to stare, and we continue to stare at each other across the dashboards. He is as stubborn as I am, but he will have more explaining to do if the police appear.

Another cigarette, a total of 15 minutes wasting time. He concedes, and starts to push his way back into the traffic, which I watch, not moving my car. As his car draws level with mine, that was the moment I wondered if he had a gun. He did not. Whilst I lived to tell the tale, life was cheap in nineties' Moscow and I later realised that I had been unwise.

Poor Tatiana would sometimes remind me that these were not safe times. It was common to hitchhike in Moscow in those days. We did it all the time when we were students, but you had to be more careful now, making sure there is only one person in the gypsy cab that stops to pick you up, that kind of thing. I needed to do this less than before now I had a car, but Tatiana would remonstrate with me for picking up people if she happened to see as I left her apartment.

THE COUP

In the early nineties, not everybody is happy with glasnost (open talking, though I would not say very open), perestroika (rebuilding), all the new cooperative business appearing, and what looks like a reduction in material privileges for the elite, with more opportunities for the masses. No, not everybody was happy at all.

Nineteen ninety-one was a year that would go down in history.

Whilst General Secretary Mikhail Sergeevich Gorbachev was at his summer retreat in Sochi, and I was brushing my teeth one August morning, five high-ranking Soviet officials announced a reversal of all that had taken place.

We are back in the USSR.

I stare in disbelief at the television screen as the "Putschisty," (the coup's organisers), as they will come to be known, have called a press conference, announcing the house arrest of Gorbachev in the southern resort of Sochi, and the restoration of order by means of the military. I choke back tears as I watch the progress of perestroika slip away for ever, because I did not recall the USSR being a very happy place. Happy on the surface perhaps, but it was where a quarter of the economy was spent on tanks so women all had to wear the same few dress styles. Where people could not travel, could not buy a car, where carpentry was the big event on television and there was no bread in the bakery. Where the elite were given cards to buy foreign products in shops that were closed to the locals on pain of imprisonment. Still, that was where we were headed once again, back to the corrupt Soviet way.

I drive into the office in sombre mood and am met by Sasha Popov, who tells me to leave the country.

"No. I'm not going to do that. Not yet anyway. Let's see what happens."

The day itself is quite mundane, with worried messages from

Washington and Woking offices, but in business terms nothing has changed yet.

You see, there was a reason I did not want to leave the country; this was not bravado. The truth is I was to get married at the end of August, only 12 days away from now. My general rule is to remain calm, not to make any sudden decisions. This would be the way I would deal with Covid many years later, when faced with a similar dilemma. In a crisis, the last thing you need is sudden, unplanned decision-making.

On day two of this new political state, I arrive at the office and the same conversation takes place with Sasha, but now my office bosses are telling me to get out of Moscow, get to the airport. I hesitate. It could be the end of my career. This was where I needed to be, even if it was to be run by a bunch of yesterday's men. Is it worth going against a direct instruction from my superiors?

That evening (under strict instructions from my fiancée on the other side of town not to leave the apartment), I left the apartment. I did this because my flat, 1223, was not in the epicentre of the protests and tanks but just a few blocks away from what the Russians call the "White House", the seat of the Russian Federation Government (as opposed to the Soviet government, which sat in the Kremlin). This was the same building that I had driven behind to take a shortcut and been caught by the police. The same building with the steps behind it that I had driven down, bump, bump, bump, to get away from more police. The White House was where much of the pro-democracy countermovement was being coordinated. It had become, in just a couple of days, a bastion of support for the continuation of reform, and a baulk against the reactionary forces of the putsch committee. This is the white building in front of which Yeltsin climbed onto a tank (as some soldiers began to renounce the coup) and made his speech to the people, urging them to come and support reforms, but that was not for now.

As I approach in the darkness, I see a lot of people on the steps outside the building and also milling around. I soak in the atmosphere. It's a warm, dry August night and a man holds a loudhailer to his lips urging support from ordinary people, not to let this be done to them, to have courage, to get onto the streets and show that we are not going back.

"Bring flasks of tea, bring blankets, bring food, we are here for you, help us and we will stay right here until this is brought to an end!"

That is what people were doing, donating what they had to the group which had set up camp. They were leaving flowers and wishing their friends well.

The atmosphere I would describe as electric. It was an embrace, a coming together, a refusal to be drawn back into the past. It was a peaceful protest, and it was right on my doorstep, history unfolding before me.

The conversation, as I arrived on day three, was different. Sasha was there, but there was a different face, a different tone.

"David, you left it too late. They closed the airports."

Well, that made it less of a tricky decision. I couldn't leave now. I was stuck.

I remember driving home that day, and down Tverskaya Street. You may remember that I had briefly done journalism before business, and there was an inquisitive streak in me.

I drive right down the main thoroughfare into central Moscow. From nowhere, a line of tanks appears behind me, heading south towards the Kremlin. They are big and going faster than me, twice the speed. My car, with foreign number plates, is now stuck between the pavement on the right and moving tanks on my left. A woman appears in front of me, and thrashes a red rose onto the side of one of the tanks.

"Guys, don't do this, please, don't," she cries at the young soldiers on board.

The tanks continue and I do not want to be in this scene any longer. I risk entering a very Russian military and civil dispute. I have to do a U-turn, between the moving tanks, and head back north to get to the Garden Ring. I get close to a tank in front, pull the wheel hard and fast down to the left and get out the other side before the next tank bears down on me. As I emerge from the line of tanks, a police car flashes by with its blue light, and I narrowly miss being hit. I drive north, and turn onto the Garden Ring.

I head west towards and under Kalininsky Prospekt, which was the scene of one of the deaths in this coup, past the US embassy to my right, and just as I want to make a turn to head towards 1223, my progress is halted by a massive crowd of people, moving towards Kalininsky and in the direction of the Kremlin. My car is stopped with the engine running. I am being jolted and bumped as people pass the vehicle. I feel highly vulnerable. I switch off the engine, not wishing to antagonise the crowd, not as a foreigner in a foreign land. This is the middle of an event that has cost several lives, I should not be here and it is my fault that I am. Now, I just want to get home.

Luckily for me, this was a pro-democracy crowd, a benevolent crowd, who have no argument with a foreigner (except that my car was in their way). They jolted and bumped past the vehicle, ignoring the guy inside, and as they moved away, I started the engine, carefully moved my vehicle forwards and headed for home.

This coup was unexpected, as coups are, but it was also short-lived. The perpetrators were arrested and Gorbachev was released, returned to Moscow and made a speech. The Soviet Union would soon cease to exist even formally, as well as informally, and Gorbachev would be a king without a kingdom. The genie was out of the bottle and would not go back in. He just did not know it at the time, none of us did.

Of course, the genie would be pushed back into the bottle by stealth, years later, by a man who spent years on his project.

The coup of 1991 had a positive side effect, marking the beginning of the end of Soviet, autocratic and corrupt rule (admittedly to be replaced ultimately by another autocratic and corrupt government). It brought about a brief period of what looked like democracy, and the beginning of the Yeltsin years. I am not going into the transition of power, the dissolution of the USSR and Gorbachev's fate; there are history books for that.

Of course, this was never going to be a democracy. Even Yeltsin said of a woman who bought bread, butter, tomatoes and ham, and made them into sandwiches to sell at Belorussky Station, that she was guilty of "speculation". No, this was going to be just a different kind of government altogether, one that in hindsight we can call the government of chaos and corruption. Putin would later get rid of the chaos.

NEW RUSSIA LIFE

The day of the wedding arrives, and my brother and his wife have made the journey to attend this event. We all pile into an old Volga taxi, very standard at the time. It's pouring with rain, and of course, we have found the car that is going to break down every few minutes, all the way to the ceremony. Even at the time, it had a certain charm to it; nobody was stressed, even though we were late. We need not have worried.

We arrive finally at the "Zags" palace of weddings. Sounds grand? No, it was just a large building with a large staircase.

Wedding day Tatiana, Author, Margarita, Misha

On the staircase are several brides and grooms, each accompanied by a handful of people. Tatiana and I join this odd queue, along with Alasdair and his wife Helen, and Tatiana's maid of honour, Elena. Very slowly, we ascend to the rooms at the top. The actual ceremony is brief – very brief. One moment I am a bachelor, the next, I have a Russian wife.

What is not brief is the paperwork that follows. We are led into a room with a dozen tables, each with a large woman seated behind it. At the first table, we sign the registry to confirm that we are now married. At the second, I am asked where in the passport the "married" stamp should be placed. I explain to the woman that we do not stamp our passports with our marital status, so she can leave my passport alone, thank you. This just seems to annoy her. The notion that a passport could exist without a marital status is to her absurd. What uncontrolled chaos the West must be, she seems to suggest! I am not going to win this discussion, so, as if I have a sudden lucid moment, I theatrically declare that here, here is the page upon which should be placed the marital stamp!

With a satisfied flourish, the woman presses her stamp onto the ink pad, hovers it above the paper and bam! She lands the stamp with vigour onto my passport.

Now I have the document that she wants me to have. She is unaware that I will be changing my passport sometime later. I am unaware that I will also be changing my wife sometime later.

Wedding day, Moscow one of many tables…

Anyway, this day appears to be more about tables and money than about the wedding. I am led from table to table to table, paying for this and that.

At one point, having paid for the flowers, I sighed, "What am I paying for now?"

"Now you are paying for the music."

Anyway, four minutes to get married, and 90 minutes, a dozen tables and 12 angry women later, I am married with a set of documents and free of my debt to the USSR.

We left in a little yellow Lada.

Wedding day Lada departure

We make our way to a small ship on the Moscow River, where there is music, dancing and a banquet, a lot of toasts, a lengthy snog by two elderly guests, cheered on by the crowd, and the captain taking to the dance floor. It was a joyous occasion, which was completed when the ship returned to the quay and we disembarked. One young guest did not get further than the quay, being so full of spirit. He chose to lie down there. That would teach him for taking on Scotland at drinking vodka.

A curious little addition to this story is this: you may recall our holiday in Thailand, when we had done a trek in the north. During that trek, we made friends with two young Australians, seeking a place to stay on their next adventure in London. I handed them my keys, which I did not regret then or now. I was living in Moscow anyway and wanted to make sure the place was looked after. The *Sun* newspaper got a hold of the story that some Brit was marrying a Russian and this apparently was interesting for them. Lord knows why. They ran a story on us, and placed it on page 3. In those days, that was right by the image of the topless model, which used to be a daily *Sun* feature. Oh, how those hacks tried to get us for their little story. They went to the flat, they parked outside, they called the office and the flat. Each time they tried calling the office, and each time they called my two Australian friends in the flat, they were given the runaround. The story would change from "they'll be back next week" to "no idea who you're talking about" and even "no, he's marrying an Inuit". As a former journalist, I can say this kind of pestering is the main reason I left journalism, because that, in my view, is not journalism at all. We beat the *Sun* at its own game.

As Russia opened up and a market began to appear, so things changed in our business and personal life. I could now find an apartment with my wife instead of having to live in a business centre. We found a lovely apartment near Barrikadnaya. It was a former "kommunalka", where several families lived in rooms off a corridor and shared the kitchen and bathroom, but this was all ours. A large hallway gave doors to the kitchen on the left, the bedroom, then a bathroom, a wonderful airy library and a lovely lounge area. It was a good apartment, in a great location. There was a small parking area far enough away to be safe but close enough to carry bags, and it was not a very long drive to the office. Opposite was one of the Stalin buildings, which made for a very big view.

Business was tough, Moscow was tough, and little things became big things, a bit like when we could turn boiling an egg into a party when we were students. While I was living in Moscow, occasionally people came to visit. I recall my friends Susie and Sarah coming to visit. They were not hugely impressed by the nightlife or the social scene, and I remember with some envy, as I drove them to the airport, how they were planning to meet next day at the Horniman's pub at London Bridge. A pub; how lovely that would have been! Richard came to see me, and we went for a beer in the hotel bar, an awful place devoid of music, décor or even good beer. Richard and I were chatting and having a pint of warm Heineken. Opposite sat a group of American businessmen. Their colleague entered the room, walked up to them to introduce himself:

"Hi! I'm Dick Cock!"

Not wanting to snigger like schoolboys, we just left.

The new apartment had one major drawback, well, two if you count the old Armenian lady whom we were never sure about. She seemed to live behind a door in the flat, but we never once opened it. I think we might have been scared to. The old woman spoke not a word of English or Russian, and we did not speak Armenian. She wore black and would just appear from nowhere. We thought little of it at the time, but looking back on it, it does seem a little weird.

Apart from the old lady in the cupboard, the problem was with the cockroaches – massive, black things that infested the place. We would come home at night, switch on the kitchen light, and the wall would be black and moving. I devised various means of despatching them, but once they were gone, I kicked them under a sofa in the kitchen, because I wanted to show this roach cemetery to the landlord.

Then there were the mice. Unfortunately, there was no bed in the flat, just a mattress on the floor, and as we would lie there, waiting for sleep every night, we would hear rustling from behind the wall, then the noise of scampering across the floor. I have no idea where they were going. One hilarious occasion, one of these things appeared to get confused and crossed the mattress on the way to the other side of the room.

In hindsight, maybe it was not that good an apartment.

Shopping was a tedious affair before I had a girlfriend then wife. Previously, I had two choices, the mini-market in the business complex or a hard currency store, the Beryozka, which was largely unaffordable in my view (even though the company were paying).

There was still not much in the shops unless you had an army of relatives to go to various different places with plastic bags and spend a weekend doing it, but at this time, other foreign outlets were just beginning to appear. Places like Stockmann were a little expensive, but they had lots of things that were unavailable elsewhere. When Tatiana appeared, shopping changed. We would drive around, ordering things, grabbing a loaf here, a fish there, it was exhausting, but it added variety. I cannot say that I enjoyed shopping for food, it always seemed to take the entire day, but it was a necessary part of life and this is where I lived and worked.

In addition to shopping, our evening and weekend socialising also changed. We would often find ourselves visiting friends or my wife's relatives. I recall with one family, a lovely time was always had over there. We would sit at the dinner table and whilst everybody chatted (very loudly), the dog would sit at the end of the table, for ever hopeful, and somewhat strangely I recall two budgerigars would occasionally swoop and flit over the table. It just became normal.

This particular table was presided over by the grandmother, whose name was also Tatiana.

I recall being designated driver one evening and watching in amusement as the diners became more animated, the stories more ludicrous, helped no doubt by the inevitable vodka shots followed by a sip of cranberry juice. Yet…

The grandmother suddenly announces with some amusement: "This isn't vodka! It's water!"

"Well, you brought it!" exclaims my wife, turning to me questioningly.

"Yes, I grabbed it from on top of the fridge as we were leaving," I explained, not entirely understanding what was the matter.

"That wasn't vodka! That was water that had been blessed by the priest!" says Tatiana junior, her head in her hands.

Anyway, they hadn't noticed until Granny ruined it. How was I to know the priest would use a vodka bottle for the holy water!

I used to love visiting that family. On another occasion, I was not the designated driver, and the vodka had come from a shop rather than our kitchen.

Dinner was lovely, toasts of course, and after dinner, we all retired to the lounge, and continued our toasts.

This property had a balcony, and various people stepped onto the balcony from time to time for a cigarette. Never more than two people because this was Soviet construction.

The ladies remain in the room whilst Mikhail and I popped out for a cigarette. I recall it vividly, despite the vodka. I recall the deep snowdrifts in the darkness below, and the icicles dangling precariously from the eves of the block opposite. We were in an animated discussion, and simply could not agree. It was friendly and civilised, but I could not understand why my point was being totally misunderstood. In fairness, he felt the same exasperation.

Eventually, Tatiana came to the door of the balcony, obviously not daring to venture onto the narrow overhang. She listened to our chat, rolled her eyes and returned to the ladies seated in the lounge.

"Couple of idiots," she announces. "They can't agree about Armstrong. David is saying he was a musician, and Mikhail is saying he was an astronaut!"

Happy days, indeed.

Meetings could be a bit odd sometimes in this Wild West environment. We met the director of the (now) prestigious central Moscow department store "Tsentralny Universaly Magazin", or "TsUM". I recall being dismayed that his card sported a black and gold font. *How am I going to copy that?* I wondered. That meeting was in the morning, which didn't stop him from pouring a large cognac for all of us, then the largest measure for himself. Three days later, I called him to follow up on the meeting, but he had died. This was not the first or only time this had happened in a country where average male life expectancy was 58 years of age. I suspect our morning cognac with him was not his first rodeo, but I did not need to photocopy his black and gold business card. So, that was a plus.

Department store, "TsUM"

It just was constantly abnormal, tense, dangerous, intimidating, and occasionally, downright absurd. Flying to London from Moscow on the Aeroflot that existed then (very different to the luxury airline it would later become), we asked for a glass of water.

The stewardess responded sharply: "You know, I need to sit down at some point too!"

1992

Boris, the company vice president, was a man I looked up to a lot. Of course, his sense of humour meant that he would occasionally play jokes, but not just a normal joke, like, say, getting the waiter to say that you need to wear a tie. No, Boris told me that there was a new possible business opening up, and could I please take a sample from Moscow to the UK office in Woking? I did. This was normal enough, except that when I agreed, I did not ask what the sample actually would be.

Let's just look at that for a second. I am flying Moscow to London, and I have with me my suitcase, my carry-on bag and, somehow, a disassembled Euro-pallet. It is 25 kg and with lengths of timber of over a metre in length, this makes for a tough taxi and a tricky trolley ride through the airport. Yet, I got it all the way from the office in Moscow to the office in Woking.

Whereupon, Boris grins and says, "God, you really brought that thing? I was only kidding!"

Super guy though, and an excellent boss.

Just on the subject of my American bosses, this would be incomplete without a mention of Judith. She, Boris and Michael were friends, and Boris was temporarily in the UK, whilst Judith had settled with family. Occasionally, she would visit the Moscow office. I had a soft spot for her because it was she who had written to me and conducted my first interview when I was applying for the job. Anticipating her arrival, I agreed to purchase some items in advance of her trip. I remember looking for what she called "diapers" (nappies), and of course, I bought the wrong thing. How was I to know that there are different types for boy and girl babies? I still do not understand this.

TRAVEL

I have said nothing of business trips within the Soviet Union. I did not really enjoy them too much in the early days. The airports were very basic, and there was no guarantee that any of the meetings you wanted at the other end would actually take place. You could never arrange meetings in advance. The stock answer if you tried was "just call when you get here". When you do, you may find they have gone on holiday, been taken ill or simply don't pick up the phone.

Particularly in the winter, it was tough. The aircraft had to be de-iced and it was -20 outside. Sometimes, it required a second de-icing it was freezing so fast. Nothing really worked, everything was in short supply and it was all just uncomfortable. There were no cafés, no warm places to sit, and of course, nobody had smartphones or the internet, so it was basically a copy of *Pravda* or read the safety instructions. I went to a number of places. Being there was fine. It was the getting there that was the problem. Aviation fuel was another issue. My colleague Tom became so frustrated after waiting at the airport in Kyrgyzstan for three days that he eventually took a taxi from Kyrgyzstan to Kazakhstan. That's how bad the waiting rooms were.

Travelling with somebody made things a little easier. I remember some good trips with Misha to Lithuania, for example, and a train trip to the Urals region of Russia. Several days on a train are easier with good company.

In fact, Misha and I became in some ways inseparable, often to be found putting the world to rights over a few beers. That's a lot of beers over many, many years.

A trip with Michael to the capital of Azerbaijan was particularly memorable. Our company was doing a good business with the air conditioner manufacturer, BakKonditioner, and Michael invited me to join him on a business trip, to which I agreed readily. Of course, this being Michael, we were also going to attend an Azeri wedding which happened to be taking place at the same time.

We had a most enjoyable day, and in the evening, Michael and I are watching the Azeri tradition of showering the newly-weds with bank notes (whilst the children are picking them up just as swiftly). One of the guests sidles up to us and asks us if we would like to try some hash. I look at Michael, and Michael looks at me.

"Well, yes, I suppose. Why not!" exclaims Michael, somewhat to my surprise.

"Great, we will pick you up at 06:00 from your hotel. Don't be late." Another surprise.

Morning comes, and sure enough, a knock on the door. A man, who may have been at yesterday's wedding (it was a long night) takes us to a Lada, and behind the wheel of this car is an enormous man with a fur hat and gold teeth.

"Michael!" he shouts in glee, ignoring me completely.

"Good morning," says Michael politely.

"You don't remember me, do you!" exclaims the improbably large man. "I was your dance partner!"

Off we drive onto the peninsula to partake in goodness knows what. It certainly was not the hash I had been thinking of.

The car pulls up at a hut. Inside the hut are posters of ladies with little left to the imagination, and in the middle of the room are a table and chairs. The table has been set for eight people, plates, cutlery and glasses. We sit, and waiters come in with things that a lot of people might not expect at 07:00 on the Caspian Sea; garlic, onion, pickles and herring, along with mustard, dill and oh, what a surprise, vodka.

I cannot help but ask, what is this all for?

This will make it all less "priterny" said our host.

Michael and I glance at each other for inspiration. This is not a Russian word we know.

Suddenly, from nowhere, and I have not checked in the 30 years since this took place: "Cloying?" I venture.

I think I must have been right. Actually, 30 years later, I just checked. "Sickly-sweet" is what my app says, but there was nothing sweet about what happened next. I am sticking with "cloying".

In comes the waiter with a massive, steaming bowl, and he serves it into each of our bowls. It glugs and slurps its way into the bowl and seems able to find a level, because this was neither liquid nor solid. This was a bizarre state of sludge. Did we eat it? Drink it? Swallow it whole? I don't know. I have done a little DIY in my time, and this includes mixing cement, and to all intents and purposes, before us in this bowl is some kind of cement. Whatever it is, we consume it as quickly as we can, so utterly revolting is it. Michael's moustache crystallises. My tongue becomes fixed to the roof of my mouth, but of course, I am British, and inherently polite. I am also apparently an idiot because I said, "That was delicious" (actually, "mwaa waa dilisha"), and a man behind me, whose presence was unknown to me, filled my bowl a second time. Michael was not so foolish.

So what is hash? First, it's thick and greasy. I do not even butter my toast. This is hell in a bowl.

They are extolling its virtues, how they eat it once a week, it keeps you strong, it helps you focus, it gives you core strength.

Utter nonsense, because I can explain exactly what it is, and how to prepare it:

Kill a cow.

Throw away the meat.

Collect the eyes, the anus, the ears and entrails, anything that glistens and wobbles.

Place in a cauldron and set gas to low.

Leave it for three days.

When fully melted, serve it to the foreigners that just landed from Moscow.

It may have been this trip or the next, I don't recall, when I had a minor timing problem with the flight. You see, in those days everything was relatively simple. There were not many designs of dresses, very few options when it came to choices of brands, places to eat and so on, and it was the same with airlines. There was one, Aeroflot, and it was not great. Preparing a trip was pretty straightforward. Flights going south leave from one particular airport, with the catchy name of Domodedovo. This was at the time a very basic airport, now totally refurbished. I head out to Domodedovo and here I realise my mistake. A new airline has emerged by the name of Transaero. On closer inspection of my ticket, I am on this new airline, and I am in the wrong airport. The woman at the airport desk is unhelpful, assuring me that there is only one airline in the USSR and that is called Aeroflot. I finally hear some sensible advice from a passenger who advises me that the new airline flies not from Domodedovo but from Sheremetyevo, another zippy airport name by the way. The problem is that the two airports are in entirely different locations, one south and one north of the city. There is no way I can make it.

Of course, I am going to try. Just whilst I am negotiating with a taxi driver about how I would pay more the faster he drove, a man comes up to me to tell me that, if I fail to make that flight on time, I can come back to this airport and, for a small fee, he will take me on a Yak propeller plane, leaving at midnight – heady days. Fortunately, I did not need his services because somehow, and to this day I do not know how, I made the flight from the other airport after the scariest drive of my life.

It was a happy time, a happy company and I could not have asked for better colleagues. Tom, for example, who famously said (after messing up a contract) "But I make a great seafood salad!" and nothing more was said about it. These were really good people to work with and I look back fondly on those times.

A slightly similar experience to the Azerbaijan trip took place when I travelled with a colleague to Kazakhstan. The poultry processing factory we were going to see needed new equipment and there we found ourselves in the early morning, being invited to a pre-tour breakfast with cognac, together with the smell of 80,000 chickens and tiny feathers floating around in the dusty sunshine around our table.

Russian trips could be just as colourful, though. You did not have to go to Azerbaijan or Kazakhstan!

A visit to Voronezh with two Scots American clients was uneventful except for the Russian director's comment, as he put us back on the train to Moscow: "Guys, thanks, but please send the specialists next time"! I say uneventful; it was apart from the bit where we all got naked in the sauna after dinner, but business trips and saunas had become more or less standard practice. They are not as much fun as they sound either. Although in fairness, six naked men in a sauna full of vodka and discussing contracts in Russian possibly doesn't even sound that much like fun anyway.

The city of Voronezh was where I would have been living as a student if at the last moment they had not decided to place us in Moscow instead. I have to say, from what I have seen of the city, I am pleased they made the decision they did.

I had to learn to love Voronezh though, because I would be visiting it a lot. One factory was especially memorable; I apparently could not stay away.

I took two clients to visit a factory there by the name of NPO Energia. This was formerly part of the military Industrial complex, making military hardware, but with the changes currently underway in the former USSR, it was trying to find a new role. This was not always easy; transition can be hard, especially if you have been making what they were making.

The first visit I made to this particular plant, I was accompanied again by two American gentlemen, the USA being a significant part of what we did. They were proposing to the Russian factory a joint venture to produce "low noise block actuators" for satellite dishes. This would have been easy for the Russians, but somehow it did not work out.

NPO Energia. A meeting, with my American clients to my left

The second visit, I took a new client, and he was interested in setting up production of telephone units, not perhaps the same level of technology as before, but surely this would be an easy win. No.

On my third and final visit to this particular factory, I took a small round chap with me, who had in his suitcase some brightly coloured soft, long things. I cannot really describe them. I do not really know what they do, but I remember him, looking a bit like Danny deVito, demonstrating how you could use this orange, soft, long thing to massage your back if you held it the right way. We were politely asked to leave the building.

"David," said the Russian director to me as we made our way back to the car, "Don't bring any more investors or ideas for joint ventures. Just give us the money and we will decide what to do with it."

On reflection, that is a suggestion I would hear many times over the years.

However, it would be remiss of me not to mention a particular nuance of that first trip regarding the satellite dishes. As this was the first visit, we were treated to a dinner. This was to take place at the factory's "resort" on the river. One of my clients was a very big man. I mean, supersized. I shall call him John, not his real name. He was a very nice guy, but wisely declined to take part in what was about to take place.

We enter a timber building on the side of the river, and we find a table, laden with food and drink, a sauna, and a door leading to the river, a deep, quiet tributary of the Don River. Step out of the building and plunge in! We are invited to strip off our clothes and don towels, which is normal. This was only a male event. I do not recall ever any ladies doing a business sauna. It was perfectly civilised; we just happened to be naked in a room full of men we met that afternoon. We take our seats and are invited to eat, then come the toasts. After a toast, a quick heat in the sauna and a plunge into the icy river to refresh. John watched the proceedings all evening and filled his colleague and me in next day with the bits that seemed to go astray from our memories.

So, the evening progressed:

Food, vodka toast, sauna, river.

Food, vodka toast, sauna, river.

Food, vodka toast, sauna, river.

Food, vodka toast, sauna.

Food, vodka toast.

Vodka toast.

Vodka.

Vodka.

The Americans toast, the Russians toast, the Scottish bloke toasts, until we are all toasted out. I vaguely recall a bus taking us back to the hotel. This was the Russian way. Get you drunk and then try to get you to divulge commercial details or agree discounts or other such skulduggery! But it did not work, not once. So, what was the point?

We return to Moscow with our headaches, collective and individual, and we head for the office.

At this point, John realises that he has left his US passport on the train. That's John, the only one of our party that did not have a splitting headache, but anyway, of the three of us, it was he who forgot his passport.

Michael quickly musters us. He agrees to take John to the American embassy, a colleague goes to the airline office and I go to the station. What

I expect to find, I am not sure. Am I hoping that the train might still be there, and on a table, a shiny American passport will be lying with an *Alice in Wonderland*-type sign saying "Take me to John"? Unsurprisingly, there is no passport, no table, and even the train seems to have vanished. For some reason, nobody had handed in the valid American, highly sought-after passport.

None of us has had any luck. It's Friday. We are going to be stuck with John all weekend. We take the two clients out to the airport. One of them sails through immigration, his passport is stamped and he is fine. Then there is big John with no passport. We have absolutely no chance of getting this guy out. The passport officer, reasonably enough, tells us he cannot let a passenger through immigration with only a driving licence. He needs to see a passport.

To be fair, this would be a problem *anywhere*, not only in Soviet Russia. Then my colleague has a brainwave. She is very familiar with how things work here, and she knows that the only thing a Russian will respond to when he is denying your request and making it your problem, is if you give him a bigger problem and make it his. So she lies.

"Look at this gentleman!" she says calmly to the immigration officer. "You can see he is diabetic. He had exactly enough medication for this trip, no more. And it is highly specific medication. So, if you do not allow him to get on that flight, and to get back to where his medication is, he dies – within hours. And you alone will be responsible for his death. I am not saying this to make you feel bad. I am merely stating what cannot turn out differently."

She delivers this cold, calm and matter-of-fact. John is oblivious. He's looking around, wondering what is going on. I am in awe of my colleague, and the immigration officer has now gone pale. He has a choice. Break the rules and let a guy through on a driving licence, or kill an American by accident. Without saying one word, he beckons John through, and my colleague and I return to Moscow city centre. We would have high-fived each other, but even that does not yet exist.

This was also not the Moscow of student days. Remarkably quickly, in the late 1980s and the early 1990s, Moscow particularly became a very different place. Suddenly there would be lots of cafés, restaurants and bars, and this would continue, faster and faster. By 2020, Moscow was vibrant, also highly advanced. The Moscow metro, possibly the most efficient in the world, was growing. The bus stops came equipped with USB ports, Wi-Fi was available everywhere in the city including underground. The change would be remarkable.

Back in the nineties, it was still a bit "hit and miss" but still better than before in terms of comfort.

Not all places were to everybody's taste. I could mention the Hungry Duck, Boar House and Night Flight, but these places are a book in themselves. It may be simplest to illustrate what Moscow was like by just saying this. The Duck was opened in a dark corner of a set of buildings right in the centre of town, in fact a stone's throw from the headquarters of what was called the KGB before being rebranded the FSB.

Same entity, different letterhead.

One evening, many years later, two Russian MPs wandered into the Hungry Duck and were surprised to see an Afro-American stripper on the bar top removing his clothes to the tune of the Russian national anthem, whilst throngs of scantily clad ladies cheered him on. From recollection, it was the very next day that the two politicians raised the topic of this travesty before the Russian parliament, and very soon thereafter, the Duck was no more. Not that this bothered Doug and Marty, the proprietors, who promptly opened the Boar House near Kursky Station.

Same entity, different letterhead.

The Night Flight should have been a pleasant place, but it somehow became something different. You may remember Mark, who helped me when I had appendicitis. As it happens, Mark left our company not long after this, to pursue his career elsewhere. He joined a major US tobacco brand. He came back to Moscow and we would meet up from time to time for a meal or a couple of beers. Mark invited me to a new restaurant and bar opening up, by the name of the Night Flight.

We were not going for a meal, but a daytime meeting to discuss the possibility of Mark's company advertising in the windows of this new restaurant and nightclub. This place was Swedish, and they had big plans for offering great cuisine, a fully stocked bar, dance floor and plenty of space for chatting over cocktails. Mark was very clear with the management that his company would have nothing to do with any club which condoned any form of behaviour involving girls offering inappropriate services to clients. His brand was too valuable to be associated with anything of that nature. The management assured him that nothing of that nature would take place.

Well, Mark was no fool, and chose not to place ads in this establishment, which was just as well, because the place became synonymous with inappropriate services from a multitude of young ladies to a multitude of men in suits.

The formula must have worked because it became immensely popular, remaining open until some 29 years later, in September of 2020.

One trip I should mention, just before I leave the topic of business travel, and this time, it is two Russians visiting London.

These two were test pilots, one of the most dangerous jobs on the planet. Their task was to take a new design of aircraft up into the air and break it.

At the time, there was talk of our company becoming involved in a service involving corporate jet travel. It did not work out and was not really our thing, but whilst these talks were ongoing, these two pilots were to join meetings in London. They would stay with their UK host in Clapham, in his home with its front on the main road, and a rear garden with another street behind that.

Their host had to be away one evening and these two decided they would go out and have a few beers to soak in the London atmosphere. That would have been fine if they had remembered their keys, but it was now dark, and they got to the front of the house. Knowing there was a spare key in the back garden, they applied a kind of beery logic to solve this. They started walking along the street, counting the houses to their left. At the end of the street, they turned left and left again, going back down the street that the rear of the properties overlooked. Finally, they got to what they believed to be their friend's house. How to climb over the wall? They could use a convenient tree that was just about close enough to then scramble over. So, they start climbing the tree, and one of them managed to get on top of the wall. At this point, a police car pulls up and two officers enquire what they are doing in a tree and on top of a wall.

The Russians answered honestly in broken English: "We are Russian test pilots."

Of course.

TIME TO LEAVE RUSSIA

Argus had been a very positive time for me. I had married, learnt business, and I had great memories. To this day, I have great friends from that time.

But it was also a difficult period. I was burnt out. Around Christmas time, 1992, I called Michael, and said that I needed to move on, to leave Russia. I had no plan, and I remain proud of that to this day. Some 30 years later, only one person has left my company in the same way. Everybody else has made sure they had a plan, a new job, whilst on our payroll. Maybe that's the way it is meant to be done, to look after number one, but that was not my style. I was loyal to Michael, Boris and Argus, so I told him, and Michael was gracious about it. He asked me if I could stay for a bit longer and I readily agreed.

"How long did you have in mind?" I asked. I remember the room I was in at the time. This was big for me.

"Well," said Michael from eight time zones away, "perhaps another year?"

I had not anticipated that, but hey, life is about compromise! We agreed that we would leave Russia in May of the following year, and that is what we did.

1993

Although living in Moscow in the late 1980s and early 1990s was not the "fun" time that most of my peers had had in London (for there were no bars or clubs, and most things were unaffordable or dangerous) it was quirky and charming. I lived there as a businessman from the age of 24 until I was 28. It seemed longer because it was intense.

That intensity had burned me out. I had to leave. It included constantly having to park the car two blocks from the apartment, not speaking English near where you lived, the traffic police wanting bribes, the threats, the constant possibility of danger and female staff being issued with pepper spray by the company for their protection, because the nineties in Moscow were known as the killer years. Of course, from Michael and Boris' perspective, this was a difficult time for business. The entire economy was changing and what had been for many years relatively easy business, if niche, suddenly had become very tough. The five-year plans were gone, the budgets, gone, people were losing their positions, their ability to make decisions and occasionally, their lives. People were trying to sell you things they did not own.

I recall one man in the office trying to sell me an aircraft, and telling me it was a great deal, but I had to move fast because it would take off in four hours. I had to present these people with a questionnaire, questions such as, "What is your company name?" Mostly, I never heard from them again.

When you took a train on a business trip, and enjoyed the tea served in glasses by a train stewardess in each carriage, you would look out of the window as you pulled into a station and see the most bizarre scene, more or less all during Yeltsin's years in power. All along the platform, even in the middle of the night would be elderly men and women, clutching scarves, bags, tea sets, vases, whatever their factory produced. At this time, everybody was running out of money, and the factories would pay their workers in product, which they were then expected to sell somehow, somewhere, sometime.

A mess had emerged. Boris Yeltsin was well meaning, absolutely, but he had no idea how to preside and the chaos that ensued was exhausting.

No, it was definitely time to leave. I would be returning regularly all through the nineties, as it turned out, and beyond; I just did not know that at the time.

One day, in May 1993, our colleagues took us to the airport and presented us with gifts; I was given a dark red briefcase, which stayed with me, in a rather shabby state by the end, for some 30 years! We flew from Moscow to London to start the next chapter in our lives. I had no job to go to, but a flat in Battersea.

Being out of a job was quite a wake-up call, particularly now living in London with my wife. She took a job doing telesales to Russia and, with the time zones factored in, her shift started at 04:00. She was selling advertising space in business catalogues. In hindsight, this was a bit of a racket. A company would create a business catalogue, in the full knowledge that nobody would look at it. Then they would find Russian companies to contribute articles about their company, and a photograph of the director. These Russian guys thought that in this new world this was how business worked, and they paid a lot of money for something of no value. Of course, Tatiana and I knew nothing of this. She was simply doing her job, and it was competitive. Russia covered 11 time zones, so if it was 04:00 in the morning in London, it was definitely mid-afternoon in Vladivostok. If you wanted the business, you got up at 03:00 to get to work and you put in the hours. She did pretty well there, if you ignore the occasional squaring up to colleagues when they encroached on each other's patch!

I took work where I could find it, including a little work for my old company, but also some consultancy. An Asian company invited me to a hotel by Paddington station, a rather scruffy place, with an office in the basement. I think their family owned the hotel. They had decided they wanted to do business in Russia. It was like the Klondikers in Russia at this point. Everybody wanted in, just at the point that I had wanted out. My timing was not great, but actually, some of the business that was done at this particular time was frankly not nice. These guys were OK, maybe not my type of people, but they wanted to set up an honest business. They gave me the task of helping them to sell tea in Russia, and I had reason therefore to return to the city I had lived in, where I knew so many people. I recall conducting a survey on the Moscow streets, asking locals what they wanted to see on a packet of tea. It's an elephant, by the way. Still, it was money. There were other companies selling second-hand products, many of them tainted or damaged. These would go in by the containerload, and it was a particularly unedifying sight, to see these people at the trough. I wanted nothing to do with that kind of "business".

I wasn't enjoying this much, but I had made my decision and I would stick with it. It was a bit unstable, not knowing if I was going to have enough money the next week, but we got on with it.

THE MAN FROM THE MINISTRY

Then one day, the phone rang.

A man from the ministry of trade wanted to speak to me. Kester, his name was. He was quite high up in the then named DTI, the Department of Trade and Industry. You could tell a person's seniority there, as I later discovered, by the number of windows in their office. He had four. That's a lot. Long story short, he gave me a job. This was to be a wonderful job, which I thoroughly enjoyed, but which could only last two years, such was the system.

An export promoter was a new government concept, basically an interface between government and business. We were all business people, but we operated from within the government structure, so we had a foot in both camps. My job was to go to UK exporters and extol the virtues of doing business with Russia. There were lots of us, covering all the major markets across the world. Mostly they were retiring business people from big corporations, but at 28, I was the youngest.

I didn't have an office as such, so, we came to a "hot desk" system, which I called the "no desk" system, but which worked somehow. I received my first mobile phone, a small brick but new technology at that time. I received a really good Toshiba laptop, but best of all, budgets! I was basically given access to a travel budget, an entertainment budget, a subsistence budget, a special event budget and of course all this on top of a salary. In fact, the only thing I did not get was a window! I had not experienced this kind of money before, and come to think of it, I have not experienced it since.

This job was going to be a breeze compared to the last few years, budgets, no money worries and having an actual mobile phone! It was made very clear to me that I would be required to sign the Official Secrets Act. I would be privy to certain conversations, documents, and would be learning the details of how priorities are reached and so on. That was fine, because I would have had no problem in signing such a thing, but I did not sign it. Not out of principle, or any sort of high value. No, it was much simpler than that. I did not sign it because they forgot about it, despite my reminders. After a few weeks, I did not bother reminding them and just concentrated upon the job in hand.

A NOD TO MI6

That is why I can tell you about the UK government's apparent failed attempt, sometime later, to recruit me into the world of espionage. It was a telephone call, one afternoon, inviting me to meet somebody on Whitehall. I agreed to the meeting, without knowing what it was concerning. There were lots of meetings in the civil service, not only lots of meetings, but lots of moving offices. Even the organisation changed its name whilst I was there. It had been DTI, then it became UKTI, and later would become OTS. Currently it is called DIT. Actually, I am not even sure what order these name changes came in, or if I have covered them all. All I know is that it was all a horrible waste of money. There were trips to various places, with people who frankly did not need to be there, all staying at top hotels, and every time somebody changed offices, or a name, or a place, or a role the letterheads all went into the bin. Somebody would print new stationery, cards, letterheads, nameplates. It seemed a waste of money to me, but it never seemed to stop. By the way, I think all that has changed, and now the whole budget thing is very tightly controlled, finally.

Anyway, there were lots of meetings too, some pointless, some interesting and valuable. So, to be invited to some meeting or other on Whitehall was not hugely unusual, but this one would be.

And so it was that I strolled along Victoria Street towards Westminster, bypassed the square, turned left and up Whitehall. On the southern side of the street, after Downing Street, and near the original Scotland Yard, I found the address and entered a grand building, if a little shabby compared to its former days of glory. I was shown into a dusty room, with high ceilings but not a huge amount of light. Seated by a window was Mr. Mallard. I recall looking at his business card and thinking that it was an unusual name, and it only later occurred to me that this may not be a real name at all.

The pleasantries were dealt with, and the entire conversation lasted no more than ten or fifteen minutes.

He asked me if I would pass on information I came across about the Russians, and I said no.

I could have been more diplomatic and said I would "see what I could do", and then do nothing. It was not like they gave me a briefcase, a pen that doubled as a camera and an Aston Martin. There was no "mission", just a vague request.

All the same, I was aware of how dangerous it is to be dragged into the world of espionage because of something that happened to a very close family member. It started in the same way, but years later, when there were death threats, these same people, like the man seated across the desk, did nothing to assist – nothing. We sat up at night waiting, listening, because people were calling and telling us that we would be executed.

I shall say no more on this topic, but suffice to say, I did not enter that world for either side. Whilst it may have made for a better story if I had, I also may not have been here to tell it. I left the meeting and walked back along Whitehall, glancing back once.

Not long after this, I recall being at a hotel called the "Roman Camp" in Scotland, just the girls, my parents and myself. I walk in the gardens with my dad and I tell him about what happened on Whitehall. He tells me to steer clear of these people.

There is a short story by Somerset Maugham, which describes the process of being enlisted, and the process remains the same. "R." is the title of the story from a collection called *Ashenden*:

"There's just one thing I think you ought to know before you take on this job. And don't forget it. If you do well you'll get no thanks and if you get into trouble you'll get no help."

That is why I declined.

1994

Back to the job, working with the government.

We largely decided ourselves what we were to do. We could visit the market, companies, trade fairs, conferences and so on. I enjoyed this job immensely and I took it seriously. I went out of my way to help exporters and, at the same time, not to spend much of these budgets if I could avoid it. Until one day, I realised what "use it or lose it" meant, in budget terms. The more I saved for HMG, Her Majesty's Government, the less I would receive next time. I could stay in a small B & B, instead of the luxury Kempinski to which I was entitled, but then my travel budget would be cut. So, if I was helping companies, and I believe I was, then that help would be curtailed by my attempt to reduce cost. We were encouraged to spend our budgets. There was something wrong with the system at the time.

Be that as it may, it was good to have less stress. The only thing that was irksome was when some people, usually not directors, found it difficult to understand that I was handing them a ministry business card but was *not* a civil servant. I recall a meeting in Russia with those two Asian brothers, whom I mentioned earlier. I interpreted, just to be helpful, not because I had to. After the meeting, the younger brother turned to me and asked if "the man from the ministry" had understood the discussion about payment. I could have run circles round this kid. I had done more business in Russia in the last few years than he would do in a lifetime. I had come a long way since that first day when I did not know what an L/C was, but I smiled, and said, yes, I think I understood.

I travelled a lot. This was difficult for my marriage. I was always thinking about the future, what was around the corner. I should have been focussing upon the present.

However, that was the job. I became pretty good at it. Fairly early on though, my zeal got me into trouble. I was at a trade fair in Moscow visiting the UK exhibitors' stands, asking how things were and how we might help.

As a brief aside, I think this may have been the exhibition where one particular company could not understand why their stand, and only theirs, was so popular with the visitors to the show. Each of the first two days, their stand had been overrun by Russians who were not only looking for free pens and bags, as was the way back then. They seemed to make a beeline for that stand in particular. Anyway, it was on day three that I finally broke the news to this insurance company that their corporate name in English means fellatio in Russian. To their credit, they did not even consider changing their signage but decided they should somehow embrace this reality and make it their corporate unique selling point.

Exhibitions could be a nightmare because of those Russian visitors looking for souvenirs. I remember one in particular because the German exhibitors abused the situation; this had been some years before. They decided to tease the locals by suddenly dumping on the front of their stand a large number of bags or pens or badges, all the usual corporate giveaways that companies hand out at events. Each time they brought out a pile of items, a crowd of souvenir hunters would descend on the German stand in a frenzy. It was horrible to watch, because it was condescending and insulting. What was not horrible to watch was when finally, as they brought out another bunch of corporate tat, their stand was literally demolished as the crowd surged. Suddenly, their amusement turned to dismay, as they had to rebuild their stand.

1995

In my role at the ministry of trade, I attended a lot of these trade fairs, some in the UK, others in Russia. At one such event, I was walking around the stands and I became aware of an undertone of resentment amongst the exhibitors at what they regarded as a lack of support from "Her Majesty's Government". They showed me the Italian, German, French pavilions and their stands were impressive compared to the UK companies'. As a result, I questioned them all about how we could improve our level of support. I did my job.

I later took my findings to the then second secretary at the British embassy. He listened carefully and thanked me for my time and effort. I thought little more about it until, back in London, I was called into Kester's office, placed in front of the four windows, and grilled. Why was I working against the team? The second secretary had not only failed to do anything, he had misrepresented the situation to suggest that I was stirring things up. I was not; I was reflecting opinion. This was not to be the last time I got into trouble for telling the truth. The problem was, as I could see from the inside, that there was a small minority in the establishment who considered themselves to be some kind of club members, an elite, which they were not. They were there to serve the needs of business, not the other way around. The majority of them were hard-working, enthusiastic and effective. Cliff, Gary, Andrea, Keith and John were all good people, who cared about their job. The other guy was a minority. I have other words for him, but let's stick with "minority".

One of my little theories is that the tougher the place, the tougher the industry, the nicer the people. I would sometimes be in a dinner or a luncheon, where there were toasts, as is the Russian way. Russians simply do not understand us in the UK, where we go to a pub and drink beer. They drink with food. Anyway, somewhere out in Siberia, I recall, from the heart, combining in my toast the notion of the cold, cold climate and the warm, friendly people, and I meant it. Well, the oil and gas industry was the industry that could match the climate for being tough, and the oil and gas business people whom we would meet were just the funniest, toughest guys. I will not name them all, but they include Gus, from my days working with Michael, and Tom.

Now I was quite hands-on in this role. I had been given a budget to do a job, and I was determined to do it. I was highly motivated, and so it was that I came to be with Tom, from Aberdeen, in the city of Nizhnevartovsk in the spring. You did not need a car. You needed a canoe.

Everything was waterlogged, on account of the thaw, and despite Tom being the CEO of his company, he too was motivated. He and I were on this aircraft, a Tupolev 134, the workhorse of internal Aeroflot flights, where everybody always seemed to be checked into seat 10B and goats could occasionally be seen on board. We descend the steps, but only after the captain and first officer have disembarked and the passengers have clapped at their skill (yes, Soviet travel was a bit weird; nobody ever claps for me when I arrive somewhere in a car).

We would step onto the wet tarmac, towards the wet terminal building, where we would meet some poor soul in a wet suit, who would take us to a hotel where all the rooms can be opened with the same key and the curtains don't quite meet in the middle.

On one occasion, my friend arrived at his hotel, unpacked, went for dinner downstairs and found the mafia in his room when he returned, all in shell suits, drinking cognac, smoking and having a meeting. You don't mess with these guys; you change rooms. The key will work anyway.

Back in Nizhnevartovsk Airport, Tom has descended the aircraft steps and is making his way across the tarmac with a suitcase in his left hand and a briefcase in his right. I am just a few steps behind him. It's a bit of a crush getting out of the aircraft when you are all seated in 10B.

Anyway, the point is, Tom is trudging towards the terminal building, under a leaden sky. I am a few steps behind.

Suddenly, Tom stops, places his bags onto the ground, and without turning around, or checking to see if anybody is listening, he mutters to himself: "There must, there must be easier ways of making a living than this."

He then picks up his soaking wet bags and carries on trudging to the terminal.

1996: TIME TO MEET THE WINDSORS

After two years, it was time to move on. That was the deal. There was an opportunity that came my way by total coincidence. The position had come up of executive director of the Russo-British Chamber of Commerce (RBCC), based in Southwark, London. I thought about it for a while, weighed up the pros and cons, had a few chats, and went for it. Had I known at that time what the reality was, I would not have touched it with a bargepole, so to speak.

1996 first day, RBCC, 42 Southwark Street

As life goes on, it seemed to me that decisions started becoming more complex.

A few little things were not made clear at the interview; the imminent closure of the Moscow office, the massive debt, the rapidly dwindling membership and the lack of up-to-date systems. Even then, nobody seemed to be using "386" computers except the RBCC.

These were little things that were to cost me dearly.

I took the job on the proviso that they would not object to my setting up my own company, which I had had in mind some years. They were OK with that, and even suggested this would be the first time they had in the position a young Russian speaker with actual business experience. I think, by and large, their directors had in the past been retired bankers without language skills, and possibly not the skills needed to run a *small* company.

March 1996, I walk into my new office on Southwark Street, London. Having been the youngest export promoter, I now became the youngest executive director, and I think the first who spoke Russian. I waited a few weeks, and then I started making some changes – new systems, new people, new services and a new approach. We updated the regular bulletin, produced some online services and purchased a modern CRM system. This took time of course, and it would not have been possible without a good team of people with me.

Author with the chairman of the RBCC Ralph Land CBE

A new concept, which I was keen to promote, was to appoint a patron, in the form of HRH Prince Michael of Kent, cousin of Her Majesty the Queen. A Russian speaker, with an interest in the country and of course related to the Russian Romanov dynasty, the prince also happened to have a striking resemblance to the last Russian czar, Nikolai II. On one occasion, when he was in Saint Petersburg, an elderly lady crossed herself and dropped to her knees, so convinced was she apparently that she was seeing her czar.

It took a while to clear because Sir Norman Wooding, our president, had to consider our position carefully. The prince has always been utterly charming in my many subsequent encounters and conversations with him, but Princess Michael, she seemed to me to be rather different. I can only go from my personal experience. It would be a while before this would take place, but I recall a luncheon in Moscow, where I was seated beside her. She was insufferable. Everything seemed to be about her. I recall almost dozing off, as she discussed a birthday celebration for her son. She went into huge detail about this lavish affair at Kensington Palace. The most vivid part for me her description of little ponies with carts tethered to them, in which were fresh strawberries for the guests. She seemed to me to be totally out of touch with the real world. I stopped listening.

I am pleased to say that HRH Prince Michael did indeed become our formal patron, and I believe this was a pivotal moment, after years of apparent decline.

I also "poached" a friend of mine, Sergei, from another company, where he was not properly valued and his skills seemed wasted. We agreed that he would put his skills into a regular exhibition to take place in Russia each year, under the RBCC brand.

With these major changes implemented, along with a number of other new additions to the company's technology, services and PR, we set about trying to improve things.

Both these initiatives, the new patron and the exhibition "Britain in Russia", along with the other changes, became successful in helping to rebuild a severely tarnished image. The way I saw it, I could get down into the engine room whilst Sergei remained up on deck.

Sergei could charm anybody; he was amazing to watch. He quickly brought people aboard to help, and he and his team created additional opportunities for the brand, lunches with dignitaries, receptions, high-profile visits and a conference in London. Sergei was good, and it seemed that whatever he touched turned to gold.

1997

The very first exhibition over there was nearly a disaster for the RBCC, because I was not used to conducting this type of event, and my mind was on the finances, ensuring we had enough exhibitors, and that everything had been thought of. I was so focussed on all that, that I forgot about the stand for the RBCC, the actual exhibition organiser in the middle of the trade fair, receiving guests on a bit of linoleum with no walls. In some panic, I quickly arranged for a stand to be built.

What was more difficult was how on earth to get this stand to Nizhny Novgorod, some 300 miles east of Moscow, by Tuesday. I looked at my desk diary glumly. Thursday, there was not a chance.

One or two of the Chamber's members were in the business of transport, and somewhat discouraged, I picked up the phone and called a guy named Gary. The conversation was brief. Gary agreed to do it and gave me a figure which was roughly half what he could have charged me, a fact that I have mentioned to him on a regular basis in the many years since.

Not only did he arrange for the items to be taken to Nizhny, he actually did it himself. He described later how he manhandled a considerable number of outsize boxes, going up the platform several times under the scrutiny of armed soldiers, and loading the boxes onto a train whilst being shouted at by a stewardess.

You see, Russian trains are never late. In all my decades of visiting the country, I have not once known a train to be late, and this stewardess was not going to allow her train to be late either. Gary sweated and heaved the cumbersome load onto the train and when he arrived, we went to the station to help him off. I have to this day no idea how he did that.

We would go on to conduct this exhibition several times in different cities in Russia.

During this period, part of what I would do, as the director, was to conduct a reconnaissance, or "recce", of the various places where the events were to take place. Our first, as I mentioned, was in the city of Nizhny Novgorod, a beautiful town on the Volga River, with a pretty kremlin (many cities in Russia have a kremlin, which translates as fortress).

In Nizhny Novgorod, I met Boris Nemtsov, then the youngest governor in Russia, reporting of course, directly to President Boris Yeltsin. He was charming, personable, and Sergei in particular developed a friendship with him. We needed to deal with the city administration and he seemed to get things done. I would say Boris Nemtsov was possibly the first senior politician to understand public relations. He wanted to put his city on the map, and he succeeded. People talked about the city, and they talked about him and his progressive views. Years later, I recall how he would always make a point of visiting Margaret Thatcher at her London residence for tea. He was a positive voice for Russia, which of course may explain why he met the fate he did. I would not at all say that we became close, but he was a nice guy. Sergei was the one who really hit it off with Boris, but I recall a happy day fishing with him and Sergei in England, and enjoying a pint in the pub on the way home.

Akunin, Author, Nemtsov, Ignatiev, Kolushev

Boris knew he was popular, and he had charisma. He was a great reformer and would subsequently become an opposition figure when Putin took charge. He would end up being shot in the back one evening some 17 years later, as he strolled across the Moskvoretsky Bridge in central Moscow.

Boris' great friend, Valerii Akunin, on the left in this picture, also of course to become an opposition figure, would also meet an untimely death, crushed in his car under a truck on the Minsk Highway in Moscow.

With Valerii Akunin, who would later be crushed under a lorry in Moscow

Being in opposition in this regime seemed to be quite a hazardous endeavour.

Navalny's poisoning, incarceration and sudden death whilst out walking in the prison, that is a recent and well-known, untimely end. There are many more.

Nobody can prove these were political assassinations.

Yet.

1998-2002

It was at this time that our first child was born. I remember it vividly. She helpfully arrived around 8 p.m., unlike her sister, a couple of years later, who would turn up in the middle of the night.

Being a father was a whole new world to me. In hindsight, I should have given up my job or at least found a deputy, but I did not. As a result, I was more absent than I should have been, not because I did not want to be at home, but because I was genuinely concerned that my career was going to be marked by accidentally destroying the company that had hired me. I stayed late, left early, and the more this happened, the more my wife called in for assistance from friends and relatives. This made me feel a bit of a stranger in my own home. The cycle became more pronounced, which was pretty much entirely my fault. It's one thing I would change if I could do my time again.

Russian parenting is a little different to ours, some would say, perhaps a little overzealous. With these various Russian relatives in our home, we were occasionally bound to disagree on how to do things!

On a normal March afternoon, my mother-in-law would dress the girls. I was taking them to the park for a walk and a play on the boats in the river. When I came down to get them, I discovered that the girls had become spherical, so many layers having been added by Margarita. A vest, a top, a pullover, a fleece, then a coat, a woollen scarf, a hat, possibly a duvet for all I know! Discreetly, I removed these layers, perhaps necessary in Moscow at -12 degrees, but on a crisp, spring day in Tonbridge, less so.

There was also the time I was on a business trip, and later discovered about the "scalding" incident. Baby was seated at her high chair in the kitchen, and my wife and her mother were busy with preparing lunch. At some point, a coffee was spilt and some of it landed on baby. Oh, there was a fuss. I was not there, but I know what a fuss sounds like in Russian! Lots of clucking and rushing, baby clothes removed, cold cloths applied, and advice offered; lots and lots of advice. After a while, it was suggested that the best antidote to a scald was egg white, which was duly applied, perhaps smothered, onto baby.

Two hours later, they took the child to hospital, because the skin had started to blister and this looked more serious than they had even thought.

The doctor put questions that did not entirely seem relevant to them. Was it a black coffee or was there milk in it? Had it been sitting there a while? Was the mug full?

The doctor concluded that the baby was fine apart from the dried egg white all over her, and that, by the way, the thing about scalds and egg white? It's an urban myth. And that was that.

For now, I was lashed to the wheel of the job in which I found myself. I should have wrenched free of it, but I was too worried about the consequences.

I needed to visit our Moscow staff quite a lot. The RBCC had of course closed their Moscow office as I started my job in the company, but we had a desire to reopen. I wanted to focus on gaining Russian corporations' membership.

The company (yes, the Chamber of Commerce is self-financing, not part of government) was in pretty dire straits, so the British embassy commercial section gave us the use of an office for a while, until we found a new place. We visited some really horrible places, and we set up an office in one such place in the city centre.

It was, however, a short-term plan; we had bigger things in mind.

Sure enough, following a rebranding and lots of "management" changes (a "board", which was wholly ineffective), we could finally open an office formally, not just informally.

The year was 1998, a couple of years after I had joined to watch the RBCC's Moscow office close. In hindsight, we reopened just as Moscow was about to go through some serious economic hardship.

With HRH Prince Michael of Kent now being our patron, we would need to have an opening reception. We chose to do this on the eve of our exhibition in Ekaterinburg, so exhibitors provided an automatic crowd! In addition, we invited various senior dignitaries, and the whole thing took place in the refurbished and luxurious National Hotel, right in the centre of Moscow, opposite the Kremlin.

There are some 200 people in the glittering room, a podium for the speeches, and guests include Sir Norman Wooding, our chairman, the Russian and British business communities, the prince of course and many others. The RBCC was famously founded in 1916, a year before the Bolshevik Revolution. Timing was not the RBCC's strongest suit, and sure enough, the economy was not in the best of health at this time. It was 1998, and the country was in some state of flux, with Yeltsin at the helm.

Before the speeches and the food, part of my role as director of the Chamber was to lead the prince around the room, and introduce him to guests. This sounds relatively easy, but of course, it had to be done at a certain tempo. Not rushing but keep moving was basically the technique, and of course, I had to remember the names of the people whom I was introducing to the prince and his private secretary, a charming man with a twinkle in his eye and very dry humour, by the name of Nicholas.

Around the room we go, and I introduce each little group of people – well, more accurately, I steer the prince towards the people whose names I know. One such person was my good friend Richard, the one who introduced me to orange juice, middle partings and pressed jeans. Anyway, Richard was now working for a company and using his Russian language and knowledge to good effect. I cannot actually remember what his company was doing at that point within Russia, but I can tell you that on holiday one year in Greece, the waiter asked what Richard did for a living and Richard (always seeking a business opening) explained that he was "in ladies' gussets". It was something about equipment that produces the piece of nylon that is then fixed to the front of a pair of ladies' tights. The waiter, so far as I recall, had not expected quite such a detailed response, but let's assume, for the purposes of this recollection, that my good friend Richard was still in ladies' tights.

I steer the prince towards Richard's group, which also contains another very good friend, Daren. They are just quaffing a beer when up we come.

A conversation takes place. It is all just protocol really, "what is it your company does", and so on, but not Richard. Richard has received a question and feels it only polite to give the prince detail about ladies' gussets, so that is what he does. The prince's eyes begin to glaze over, the secretary scans the room, whilst I check my watch. Oh, he's still going. Equipment. Yes, packaging. Right. Payment terms and distributor policies. Eventually, we have to stop him. It felt like it was getting light outside.

The reception had gone well. Everybody was wined and dined, speeches were made, awards presented. Time to leave. Tomorrow we are all headed for a different city.

Richard and Daren meet His Royal Highness, Prince Michael of Kent

Because after the success of the previous year's trade fair, we decided to repeat it in the city of Ekaterinburg, right on the "border" between Europe and Asia. A bigger city, Ekaterinburg used to be called Sverdlovsk, and is a sprawling, industrial city.

It is also infamous for the execution of the Russian royal family following the revolution in 1917. In the chaos of revolution, the Romanov royal family was removed to Ekaterinburg, and they lived as prisoners in the home of a merchant by the name of Ipatiev. One day, the family was taken down to the basement of the house. Footsteps followed later down the stairs to the basement. These were the footsteps of the Bolshevik assassins, who shot the entire family, one by one, there in the basement. They shot the parents, the little children, in cold blood, no chance of escape, no mercy to the pleas for clemency or the tears.

Moreover, they built the heroic USSR upon that act of cruelty.

There was talk that the young Anastasia survived, but like many legends, it was not real. History tells us that their bodies were flung into a disused mineshaft, not to be found until many years later. That was the reality of the revolution.

Years later, the house, which really should have been preserved for historical reasons, was demolished upon the orders of one Boris Yeltsin.

The Romanov dynasty had been hoping to find sanctuary in England, but they were denied this chance, because the House of "Saxe-Coburg-Gotha" (or as they became after changing their name in 1917, "the House of Windsor") was scared that if King George's cousin were to cross the Channel, revolution in England would follow. We will never know if their fears were justified, but we do know that the Windsors' decision cost the Russian royal family their lives, and Russia, their royal family.

So here we are, in Ekaterinburg with His Royal Highness, Prince Michael of Kent, near the site of where the Ipatiev house had stood. The prince quietly left our group, walked over the road and remained in silence for a long time. Nobody said anything as he gazed upon the site of the execution of part of his family. All descended from Queen Victoria: King George, Kaiser Wilhelm, Czar Nikolai.

The site of the house and the execution now has a church.

From there, we were to head to the exhibition; after the grand opening in Moscow, then an early morning flight, this was a tiring schedule, but it was all quite usual.

Everybody has furnished their stands, and donned their suits for the formal opening of the trade fair. The governor is present, along with the prince, Sir Norman and various others. This is the formal delegation, and most shows start with a walk around. What happens next, you can guess. Yes, I am once again leading the dignitaries around the room, stopping on the stands to have a brief chat, and we chance upon Richard's stand. Richard was always a sharp dresser, and there he is in his dark suit, white shirt and tie, with shiny black shoes and his trademark centre parting, and up we walk again.

With the usual pleasantries exchanged, the prince asks Richard what his company does, and off Richard goes, extolling the virtues of their underwear machinery, which is superior to the German competitor because the belt has a faster drive and the machine has a precision needle for removing blemishes and burrs from the gussets automatically. The eyes glaze over, the secretary scans the room, I glance at my watch, and we make our excuses and get away just before he tells us about penalty clauses and spare parts delivery.

The absolute best part of this is sometime later, when Richard comes up to me, genuinely puzzled, and says, "I just can't understand that; I told Prince Michael all that when we were in Moscow."

Sergei really knew what he was doing and was meticulous not only in planning these exhibitions, but in ensuring that we made the contacts needed to conduct a high-profile event. Because Sergei was comfortable moving in these circles, and he was very good at it, we would go to the exhibition venue, visit the hotel and the office of the local administration. All these regions, some the size of France, were overseen by a governor, and these guys reported directly to the president. So powerful were they at that time, that to meet them you really had to be somebody, and the role of director of the Russo-British Chamber of Commerce gave me the opportunity to do just that. I don't even know how many governors I met over the years, there were so many. My favourite was Governor Chub of the city of Rostov, coincidentally twinned with my home town of Glasgow. My least favourite was governor of the Leningrad region, with whom I had a private breakfast at the Institute of Directors on Pall Mall. His main comment afterwards was that I was very young to be the director of the RBCC. He was right, I was. So what?

Sergei worked well with these people. He enjoyed moving in these circles more than I did frankly. Many of them seemed rather "entitled" so far as I could see, but without having really "done" anything, merely being appointed.

One recce as director was rather unusual. We were considering doing an event in Rostov, a lovely town in southern Russia, steeped in history.

The governor was a super guy, very forward-looking, but not a young man. Governor Chub, whom I just declared to be my favourite, of all those whom I met, had a great team. I recall his assistant, Sapronov, and another young man in the administration, who introduced himself like James Bond, by his surname, Natarov. They were really nice people. Natarov would be headed later for high office, and much later, this would give his son a privileged position also, as assistant to a governor (before being arrested on corruption charges). Such seems to be the way.

So here I am on an aircraft to Rostov on the Don River, seated at the back as always because I can't bear to waste money on business class. I was always like that. I want something to show for it, not just a few hours of expensively purchased "free" Prosecco, which in Soviet Russia they did not have anyway. I think the only advantage of Soviet Business Class is that you were not allocated to seat 10B with all the other passengers.

I was once upgraded to Dubai (which in a way was a pity, because I was flying to Bangkok). I spent most of the six-hour flight playing with the seat positions and inspecting what business class people get in their "free" wash kit, before being returned to the back of the aircraft for the onward flight out of Dubai.

Upon landing at Rostov, a member of cabin crew approaches me and says, "Are you English?" I respond, truthfully, that I am not, and she turns to leave.

"I am British though," I said.

The lady turns to me, muttering, and beckons me to follow, which I dutifully do. On the tarmac is a black Volga "limousine". It's really just a posh version of Fifi to be honest, but it looks cleaner than Fifi ever did and it works. The car takes me swiftly to the office of the Rostov government, not to my hotel.

I arrive at an austere building in central Rostov. Ignoring security, somebody sweeps me up the stairs and I am left in a small room. Very soon, Sapronov and "Natarov, 007" enter the room. We embrace, because we already know each other, as is the way. I quickly learned not to greet a Russian whilst holding a briefcase. It's just awkward.

They offer me a whisky, which I do not want, but a refusal would be impolite, and of course, there being three of us, there are three drinks poured, and this happens three times.

We leave after a brief discussion, and walk to the river, onto a waiting private launch.

On board, a stewardess approaches our small group and asks what we would like to drink. Immediately, my hosts order white wine for all of us, and I recall thinking, *This could end badly*. The boat motors from Rostov to the small town of Novocherkassk. We alight on this beautiful, sunny evening and stroll along the quiet avenue towards a beautiful church. All the time, Sapronov and Natarov are telling me about the town and about the legend of Melanie, for whom a banquet was held on this very avenue.

We enter the church, an oasis of calm, and we are permitted to go into the area behind the iconostasis, which in the Russian Orthodox Church is a privilege afforded to the few. The whole experience is calm, peaceful. We stroll back along the avenue towards the boat, and on the way, we pass a monastery, from which comes the most beautiful singing. We enter the monastery quadrangle, and we see a choir in the garden. We listen, and it dawns upon me that the choir is singing for me. This, I did not know.

Nor could I have known what was to happen next. They place a bearskin robe upon me, and upon my head, a lambswool hat, which they call a papakha – Cossack clothing. Next, a man appears with a tray. On it are small shot glasses full of vodka, and a jug, half full of vodka, probably 350 cl. Each guest receives a shot glass. I receive the jug.

I was expected to drink it, but to make this more interesting, they also presented me with a sheathed sword, called a shashka. Unsheathing it an inch or so, the tamada or MC, placed a shot glass into the gap between sword handle and sheath, and I tightened the grip, to keep the glass in place on the top of the blade. The tamada then pours some vodka into the shot glass, and my job is to raise the sword and to raise the glass to my lips, downing the vodka in one fast gulp. I did this, and then he repeated this until the jug was proven to be empty. There followed a brief ceremony, during which I was formally made a Don Cossack. This was an honour bestowed upon various guests of the local government.

Author becomes a Don Cossack

For those who do not know, the Cossacks were fierce and proud horseback swordsmen, and I feel that is a reasonable description of me.

The sword and hat were for me to keep, along with a certificate. I thanked them, but at the same time told them I would be unable to take this sword through customs. They told me not to worry, because they would give me a government letter, permitting me to take the items out of the country. They subsequently did, although how it worked, I will never know because it basically said "this is not a weapon, it's just a sword".

We are now beckoned towards a table laden with food and drink, and there follows a banquet. A lot of red wine was consumed at this table, and many toasts uttered. I was quite sure this was some kind of test, but I got through it and apparently earned the Cossacks' respect. We now head back to the boat in the darkness, and the boat makes its way back to Rostov. I have a little lie down, because things don't appear to be staying in the same place. Keep in mind that I have not yet seen my hotel room, and never have I wanted a room more than right then! But no, because that would be too obvious. Waiting on the quay is a white Volga, which we pile into, and sure enough, instead of going to the hotel like we should, they take me to a nightclub, owned by one of the group. I seem to recall it was called Aquarium, and we drank beer, all of us. This is absolutely the last thing I want to do. I need sleep because I have an early flight back up to Moscow.

Finally, we get back into the car, it's probably 3.30 a.m., and we head for the hotel. At last, I think to myself, clutching my little bag, my certificate and my sword, with a big woollen hat upon my head. However, upon arrival at the hotel, I am told that we have to discuss our business, and we head for the bar, where he orders whisky. I already understood I would not get any sleep. The problem was rather like the famous Morecombe & Wise sketch, where Eric tries to play piano in front of virtuoso pianist André Previn. During the evening, we had consumed whisky, then white wine, then vodka, then red wine, followed by beer and finally, to bookend the whole thing, more whisky. The amount was absurd, but like Eric Morecombe, I could not help thinking that we had all the right drinks, just not necessarily in the right order!

I have no recollection of the business discussion. Around 05:30, probably, my host checks his watch, jumps up and exclaims that I must go to the airport. He orders a taxi and is astonished to learn that I am flying economy class. I find my seat, put away my Cossack regalia and fall fast asleep for the duration of the flight.

I sometimes wonder what Rostov would have been like, if I had actually seen it, I mean.

Trips to Russia would invariably start and end in Moscow, and when we conducted formal events, accompanied by the prince and others, there were invariably motorcades and outriders. There are stories about Prince Michael of Kent "selling access" to the Russian president. I do not believe that to be very credible. If only because, in my experience, his contacts did not quite go that far. I may be mistaken, but in general, the prince would conduct meetings of a more protocol nature, a lot of high-ranking politicians and businessmen, but I am unaware of there being any special relationship between him and the president or those of the president's immediate circle. I mentioned Nemtsov a moment ago, whom I knew but not that well. He would later be shot in the back, whilst strolling over a bridge in Moscow. The people whom we would meet would include, for example, Mikhail Khodorkovsky, then head of oil giant Yukos, later to be imprisoned. Governor Chub of Rostov, Governor Rutskoi of Kursk, Governor Yakovlev of Saint Petersburg, Governor Efremov of Arkhangelsk, actually, lots of governors! Also Boris Berezovsky, erstwhile oligarch and lever puller, later disillusioned, largely irrelevant, and later to be found hanged.

These were the people whom I met, and I did not care for all of them by any means.

Moscow Mayor Luzhkov considered himself to be super important. I shared a panel with him at a conference and met him several times. I did not take to him one bit. Put it this way, on one occasion, I was at an event in Moscow and noticed him leaving a room whilst talking to somebody on his mobile phone, but his phone was not in his hand as he walked (despite his hands being empty). His phone was being held to his left ear by a lackey as they walked. That is how important he decided he was. He was widely suspected of being corrupt.

As this trade exhibition moved from city to city over the course of a few years, and we continued to do our pre-show planning trip, a particular incident remains etched in my mind.

Amongst the things that Sergei did was to arrange an after-party for the exhibitors. They bring their products and brochures to a city, and each day attend their stand at the trade fair, and host various local companies which had an interest in doing business with the UK. On the evening before their departure, the British business people were given a party.

We had flown out for a few days for meetings with the local government, the exhibition venue management and various others. Travel in Russia could be quite entertaining for all the wrong reasons. I recall standing in the hotel bathroom and watching the bath filling up with a brackish, brown water that smelt of eggs. It turns out this was something to do with sulphur in the supply and it was allegedly harmless, but I didn't like the look of it one bit.

A BRIEF CHAT

Some weeks before, a nightclub in Ekaterinburg was one of the venues we visited. The venue for the after-party was quite large, with a huge dance floor and several bars, and a "Zone of Higher Comfort".

How intriguing. We had no idea what this was, but it was behind a door, and nothing makes you want to open a door more, to see what is on the other side, than a sign saying Zone of Higher Comfort.

Inside is a darkened room, tastefully decorated with a number of cocktail tables, each with a lamp, and in the middle of the room, a stage, but actually more like a runway, a catwalk. We sit down, and someone orders drinks. Mike is on form. He's a really nice bloke, Mike, from Stoke. He ran his own business, I had been to Siberia with him, and he is great company. He never seemed to go to the bar, as he was always chatting. Anyway, somebody orders drinks, and a few minutes later, music starts and a young lady comes onto the stage. Elegantly dressed, she begins to dance. It's very tastefully done, actually.

Out in the main body of the venue, the service had been rather poor, and of course, I didn't realise it at the time, but I suppose this was a kind of "mystery shopping" experience, where we went to perform an incognito inspection. My mood is not great, mainly because I need to speak to the management about the service out in the main venue, in other words, where the after-party is due to be held. That is part of my role, unfortunately.

However, the music is good and the dancing is tasteful, and we have drinks in front of us, so my concerns and my need to speak to management will have to wait. Whilst we sit, chatting and enjoying a beer, the young lady onstage removes her shoes.

And her top.

Then her skirt.

This is rather unexpected, and we begin to understand why the room is named as it is. There are quite a few people seated, having drinks in this zone, and about half of them are women, so we are particularly surprised at the dancer's next manoeuvre which is to remove every other item of clothing.

Then another young lady appeared.

And it happened again.

Here is the strangest part.

Each garment was then thrown to the floor, and each dancer was elegantly dressed upon arrival on stage.

So, after an hour and numerous dancers, the floor was strewn with clothing.

At this point, I go to the toilet, then to find the person in charge, because we could not have people waiting for coats to be taken, waiting to order drinks and so on, out in the main part of the club. In here, by contrast, the service had been fine. Was I also concerned about the zone? Not at all, for it was behind a door.

I return to the zone and ask to speak to the management. A gentleman arrives, and just before going to speak to him, I quickly don my jacket, which has been hanging on the back of my chair.

I am polite, explain to him that we are the advance party of a delegation of over 100 people, and that we need our guests to receive service considerably better than we experienced out in the main venue.

The manager, very professional, apologises, assuring me that he will speak to the relevant line managers. The discussion is brief, courteous and businesslike.

We leave shortly afterwards, and this is the first time I see chortling. Mike, obviously. Oh, how Mike can chortle. We go to the hotel, and to our separate rooms.

The discussion with the manager had been more "brief" than I realised. Before preparing for bed, I hang my jacket in the wardrobe. *Only then*, I notice that the pockets are bulging. I examine my jacket more closely, and find it full of ladies' underwear.

Mike. I certainly got to know his humour better that evening.

I sit on the bed, and wonder what on earth that manager would have said if he had known that the director of such an august entity, currently admonishing the level of service in the establishment, was doing so with a jacket stuffed with other peoples' knickers.

Sergei had been very successful in giving the RBCC some presence, some gravitas. Whilst I was not a fan of Russian power individuals, I recognised that in Russia, you need to woo them and Sergei could do this admirably. Whilst working together, he put on events in several Russian cities and then created a London event, which was equally successful, until the Russian president declared that the Saint Petersburg Forum was where Russian dignitaries should be. Of course, they all followed what the boss told them to do.

To be honest, Sergei was too big, too ambitious for the RBCC and we were forced to go our separate ways when this became apparent. We fell out, which I regretted, but I just thought he was made for bigger things, and deep down, I think he agreed. I am glad to say that we got back on good terms 20 years later!

Some while after our relationship had ended, politically, things too had changed, with the installation (not election) of Putin to the office of president. Yes, Putin was put in.

I recall being summoned to Berezovsky's office, just off Piccadilly, when he was effectively living in exile, no longer the kingmaker that he had once been. He was bitter and angry. He wrote to a lot of people around this time.

Berezovsky was an oligarch, and in the rather unpleasant nineties, he had made his mark as a kingmaker. He would consider himself largely responsible for ensuring that Putin would become president, and there were few high-level, power-broking meetings without this man, but the man whom he believed he "installed" as president would turn on these oligarchs, who had carved up swathes of the Russian economy for financial gain. His power dwindled, and whilst he avoided prison unlike some, Berezovsky was no longer in favour. The revolution had eaten her children, as they say.

Deeply embittered by his overthrow and now apparent irrelevance, he moved to the UK and lived in Berkshire.

Berezovsky, at this time, had a desire to meet with me in my capacity as director of the Russo-British Chamber of Commerce.

I had met him briefly a couple of times and I can't say I was fond of him. There were some of these power brokers who remained personable characters, pleasant to others. He was not one of them. With an appearance of a squat, sullen man, he now had bitterness to add to his arrogance. I was not in a mood to do business with him.

He asked if I could put on a conference in London, somewhere near Heathrow. I asked him how many people and over what period, one day, two, along with a few other questions. He asked me how much it would cost. I gave him a cost, which I made up on the spot. He asked dollars or sterling.

> # BORIS BEREZOVSKY
>
> 14 March 2003
>
> Mr. David Cant
> Director
> Russo-British Chamber of Commerce
> 42 Southward Street
> London
> SE1 1UN
>
> Dear Mr. Cant
>
> I wanted to share with you an important announcement made earlier this month (6 March) in High Court where Forbes accepted in court that allegations made against me in its magazine in an article entitled "Godfather of the Kremlin?" were false.
>
> I have enclosed a copy of my statement setting out what Forbes agreed in Her Majesty's Courts of Justice were false allegations and erroneous assertions as well as a correction notice Forbes agreed to post on their website (www.forbes.com).
>
> This has been a long six-year legal battle, which included a thoroughly balanced decision of the House of Lords, to clear my name and vindicate my reputation. I am pleased that Forbes accepted it was wrong and the case has ended.
>
> I am confident that the image of Russia and reputation of Russian businessmen will be strengthened following this court agreement. For many years Western media have portrayed Russian business leaders as corrupt crony capitalists. The acceptance by Forbes of its wrong-doing should contribute to more informed and accurate reporting on Russia's emerging market economy and business.
>
> Interpark House 7 Down Street London W1J 7AJ
> Tel: +44(20)7 647 5080 Fax: +44(20)7 647 5090

Letter from Oligarch Boris Berezovsky to the author.
He would be found hanged by the neck some ten years afterwards

"Sterling," I responded, again, just on the hoof.

I then asked the nature of the conference, and he explained to me that he wanted to put together a conference of those opposed to the current Russian government. I had already decided not to become involved before he had finished his sentence. I have never involved myself in Russian politics.

The following day, I happened to be at a London event and was chatting to the Russian ambassador, His Excellency Mr. Fokin. He was more approachable than most ambassadors whom I have known over the years. I mentioned my meeting the previous day with Berezovsky and the nature of the discussion.

"Put it this way, David," the ambassador said to me. "If you were to organise this conference, there would be people in the Kremlin who might feel quite emotional about it."

On the left, Sir Norman Wooding and HRH Duke of Kent, whilst Russian Ambassador Evgenii Fokin is in conversation with the author

It was rather academic, because I had no intention of working with Berezovsky, but I noted the ambassador's turn of phrase, kind and chilling at the same time. Berezovsky would be found sometime later in his Berkshire home, hanged by the neck. Yet another Russian "mystery".

Going to Russia was often eventful, and particular trips are etched firmly on my mind. The London experience, however, was a different thing altogether. The office on Southwark Street was a fairly dusty, lacklustre environment in the former Wilcox building. You can still see the building as your train goes from London Bridge towards Waterloo East. The landlord was an absolute nightmare and had quite a reputation. He was fabulously wealthy, but drove a clapped-out Merc and wore shorts and a T-shirt. He was not a nice man.

The office and even the landlord were tolerable. Having started working there in early 1996, just over a year later, with my wife now pregnant, we had moved to a property in Kent. One problem; I had to learn to commute and that is what I did for years. The 07:22 from platform two, to be precise.

That said, London was not all bad. The commuting was bad, the executive council meetings were pointless and sometimes worse, but there were good times also. Barry, for example, who had been doing business in Russia long before me. His company was named "The Russia House", which was a gentlemen's agreement, as I understand it, between Barry and the author John Le Carré, whose novel of the same name had made a brief mention of Barry's employee (with whom I would later work). Barry had become a kind of statesman of business in Russia. He was one of those people who just refused to give up. He was always coming up with ideas, and he was supported all the way, all those years, by the lovely Margaret, always right there for him.

Then there was Paul. He worked for a bank. He was a really nice guy, highly intelligent, and great company too.

One Tuesday afternoon, I bump into Paul somewhere around London Bridge, and he tells me that I would be a welcome guest on a wooden, full-size replica of a ship named the *Shtandart*, which is sailing back to Holland, having been berthed briefly near the HMS *Belfast*. It's sailing east along the Thames, under Tower Bridge, and it will make a stop at Tilbury. From there, a ferry could get me back across the Thames to Gravesend in Kent, which my head told me would be easy because I live in Tonbridge, Kent, a mere twenty miles.

The ship was a replica of Peter the Great's fastest frigate of its time, built in 1703, the first ship in Russia's Baltic Fleet. The czar was determined to create a Russian navy to compete with anyone.

"That sounds great, Paul. I didn't know about this. When is that happening?"

"We leave in about half an hour."

I had not expected that. After a nanosecond, I ran to the office, told my long-suffering secretary, Dee, that I had something urgent I needed to do, and ran back to the quay just by the Horniman's pub and the HMS *Belfast*.

Possibly, the reason I had not known about this private event was that nobody seemed to know about it. When I boarded the beautiful vessel, I was astonished at how few people were on the deck. We were shown around, the Russian crew greeted us politely, and we cast off.

We start heading east and as we go, the river gradually widens. We go past the O2 Arena, out of the City of London and we head for the Queen Elizabeth Bridge.

There is a bar at the stern of the vessel, an impromptu affair, and hence, nobody is at the bow of the ship. It was a sunny afternoon and an experience which could not be repeated. We made our way under the bridge, and finally, made fast in Tilbury. It was a great and totally unanticipated afternoon.

A couple of weeks later, I bump into Paul again, and we start chatting. The chat turns to the boat trip, and Paul's face takes on a pensive expression.

"Yes, there was a bit of a misunderstanding about that trip," Paul mentioned. "I was asked to speak to the chairman of the bank about it. The chairman pointed out that the bar bill included four bottles of vodka, two cases of beer, five bottles of white wine and a carton of orange juice."

I was not sure what to say, so I asked him how that went down. "What did he say?"

"Well," he replied, "I told him, I was totally at a loss as to who had been drinking the orange juice!"

Travelling was altogether more enjoyable, and also very necessary, because one thing I learned to my dismay was that Russians need strong leadership. Initiative can be in short supply, and when there is initiative, it has a habit of being used for the wrong purposes. It was frustrating. I had left my previous role, with the American company's Moscow office, because the cook asked me how many potatoes she should buy at the market. That was one step too far. I said nothing to her of course, but it was a significant moment in my exasperation.

I always liked the prince, a thorough gentleman with a sense of humour, despite his titles. Our meetings always took place at Kensington Palace, which sounds grand, but they were in a small basement room.

Working with royals is fun. We would arrive into Moscow and a cavalcade of limousines would take us into town, police cars, motorcycle outriders and the traffic police stopping the traffic all along the route. What takes an hour was a mere 20 minutes. The prince did not like to be driven around like this, but it is the Russian way, and whether he liked it or not, that is what the hosts did each trip. In the regions, this was even more noticeable because, of course, visits were fewer than in the capital.

Prince Michael conducted a lot of charity work, and one of his great loves is cars. More specifically, collectors' pieces, massive 1920s' Bentleys, big, throaty, 4.5-litre machines in what was then called British racing green. Several of these car collectors, owners, including the prince, came up with a charity idea to drive all the way from Brooklands race circuit, in Surrey, to Red Square in Moscow. Nigel Mansell flew in to a breakfast ceremony, and we waved these magnificent machines off. The year was 2003, so far as I recall, and they made it all the way to Red Square, where they were met by, then, Mayor Luzhkov.

Like so many Russian politicians, Luzhkov was accused of widespread corruption. Putin fired him and awarded him an Order of Merit anyway. All pretty normal by his standards.

The Bentley rally raised money for charity, with its sponsorship and a lavish event in the grounds of Kuskovo Palace, and it was wonderful PR for the UK.

Brooklands to Red Square charity rally reception Kuskovo Palace Moscow

The prince was always a good figurehead for the RBCC and, as a royal, he required security, in the form of a gentleman called Chris – a police officer, who carried a gun, concealed discreetly. Russian security was the polar opposite. They wanted people to know they were security, so they were massive guys, with earpieces visibly protruding because of a cable. They wore their guns visibly, but in a dangerous situation, Chris would have been more effective.

On one occasion, we were all together, and I think we were opening the Wedgewood store.

It is morning, perhaps 08:30. We are all turned out in our suits, and the atmosphere is quiet as we wait for proceedings to commence. Well, unannounced and absolutely unexpectedly, two young figures, about eight years old, rush into view in the room from behind a wall, dressed in full flamenco costume. They dance energetically and beautifully, but the music they chose had a loud and sudden opening. I can still hear it today. On that quiet morning, it was unexpected. Chris, thinking the prince is in danger because of the sudden loud bang, grabs his gun and leaps into the air before realising that the danger is a couple of eight-year-olds. He resumes his composure quickly, but will be reminded about this for a long, long time afterwards.

I recall having breakfast with Chris and a couple of others in the Kempinski Hotel in Moscow, and the conversation turned to working with the royals. Chris explained it eloquently: most people do not become "friends" with the royals when working with them. There is no long-term contact. He likened it to walking past a window, and before you know it, you have passed it. That was the same with me, working with them. I walked past the window, had a brief insight into the family and how they interacted, and then it was behind me, with no further contact.

I mentioned Princess Michael previously, somewhat different to her husband in my experience. They travelled together to Moscow on one occasion only (at least, I was only personally involved in arranging one trip). We accommodated them in the best hotel available, and this was a suite in the Baltschug Kempinski.

This hotel had been one of many crumbling old relics just a few years before but was now truly a sumptuous hotel, thanks to investment. Right on the river, opposite the Kremlin, the ground floor was massive, with shops, lounges and of course, attentive staff everywhere. I stayed there once or twice only, when I had the budget for it, and I recall that the bed felt like an ocean of eiderdown, the size of my entire room when I was a student.

Up on one of the top floors of the building, the suite for our royal guests was sumptuous, basically an apartment.

Stationed outside the suite for the duration of their trip, some three days, would be two FSB officers, day and night. KGB, as they were previously known. The Russians demanded their presence to ensure the security of the VIPs.

Being the director of the RBCC, I wanted to make sure that these guys were catered for also, because their Russian bosses would certainly not be thinking about that. I suggested that they should be allowed to use room service. They abused this gesture in the most grotesque manner.

The trip went well enough. I learnt a little more about the dynamic of the relationship between the prince and princess. She did a lot of talking. He did not really need an interpreter, being a Russian speaker, but she did, so I translated on various occasions. I recall visiting a monastery, and being offered tea. It was all very pleasant, but I think at some point, she must have become bored. She says quietly to the prince one word: "aufstehen", which means to "stand up", in other words, it was a brief suggestion to end the meeting, and she probably thought she was being discreet, but she was not. We all spoke German. The prince concluded the meeting.

At the end of this trip, I escorted them out to the airport. Upon checkout, to my immense dismay, I had discovered that the two FSB officers had racked up so many room service orders that the cost of their bill, over three days, was actually *greater than the cost of the royals' suite*. It was a cynical, actually childish abuse. I had called their commanding officer to complain; I recall asking if they had been filling their boots with caviar. I was furious. Why is it not possible for someone just to accept a kindness without feeling the need to fill a bag to take home to the family? On the way out to the airport, I received a call to advise me that the officers "have been dealt with", whatever that meant.

March, 1999, I am in the basement restaurant of a luxury hotel in London, hosting a delegation from the city of Arkhangelsk. Governor Efremov is sitting opposite me. I cannot stay for the entire dinner because I leave the following morning to lead a trade mission to Saint Petersburg, but I liked this governor; he did not seem to have an issue with my young age, and I wanted to hear more about his region of Russia and what he did. Towards the end of the meal, I broached a topic, and I am somewhat ashamed to say that I did not really know enough about what I was asking.

The delegation visiting London had a busy schedule ahead, with protocol visits including Kensington Palace and business meetings. A call had come into my office earlier that day, and I explained to the governor at the table about the request from the Arctic Convoy veterans to meet his delegation. No sooner had I mentioned the veterans than the governor jumped to his feet, called for silence in the room and announced to the Russian business community in the room that the actual Arctic Convoy veterans had expressed a wish to meet their delegation. There was a cheer and a toast. The governor turned to me and told me to be sure to include a meeting with the veterans in their programme. I was only later to understand why these people were so important to Russians, and particularly to those from that part of the country. The veterans had played a significant role in keeping Russia supplied in some of the fiercest conditions of World War II.

Next day, leaving the delegation with my colleagues, I head for Saint Petersburg to lead a delegation of UK exporters on a trade mission.

Saint Petersburg is an interesting city. Built on a swamp by Peter the Great, it is known as the Venice of the North, with its canals and its beautiful avenues and grand buildings. Trade missions remained useful for companies with little or no previous experience of a market. I have been on a trade mission myself when I was entering the Croatian market on behalf of a client. They definitely have their place for companies new to a market. Russia was my patch. I don't recall how many UK companies were on this trip, probably a dozen or so. The local Chamber in Saint Petersburg was our partner for this trip, and the week's meetings were marked by a brief breakfast reception at the local Chamber's head offices, with the inevitable speeches. In the evenings, we would usually offer to take the delegates out to dinner somewhere, everyone chipping in to the cost of the meal.

St Petersburg Chamber of Commerce mission

British companies preferred informal places, with atmosphere. Russians tend to think that business people should fly business class, the restaurant must be expensive and quiet, and preferably where a waiter stands by the table throughout the meal, with a serviette draped over his arm. I can think of nothing worse.

Over the course of the next few days, I came to know some of the business people on this Saint Petersburg mission. I remember in detail only one of them, because he was an interesting guy, and as it happens would become an important figure to me.

Ken owned a factory and was a very nice man, with an amazing wit; I pity anybody who caught the sharp end of that! Ken had received some orders from Russia, had travelled out to learn more and, of course, to find more business. For that was Ken, a go-getter, a self-made man; as he used to say, "You make your own luck in life".

One of the people whom Ken met on that trip was Sergei Tsivilev. Sergei was a lawyer with an office opposite that of the local Chamber on Tchaikovsky Street. We shall see a lot more of this man later, because he turned out to be headed for high office. We just did not know it at the time.

When the mission was over, and the business delegation was ready to go, I bumped into Ken in the hotel corridor.

"Hi Dave," grins Ken. I have no idea why he always called me Dave, but that was OK. "Listen mate, I'm not going to fly home today, I'm going to go to Moscow."

"How? You don't even speak Russian…" I was puzzled. Impressed, but puzzled.

"Not a problem, I'm all sorted; I'm going on the overnight train!"

That was typical of Ken, very independent, and always on the lookout for a way of creating an opportunity, a true entrepreneur.

Off he went. Ken later told me he was picked up in Moscow, taken to a meeting and could not help noticing a baseball bat lying on the back seat. He also later told me that the Russian company owner, whom he met once on that trip in Moscow, was poisoned shortly afterwards and died, but that did not stop Ken, oh no!

Time would roll on and regular council meetings would take place in the offices of a large city law firm in London. They were always unpleasant and had very little to do with the business, because not one of the members of the council was a current or relevant business person. They were all retirees from big corporations, with zero experience of small business. I believe that has been resolved now, not before time. I used to wear this tie to every one of these meetings, a small protest at the waste of time. Nobody seemed to notice the pig baring its backside at everyone.

Not long into this new role, I received a request to attend a Foreign Affairs Select Committee hearing on the role of the embassy in supporting commerce. This made sense; after all, I had been in the ministry and in business and had become fairly knowledgeable on Russia by this time. Apparently, I "didn't get the other memo" as they say. The one that said the real purpose of this hearing is "keep your head down".

I garnered views from the British business community on their experience of support (or otherwise) from the commercial section of the British embassy in Moscow (whose function was *to support business*). Some business people with experience of dealing with this commercial section at that time had views that were not positive, and my duty was to include this in my submission. I was simply doing my job. Not only that, but my then chairman saw my report and suggested I make the points more strongly: "Spike it up" was the expression he used.

Off I go to Westminster Palace and take my seat along with the big corporations. It was one of those lovely rooms with wood panelling on the walls and before us sat the committee, representing various parties and disciplines, with some knowledge of business and, of course, foreign affairs. Each corporation invited to this committee took this opportunity to praise the commercial section of the British embassy for their sterling work in supporting big business, and then it was my turn. I took the opportunity to repeat the experience of "SMEs," small and medium-sized businesses.

The experience that I recounted that day, directly from the mouths of exporters, was a little less gushing than that of the big corporations. In fact, it was not positive at all, because the companies whom I was talking to felt that the government at that time was not helping them. I had every reason to believe that the views expressed would be received in good faith and acted upon. I was wrong.

You may remember that I had had this once before in a previous role. Where somebody within the system could not take the critique, and instead of doing something about it, "shot the messenger" as it were.

Not long afterwards, I would receive a handwritten letter from the outgoing British ambassador, which I will liken to a child throwing his toys out of the pram. He claimed to be disappointed in my comments to the select committee, stated how he had always been proud of his achievements and that this kind of commentary in Westminster was uncalled for. I shall not name him here. It was astonishing. The points the companies had made through my report had been ignored, at least by him; the ambassador decided this was a personal attack upon his stewardship at the embassy. It was not. I did not mention the ambassador, because my brief was to talk about the commercial section. I can only imagine that at the end of an ambassador's career, something happens a little bit like the allocation of windows I had come across earlier in the London ministry. You rise in the ranks and you get more windows, as you retire, if you get a black mark or two, something bad happens, though I cannot imagine what. Nothing else could explain this man's outburst.

Now the same chairman, who had urged me to "spike it up," to hold nothing back, suggests we meet the new ambassador to explain everything. We did this, three of us in the Reform Club on Pall Mall, and to be fair, the new incoming ambassador listened and seemed quite relaxed about the whole thing.

The Reform Club, scene of many meetings

Cabaret Rehearsals    *Performance of Cabaret*

Our Student Room

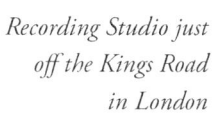

Recording Studio just off the Kings Road in London

Soviet Taxi

Street Newspaper Pravda

The fun of the Soviet Trolleybus

The sign that met me every day saying the lift does not work

Volgas and Ladas

Bored Soviet Soldiers

Guarding the Mausoleum

May Day Moscow

The Chicken in the Hotel Foyer

2002 author with football cat Zhulik

AGM Chesnokov Scallon Smith Wooding Land Author

"Britain in Russia" exhibition with Sir Norman Wooding CBE and HRH Duke of Kent

HRH Duke of Kent and Author

Governor Rutskoi of Kursk Region in London with the Author

Baroness Smith of Gilmorehill, HRH Prince Michael of Kent KCVO and Author

Sergei Kolushev, Baroness Smith and Author

Ralph Land, Sir Norman Wooding, Boris Nemtsov, Author, Catherine Revill

With HRH Prince Michael of Kent

Speaking at National Hotel Moscow

With colleagues, friends

With the Chairman

Speaking in Saint Petersburg, 1999

Katya Drozhzhina  *Albion Stand*

Another Albion Stand  *Dasha at a trade fair*

One of many factory visits

With Grigory, Christmas Day, Moscow, 2020

Katya food factory visit

Kremlin Banquet

Wedding of Author and Lorraine

Moscow Bridge

Moscow City

Moscow Snow Piled up

Moscow Streets

Spassky Tower and St Basils at night

Trade Fair

With Katya and Grigory on a train leaving Moscow for meetings

Wham plant

Covid Pub "Ulysses" Moscow

Cuba

Gorgeous Cuban Cars, oh and my family

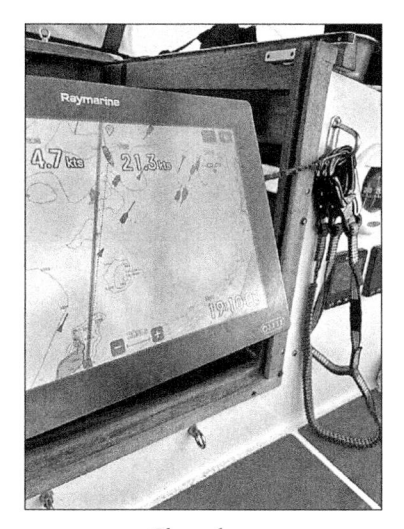

Chartplotter

Ocean Blue

Dolphins in the Ocean

Katy

DC at the wheel

"Hoist the Anchor! All the Russians are in the water"

Richard and Gary

UK Russia Ukraine France

However, I couldn't help thinking that I had been somehow used as a pawn in a real-life game of chess…

Whilst I busied myself with work and commenced the process of destroying my marriage with all these early departures, late arrivals, travel and financial stress, the company that my wife and I had started was beginning to show signs of life.

There was another reason for the stress. We had been talking to two people about doing some business together, and the long and the short of it is we lost money by investing in them – thousands of pounds, money which we could not afford to lose – and we had tried so hard. My wife was essentially working for them without charge, whilst I was assisting with time, language and experience, where I could, usually at weekends. It was going nowhere, this project, for reasons to do with people, which I will not go into here. Money was being thrown around and whilst one was supposed to have industry contacts, he did not, the other, useful financial contacts, and he did not. In exasperation, we took legal action against them in the form of a legal "Winding up Petition" to their company. Just in time as it turned out, because they were attempting (I think the following day) to close their company, which would have meant that the court action would not have been filed, and nobody would have known about the complaint. The one supplier we had through the project above was effectively lost. Tatiana and I visited them; they listened, understood, and we agreed that Albion would service their export requirements. That business continues to this day. Albion was born into fire.

Our second child was born in March, 2000, a little sweetie pie who arrived late, as she would do for the next couple of decades! We named her Natalie, but would come to call her Natasha within minutes. We now had two little bundles of joy, and life was a busy affair!

In hindsight, every time I have attempted to invest in anything I have lost. I always had an appetite for risk, building materials, corporate governance, classic cars, all of it went bad, even when I took professional advice. Do I regret that? No, I do not, because I might have won. That is what risk is about. There were lords and knights involved in the corporate governance project, and I thought it was a relatively safe bet. I was not going to bet the house, don't get me wrong, but the thought of waiting years for an ISA was not for me. There is a place for the risk-takers; we accept that we may not win.

2001 Seminar

If I changed anything, it would be the RBCC. It was stressful, governed by people who seemed to me to be clueless, up to its neck in debt, outdated and largely irrelevant. We changed all that and it is very different now, but it was a heavy price to pay.

My time at the RBCC had been an interesting one, but not joyous. Had I known at the interview the state of its finances, its services, the opinion of its dwindling membership, and that large corporates occasionally tried to join as "sole traders", I may not have taken it on. Yes, it had interesting elements, the receptions, the venues, the travel, meeting people in high office, but it was a constant struggle. Many was the night I lay awake, anxious that this entity, founded in 1916, before the Russian Revolution, could go down "on my watch". I had not been given full disclosure even at the original interview. Their so-called executive council demonstrated at every meeting their lack of knowledge. One claimed the internet was a fad, another asked if meetings could be later so he could get a cheaper rail ticket, and the nasties would tell jokes in the meeting about my predecessors and what had become of them. These people more specifically were Telyatnikov and Trofimov, from the Russian Trade Delegation, Highgate. They were particularly odious people whose principal interaction seemed to be based upon an attempt to undermine.

No, it was definitely time to move on, for the sake of mental health, family life (which had taken a particular beating at the very time that I should have been there) and for career. Mostly, they considered a 36-year-old to be too young for the job, so I had nowhere to go here. What I did not know was what was to happen next.

I recall sometimes sleeping in the office, pulling two chairs together and trying to get some sleep because I had to finish something or start something, prepare something, and it cost me dearly; my marriage, perhaps.

I have not told many people this, except my late father. I was in the running to get an MBE. Two people had said they would like to put my name forwards, but I suspect I had ruffled too many feathers in Westminster and Whitehall.

I didn't need an MBE. My work here was done.

2002-2004: ALBION

It was time to jump ship, onto Albion, full-time, no going back.

It is fair to say, following the founding of Albion in 1996, that 1997 was a good year. The problem was that this was to be followed by a quarter of a century of bad years and, whilst that may sound slightly comical, it is true. I watched as companies went under, colleagues and friends left the market, changed careers or diversified, whilst I lashed myself to the wheel and stayed with Russia.

Was this a mistake?

Yes. It was a mistake.

I should have abandoned Russia.

I should have seen where it was headed.

Many people saw what I did not want to see. John, one night in my friend's place in Melfort, he told me, "Russia under the current leadership is toxic. Get out". I didn't listen, because it was my life's work. Maybe I just didn't want to believe what I was seeing.

Anyway, here I am, running Albion with Tatiana, and I set up the consultancy side of the business. This would work to complement the trade and export that Tatiana was handling.

My first client was a company then owned by Rolls-Royce group, based in Pershore. At the beginning, there was only a handful of consultancy clients, and of course, we had the export business. This led to further clients, and I gradually became better at refining our offering, so we gave the client what they wanted, not just what I could do. Soon we had a good list of good UK manufacturers, who wanted help, not only with language, finding partners, distributors and contracts, but also, help with how business really works in Russia, the importance of culture, understanding hierarchy, mores and values. They wanted me to accompany them to and around Russia, to explain why the Russians close their eyes during meetings, to explain how meetings work, who speaks first, what to talk about before talking business – to *interpret*. Interpreting has little to do with language. That would be translating. By and large, Tatiana was running the export side and I was dealing with the consultancy.

We actually became really useful, and I don't know how many hundred companies we helped to get into the Russian market. Not every project worked, and we were not perfect, but we certainly tried hard and we achieved results.

The cultural differences alone made for fascinating interactions, and explaining some of these issues became a (minor) part of what our company did. So why do Russians close their eyes during meetings? It is not intended to be rude. It is usually a mark of listening intently. Taking calls during the meetings or arriving late, that seems rude to us, but in Russia, it is more or less normal. The thing to remember is they do not expect you to behave any differently, so it is actually wrong of us, in that environment, to "over-apologise" for a late arrival.

We covered a lot of ground in these cultural sessions, conducting meetings, women in business, communication, customs, hierarchy, alcohol, dining out, all sorts of things, and it taught me a lot. Well, it taught me how to prepare a soft-boiled egg for a start, which I used to joke was a bastion of Russo-British cooperation! Boil the egg the Russian way (straight into boiling water, remove 6 minutes later for the perfect result). Eat the egg the British way (decapitate it, instead of tapping it on the head with a spoon whilst bits of eggshell fly around the kitchen). However, there is a whole different book in there, so let's not go there right now.

For the most part, our role was to find companies with a potential interest in Russia, and, put simply, to find partners for them and start their business. It was a real buzz to get a company up and running, and it was a wonderful chance to meet interesting people and to travel.

It was not glamorous. I recall in Saint Petersburg, walking to my hotel, with an envelope in my pocket containing cash payment for a client. I was stopped by a police officer, who frisked me, very politely, and robbed me of the envelope. It was very professional.

I have been robbed several times in Russia, but it has always been done very nicely; unlike Gopal or Dima, they did not beat me up.

I shall not expand upon the detail, but years of tough decisions and circumstances followed. In the fairly early years came the divorce, and I played a large part in that coming about. With young children, I did not agree that divorce was the right thing to do, but in hindsight, it was. The problem was that, whilst there was no animosity, nor even a lawyer involved, it created a difficult parenting path. Probably not deliberate, but we had different views on what was the right thing to do, and that created tension.

Oddly enough, carving up our estate was the easiest part. Everything was halved, including the company. I took the consultancy, and my now ex, Tatiana, took the trading. I didn't want to lose the house so took the biggest mortgage I could afford and we stayed in the family home. Both parents saw the girls half the time, and we did parties, school events and so on, together. We got on pretty well and the girls were our priority.

My sister Fiona and indeed Alasdair, my brother, were real stalwarts at this time. Fiona scooped me up and took me sailing around the west coast of Scotland with a couple of her friends, and this was exactly what I needed to clear my head. She gave me a vegetable peeler, laughing that I would need to do more cooking, but not to worry, that I would be happy again. These acts of kindness and humorous quips were what I needed. She maintained that I would not end up alone, and often it is the other way around, and she was right of course.

Whilst it is difficult for me to say whether I was close to my siblings, we shared a childhood, so we could support each other when needed. We all supported each other within own immediate families of course, but I think in hindsight, I tended to disclose more.

I would later learn to call this the Silo, partly because this closed circuitry took on a less than positive dynamic. In its most basic form, the Silo is simply the notion that immediate family is core. There is nothing wrong with that, but it seemed then to become rather exclusive. I always wanted our three families to interact more than at occasional events.

We had spoken about this in early years, before we all had young families ourselves, but whilst my siblings and I did not want that to happen, it happened. If only for geographical reasons, these things don't always work out as planned!

I remember driving some eighty miles or so, from Tonbridge to Cambridge so that my girls could enjoy a party with their cousins. I did this happily, but was a bit surprised when the party, which took place in a church, came to an end and there was no suggestion that we might join them at home for a cup of tea before the drive back. So, we drove back.

Families are complex of course. I had to focus on the business, following the divorce, and making sure things did not unravel there or at home.

I ran the entire business from a small room at home, and it worked, but after we divorced, I needed focus for my mind.

I became a Samaritan. I learned much from this. The training seemed to go on for ever, the practice phone calls, role play, scenarios and examples, but it was necessary because, quite literally, lives were at stake. I will not go into detail, but some of the situations were harrowing, and when I got home, sometimes in the middle of the night after a shift, I would need to decompress. This could be crying into a pillow or having a beer, or crying into a pillow with a beer. That was about it, limited choices. It qualified me on the topic of suicide. We were allowed to tell others that we were Samaritans; I am allowed to say so in this book. The reason for that is that the phone numbers are now not local, but national. You could be in a difficult situation, call, and you would never know with whom you were speaking. We were dedicated and we kept our lines open always, because one day, you might need these guys yourself. The one thing we did not do, was to disclose anything of the discussions that took place. Sometimes we had to talk to each other at the end of a shift, but never to somebody outside of the charity.

I did not therefore speak to anybody about my time there. To do so would have been to go against everything that the charity stood for, but it made an impression upon me. Some of the conversations remain in my mind even now.

One of our early clients, and one whom I had known since I worked at the RBCC and met in Saint Petersburg, was Ken. You may remember Ken from the trade mission, the one who went to Moscow to find more business instead of flying home.

Ken became a real good friend in the years to come. He was highly successful in his career in the food industry, and he had come back from that Russian trip with plenty of business. This was a time of great change in Russia and with change comes hardship. Not all Russians at this time were driving Ferraris. Ken told me that his product was a means of providing protein to a market at an affordable price.

He had approached me as I was preparing to leave the RBCC and asked me if I wanted a "proper job" – always the diplomat, Ken! So it came that Ken worked with us. I did not go on his payroll or relocate. It was better for both parties if we provided this as consultancy, particularly as we were picking up other client work.

There could be another book, just about travelling with Ken. It was always an interesting experience. We became close to Sergei, the lawyer with the office in Saint Petersburg. He helped us immensely with some product that had gone astray. I recall somebody ended up being taken away by the police whilst we were actually talking to him. We had not realised it, but we had been talking to a customer who had stolen from us. It was all sorted, but the relationship was not always easy.

I am in Sergei's office with Ken when the topic of remuneration comes up. The sum desired is not the same as the sum on offer, and no amount of diplomatic interpreting on my part is going to avoid a collision between these two business giants. Sergei, face like thunder, stands up, glares at me and Ken, and just when we think he is about to throw a punch at us, he storms out of the room and slams the door behind him as hard as he could.

"That went well," says Ken to me, chuckling, his trademark twinkle in his eye.

Seconds later, the door opens and Sergei reappears.

"I forgot. This is my office."

Both men burst out laughing, an embrace follows, compromise is found and we go for lunch. That is a standard way of conducting business in Russia.

I actually often mentioned these exchanges when I used to do cultural training to companies, how to work with the Russians. Ken understood this nuance very well. It's all about trust and sequence.

Sitting in the Sheraton in central Moscow on a cold November morning, I am interpreting again for my two friends, but the conversation is not about business. It's about family, sports, weather, cars, anything, just not business.

Only after the coats go on, and we are through the revolving doors and back on the street, Ken says, "So, mate, how much are you going to buy?"

"Let's say three containers."

Simple, but effective, but most people did not learn this art.

Sergei, over these years, came to be a good friend. He was a man of few words, and when he visited the UK, he would stay at my house. We would be sitting, having a conversation, but he had a habit of not answering for quite some time, I suspect, pondering his response. It was something I became used to, as well as his tendency to raid the fridge in the middle of the night.

Ken invites us fishing on the River Ness. Sergei fancies buying a kilt, and I fit him out with the full works in a small shop on the Royal Mile, Edinburgh. He is delighted at his Stewart tartan, and Ken's wife and her friend are given a bit of a surprise that evening in Inverness-shire when it becomes clear that Sergei is wearing the kilt in the traditional way, but is unfamiliar with the issue of "manspreading".

Fishing is better on the other side of the river to Ken's rented bothy. We use the bridge, but Sergei, being a large guy, simply wades straight over.

There were many times when he used his connections in Russia to solve problems. I had connections too, and I recall making a phone call to the Russian Chief Veterinary Officer, whom I knew and, within seconds, fixing a delay with a container stuck in Russian customs. But Sergei's help was more critical than mine.

We had happy and unhappy times together, which forged a deep friendship between the three of us. Over dinner one evening, in a well-known steakhouse in Moscow, Ken sends his rib-eye steak back and finally the chef emerges to put Ken in his place. Ken's issue is not that the steak is overcooked or undercooked, but that it is not a rib-eye. The chef swears blind that it is a rib-eye until Ken tells him that he works in the meat industry. At which point, the chef bursts into tears, and is very apologetic, explaining his supply problems. Most people would not have been as persistent, but of course, persistence was why Ken was successful in this turbulent Russia.

We take a ride in a pony and trap one summer's evening after dinner. It is beautiful, even if Ken is not his usual chirpy self. We are dropped at the hotel, and I say goodnight to Ken. Back in my room, I feel something is not right and, when I call Ken, he agrees. I call the hotel paramedic, and it becomes clear that what had happened to me in Moscow is now happening to Ken in Saint Petersburg. We go in an ambulance to the hospital, made complicated since the multitude of bridges, connecting the network of islands that is the city, are raised at night so few routes remain. In the hospital, they explain the procedure, which I convey to Ken, who is concerned but still trying to make jokes. I call his son back in the UK, and I suspect they spend a sleepless night.

Ken's recovery takes place in a private room at this hospital. His procedure has been absolutely smooth, and Russia has another British appendix to add to their collection. Sergei is upset that he has not been told about this, but I had it in hand and saw no point in waking him in the middle of the night.

"Ken, is there anything I can do?" asks Sergei out of concern for his friend.

"Well," said Ken, "I don't suppose there's any chance I could get the cricket on this telly could I?"

The television had only a couple of channels, but Ken is told not to panic, just to wait in bed. Ken has no real plans that day apart from looking at his scar.

Sergei makes some calls on this Sunday morning and, within hours, we are seated at a pavement café, on the other side of the road, watching two engineers, abseil down the side of the hospital, installing a satellite dish. That would not happen in the UK. Ken got his cricket.

Not all trips were as dramatic, but there was usually something funny to relate afterwards. I was invited to go fishing on Sergei's speedboat on the Gulf of Finland. I thought this would be a relaxed affair on a summer's evening, a little fishing and a couple of beers. What actually happened is that we spent two hours preparing rods, which were then placed in designated metal sockets around the boat. We headed out to sea, and fished until it got dark. Sergei then announces that we will have to sleep on the boat because it is too late to return that evening. It was all rather odd. We came to some weird installation at sea, big metal columns rising out of the water, with rather scary Russian writing and warning signs stamped all over it. This is what Sergei tied the boat up to. After a very bad night's sleep, there comes a dawn knock on the side of the boat, as a man in uniform enquires from his metal platform what our business is. I do not know what was said, but I was to remain below until this structure was well behind us. It was not the first time I was to see him dealing with people in uniforms. He used to love driving his black Saab around with the music turned up high. That in itself is OK, but on one occasion, we had picked up a few British crew members from a yacht that had just moored up. These young guys were treated to a night out, but by morning, we are all still out and about, now driving them back, when the police stopped us. There must have been seven of us in the car in total, which is what caught the police's attention, but as always, Sergei seemed to deal with this with ease. I probably should have guessed at that time that he was higher up than I realised.

Just writing this brings back buried memories. Strange that you would forget being taken to a Russian police station in the night and searched, but on recollection, this was not as scary as it may sound. I knew that standing by the road and having a cigarette was not a crime, and that a search would reveal nothing. Not that that stops them finding things that suddenly appear. No, I was calm because I knew that when I was removed from the roadside and bundled into a Russian police car, the car behind pulled out to follow us. These were our partners and protectors, as they used to call it at that time, our "roof". Anyway, within a few minutes of me being brought downstairs to empty my pockets, four blokes came downstairs into the police station and told the police to apologise and release me immediately, and that is what they did.

Fishing had not been successful that evening though, so the next time we went to a fish restaurant, where you caught your fish from a pond behind the building. Sergei and I stood there with other would-be diners, holding our fishing rods and wondering when dinner would bite. After about a minute and a half, Sergei decided fishing was really not our thing and spoke to one of the staff. The staff member knelt down and started pulling a net upwards from the bottom of the pond. He then had his colleague pull from the other corner until they had created a little isolated area in the corner of the pond with fish trapped in that part of the net. We pointed to dinner, the staff removed two fish and we went inside for a beer whilst they prepared it.

Ken, like Michael previously, was an important part of my career, which is why he gets a mention, but one final word on the man that was Ken. Russia was gradually trying to bolster its industries, and it did so in fairly brutal fashion, blocking imports of products whilst telling its own factories to raise their game. Now it was the turn of the meat industry. They started to control imports through quotas, each country getting an allocation, reducing annually until Russia had its own quality herds and infrastructure which, by the way, they now do.

At the time, it was very difficult for exporters to Russia. Together, we found a solution to one of the issues that was bothering the Russian government. The UK would give a pledge that they would host a Russian government vet, who would oversee the quality of production, and check the items destined for export to Russia, stamping each transaction. This was a way of ensuring that one obstacle could be removed, giving more leverage to the exporters. Of course, what actually happened was that other UK exporters declined to contribute; after all, their exports to Russia were tiny by comparison to us. We were doing around forty containers of product per week, so we rented a house and arranged for the vet to be placed near Ken's factory. Each vet came to the UK for three months or so, and if another exporter had a shipment to Russia, Ken would charge them for the privilege, because he covered all the costs. Ken always said, "You make your own luck in life."

Frozen Patriarchs Pond

Sometime previously, whilst consulting for the DTI, the Ministry of Trade in the UK, I had written a Russia business digest, entitled "Russia: Market Approaches". It was aimed at smaller companies, because, as you may recall from my Westminster appearance, I still firmly believed that the help is mainly directed at large corporations.

This digest became popular, because it explained what grants were available to business, contact details, programmes and events. Because of the nature of what it was trying to do, help smaller companies, it became the best-selling business digest on doing business with Russia. It went into four editions.

If I had my time again, I would focus on that type of help, and less on one market.

I always enjoyed public speaking, which is more than I can say for receptions, which make me nervous. To ensure a constant flow of consultancy activity in a market that was, let's face it, not known to most exporters, we had to seek business constantly. We were always talking to companies about the opportunities in Russia, and almost all would tell us they were happy selling their equipment to Croydon, or maybe to the USA, and that was that. To secure one discussion with a company about Russia, we would have to talk to one hundred or more. For that discussion then to develop until the company became a client, well, the odds were about one in fifty, no exaggeration. I think that means that we had one chance in 5,000 of securing a client. Now, repeat that process for 25 years.

2005-2006

Generally, the environment for doing business with Russia was slightly picking up. With the success of the book and our smaller events, it was time to so something bigger, and thus was born, in 2005, "Russia: Practical Solutions", which would go on to become an annual event.

The idea was simple, similar to the book, pick the relevant topics, find a sponsor from that industry and include them in the content. This event was never to make money; it was not really big enough for that, though on one occasion we had 230 people attending and it felt more like a conference than a large seminar. This event primarily was about informing companies about the market, and promoting certain specialist companies, including our company, Albion, to help them.

We were very lucky to have persuaded the wonderful Bridget Kendall to chair the event each year, which would go on to take place each November. Bridget was then the BBC's diplomatic correspondent, and she spoke with the most wonderful Queen's English, very Joanna Lumley!

I remember my first meeting with her at BBC Broadcasting House, with a young Russian lady who was with us at the time. I was rather nervous because Bridget is a big name, very well regarded, but she could not have been kinder and more interested that day in what we were doing, and to my immense relief, she agreed to be associated with our event.

She was also very good at chairing this event, giving a briefing first, then hosting the entire range of speakers and Q & A, and she refused to take a penny for it. It was all we could do to cover her expenses, which fortunately she did agree to! I have fond memories of Albion always giving her a massive bunch of flowers, which would invariably be too big to take on the train without needing a separate seat!

Our first conference took place in the Glaziers Hall, London Bridge. The venue was good, and although we were not accustomed to running events of this size, we were pleased with the turnout and with the speakers and content. What was of course not visible on the day was the hard slog that we put in, trying to secure sponsorship. We got it done, and to be fair, the sponsors were pretty good at making a quick decision in coming on board. We were most grateful for the support they gave us.

That first conference, we organised a Thames river cruise for delegates, speakers and sponsors in the evening after the event. One of the activities on board was an auction of a lot of greatcoats, badges and Soviet posters, which seemed to have come into my possession. I have a lovely memory of two colleagues bidding against one another for the greatcoat because of the captivating appearance of the lady modelling it. The charity made good that evening!

The annual conference and seminars, roughly every month, plus the business that we gained from all this, kept us pretty busy, but there was a part of me that thought this is exhausting – if I just had some trading activity.

2007-2012

An opportunity arose if not to trade specifically, then at least to do so peripherally. My old friend from student days, Misha, had joined Argus, when I invited him to meet my boss, who had flown in from the USA. I left pretty soon after that, around May, 1993, so I did not actually work with Misha, but he remained there for years. Just before I left, I had opened a company for Argus, to which I gave a temporary name. To my immense surprise, many years later, I discovered that nobody had bothered to change this name, in fact, they registered the company with it. It seemed a bit like calling a website "site under maintenance"! Soon after I left Moscow, Argus' business really took off. I should have stayed, but I was burnt out.

Around 2007, having maintained contact with Misha the entire time since we had met as students, he suggested that I become involved in this business. His reasoning was that the people they were using in the UK were not that bothered, and that it would be easier for everybody if he found somebody else to conduct this UK work, liaising with exporters, organising shipping and so on. I knew these people, in fact, one of them had conducted my first interview for Argus back in 1989. Misha assured me that this is what everybody wanted.

A slight fly in the ointment, given the volume of work, was that he offered me a paltry sum in return. I remember this well; I was driving in the UK. It was so small that I pulled the car over, and I said to his face that the offer was worse than unacceptable, and I declined. We agreed a more sensible sum and we got going. It left me with an odd impression though. Why would he try that?

In 2007, I took on a young Polish chap, and we opened an office. We had to move into larger offices after a while, as business picked up and I needed help with prospecting and administration.

After four years of doing the conference in London, we moved the event to Birmingham. The real home of the small and medium enterprise in the UK, the SME, was in the regions.

Birmingham was great. We were generously hosted by a law firm right in the centre of town, and in fact, many companies found that Birmingham was easier to get to. They were generally manufacturers, our clients, and they had no real reason to visit the capital. This was more their turf.

Sometime around here, 2009, I was asked by Sergei to help him with some translation work in connection with an oil refinery project he was working on. The politics of the meat industry had had an effect on the volumes that Ken was exporting from the UK to Russia, as the effect of the quotas bit deep. It was quite a blunt instrument to use, given that the local Russian meat products were of inferior quality compared to the imported products, but that is the Russian way, and eventually they had a meat industry. Either way, it meant that Sergei approached me on this oil refinery project.

The thing with this job was that the discussions were to take place in Thailand. I had no great problem with being flown out there to help. The deal was big, very big. It involved transmissions of oil across much of Russia, then the construction of a sea terminal and a whole host of other things. As with most Russian projects, the more they talked big numbers, the less I believed this would actually happen. We had meetings in the Institute of Directors, where cobwebs of company relationships would be drawn on sheets of paper, with descriptions of how the business worked and how this could be monetised. It involved a strange world of financing, more specifically a "Certificate of Deposit". The project was, as it transpired, a load of nonsense, which corroborates my experience that, the bigger the numbers, the more time spent on it, the less chance there is of it all being actually real.

Nevertheless, I was flown out to Bangkok, checked into Sergei's hotel, and we awaited the arrival of a delegation from the Philippines. After several days of waiting, it became clear that these people were not going to arrive. Sergei flew home to St Petersburg. I stayed on a few days, just because it seemed a good idea to look around. I had not been to Thailand since I was a student with Jon, and I'd taken a holiday there, with disastrous results!

I recall sitting in a bar. I am now alone in Thailand and that suits me just fine. The beer in front of me is cold, as I gaze at the passers-by and listen to the music. I recall looking at the overhead fan as a song came on, and thinking, *Why, oh why am I doing business with Russia?*

Here was sun, smiles, great cuisine and a potential business. In Russia, I needed to get pizza heated on the carburettor of a Volga because it is -18 degrees and dark…

It got me thinking.

Very soon after this trip, I was approached by a chap called Paul, who knew that I had recently been on business in Thailand. Paul needed somebody to travel to Thailand and write a report on the Thai banking industry. It would involve researching and conducting meetings, then compiling a report. I booked accommodation and off I went. I could get used to this, being flown out on all-expenses-paid trips!

I rented a motorbike and, each day, would scoot across Bangkok and do my research and report. This made me feel alive, not the report writing, but the independence, the bike, everything.

I resolved to do something about it, because regrets are pointless unless you tried to do something about it. I returned, spoke with friends; we returned to Thailand and bought a load of furniture. This coincided with a world economic downturn, a collapse that had a slow burn start, but a swift deepening into recession. So much for getting away from my Russian business, it was back to the wheelhouse.

As the recession bit deeper, I was invited onto the BBC's *Today* programme hosted by John Humphrys. I am in a BBC studio in Tunbridge Wells, not actually in the room with John Humphrys, but of course, this is radio, so it did not matter. I had my headphones on and I listened to the opening refrain, the remarks and the introductions. I was one of several guests. I would appear on various radio and television programmes from time to time over the years, and was not particularly nervous when John asked me if in my experience, and with my knowledge of Russia, the world was entering "global meltdown". This had become something of a cliché to be honest, a bit like when bombs "slam" into buildings, or cars "plummet" off the road, all very sexy but a bit tiresome. So, a bit like when I was invited into Westminster to speak to the Foreign Affairs Select Committee, I thought an honest answer would be helpful, and I told John that I did not think there was any evidence that this was global meltdown, whatever that might be, and that was that. I was faded out and they did not come back to me. Had I told the BBC what they wanted to hear, Armageddon, meltdown, poverty, unrest and possible civil war, perhaps I would have lasted longer, but I was open in Westminster and open to the BBC. Perhaps I had the wrong playbook all those years.

Years later, I was at an event hosted by the Royal Bank of Scotland at which he was keynote speaker. He asked if there were any questions from the guests and I made a comment about being faded out, of course with a smile on my face, because I was not being particularly serious. He was utterly charming about it, we had a good laugh, and I received a signed copy of his book, which I retain to this day.

That said, it changed my view of the BBC somewhat. I started taking my newsfeed from other sources, as I became increasingly convinced that this was agenda-driven journalism. On a very well-known chat show, I was invited on to be part of a panel, and made a comment about politicians, journalists and business people, suggesting that in actual fact it is the business community that tends to find compromise. I did not last long. It was like John Humphrys all over again.

At this time, I had ventured into dating online. I don't recommend it, though it is a bit more sophisticated now than it was then! I just didn't want to wait for the girls to grow up and to be left with the cat, though Zhulik was an amazing cat. He played football, caught flies, and loved headbutts, but he wasn't relationship material. Off I go online. It was exhausting. How many women are there out there who "like to curl up on the sofa with a good film and a bottle of wine"?

I added that to my profile, "Please don't contact me if you like to curl up on the sofa with a good film and a bottle of wine". That made the job easier. I met a lot of people, and again, I will not expand upon this, but I had a mainly good experience. People are people, and not every meeting is going to be good, but just at the point that I had decided I was not going to meet "the one", along she came in that year.

This first meeting with her, I really enjoyed, and this lady was to become my wife. The very first meeting was in central London. It was nerve-wracking, meeting. I was her first meeting, and she was not my first, but, oh, she was different! Firstly, she was gorgeous, and perhaps more importantly, she laughed with me and she laughed at me. That was exactly what I needed. We went for a few drinks, we went for a pizza near London Bridge, and her friends were speed-dialling her the entire time to make sure she was OK. We spent the evening laughing, and we shared heritage. We were both from the same town, from childhood, even if we were in London now.

After some weeks and telephone calls, then came the time to introduce her to the girls. She had no kids, and it was important to me that she got along with the girls, and she did. My daughters arrived with their badly brushed hair, and their slightly too short trousers and the dog that didn't ever do what you asked it to, and Lorraine cared for them all, straightening their hair, taking the dog, laughing with them and walking.

That was it. I wanted to be with nobody else, and that is true to this day.

She was OK with me being a Samaritan; she had done a lot of work on addiction, visiting prisons, and she had supreme knowledge on these issues. Between us, we had suicide and addiction covered!

Lorraine became an immense support to my family. She was constantly doing little things for the girls, and finally, in Rogano's restaurant in Glasgow, she met and fell in love with my mother, and my mother, with her. She did everything possible for me and for the girls, it was as if she was always with us, and I did my best for her and for the girls also.

It was not always easy. Sometimes there were disagreements, but that's how families are.

My father had died four years previously. Lorraine had not met him, and I had not met her father, who had also passed. I think we would all have got on famously. The roses, which my father bought for my mother on their anniversary, ended up on his coffin, as he died suddenly.

Lorraine moved into our family home, and we began our new life together. She, at that time, worked in an industry about which I knew nothing. I still don't fully understand it, but it involved mystery shopping for some big brands. You go into a car showroom, or a high-end perfume department, and you pretend to be a shopper. You assess the sales team, and their performance, and you report back, but that's not all. You have a microcamera clipped onto your handbag, recording everything. This is a brand's way of assessing their partners, retailers, distributors and agents. More importantly, it's fun. I was invited to watch Lorraine at work. I entered the car showroom and watched her engage with the salesman. Something in me made me hide behind a pillar, before I went to the next pillar, undetected. Needless to say, whilst the car dealership was oblivious, Lorraine was not, and she did not invite me to a meeting again.

In fact, she joined the company, moved our office, made some personnel suggestions and became critical to the business! Very quickly, she put us in a new office and replaced our ineffective salesperson who, in hindsight, just annoyed people!

As an example of Lorraine's positive attitude, she could order a coffee and if for some reason, she received a phone call and the coffee went cold, she would add a little sugar and declare it was now an iced coffee. That is how she was.

On the other hand, she would be sitting beside me on the central reservation of a road going through an industrial estate, with a couple of Thai rattan chairs, which we were still trying to sell, without success ultimately; we had to let it all go and write it off. That was the impact of recession upon our little start up. I was lashed to the wheel of Russian business and that is where I would stay.

You see, each time I tried to do something different, to get out, the project failed, sometimes my error, sometimes not, but every time.

The year 2011 would be an amazing and life-changing year, because I would get to marry the gorgeous Lorraine, absolute light of my life by now. Lots of our friends came, including Misha, and we had not only a wonderful day but continued the next day with a barbecue on the banks of Loch Lomond. In hindsight, some people should have been there who were not and some who attended perhaps need not have done so. I foolishly asked my sister's husband to be best man, and it was only as I listened to his speech that I remembered that public speaking was not his strongest suit. Oops…

Lorraine and I would later go on a honeymoon to Costa Rica, where, amongst other things, we built a house for a man called Jesus, went up into the Cloud Forest, and became convinced we saw Nigel Havers working as a barman in Puerto Viejo. Well, I became convinced, but all that is not for now.

In general, things were going OK. The business was going forwards, and we now had seven people in the UK and four in Moscow. In 2011, we conducted our last annual conference in Birmingham, because it was time to move on, we felt.

By happy coincidence, Albion had been established in the year November, 1996, and our conference took place each year also in November. The reason for the latter is that we wanted it to be far enough apart from holidays, and during a busy part of the business year. However, it did mean, in this year, we could celebrate our 15th anniversary, and Lorraine proved more than up to the task. She selected Bolebroke Castle in Sussex, a delightful, listed castle, built in 1480, and used frequently by King Henry VIII as a hunting lodge and, of course, a base for when he was courting the ill-fated Anne Boleyn. It was very pretty and surprisingly affordable.

In addition, because Misha was already in the UK for our conference, we could invite him to this event, along with a number of people who had been close to Albion. Lorraine quickly discovered the reason for the castle's affordability. The elderly owner was trying to maintain it against all odds. He was contacted frequently by a television company which wanted to make a documentary, part of a series about how expensive stately homes and castles can be rebranded and survive by adding nature trails, hotel rooms and so on, but he just wanted to be left to run his castle home and business. Lorraine decided that she would don her Marigolds and help this man to prepare the rooms for our anniversary stay. We had a lovely stay and a great dinner, but my main memory, as the rain pelted down, was all of us placing buckets all over the room to try to catch the many ingresses of water pouring through the ceiling. It was a real pity. Particularly so, as the gentleman who owned the property was to die soon after, and I am guessing it is because the stress and worry were just too much.

We conducted lots of events, promoting not ourselves or our capabilities, but the *market*, not even just talking about *Russia* but *how to get things done*. These events were popular and they were hard work. We invited guest speakers, perhaps the Ministry of Trade, RBCC, a law firm. I recall hundreds of these events, and occasionally they gave rise to curious little situations.

Such as Glasgow, where, within my speech at the Chamber of Commerce on George Square, I mentioned that Russia is the biggest country in the world.

"No, it isn't," came a voice from the audience. "That's Canada!"

"I can assure you, Russia is the biggest country in the world and by a long way," I replied.

She would not stand down and argued until finally somebody googled it.

Around this time, we made one further change, which would have an interesting effect upon everybody. We moved into a smarter office, with reception staff, a meeting room, parking, everything an office should have, but we had never had. It was also time to bring on a new team member, somebody to be on the telephone, talking about how we could help. I had interviewed and employed numerous people, and it just was not working. For example, the lady who asked to be more than just a PA, so I created a job for her and trained her in sales, and on the day she was to start this new role, she left. The girl who stole and lied was another. The lad who claimed at interview to have a deep interest in Russia, and after he started, did not actually know where it was, although, to be fair, I had done something remarkably similar in order to get onto my university course! The delightful and charming young man who had a tendency to fall asleep at his desk. The Russian lady who turned out to be having an affair with a married man and just wanted to be near him. As I fired her, she sat down at the PC to copy our database, right in front of me, so I unplugged it. The woman who, when she was let go, took the letter of dismissal, ripped it up in front of me and threw the pieces in my face. As the pieces fluttered to the ground, I suggested she should have bunched it up and thrown it at me without tearing it first. That annoyed her even more.

In autumn 2012, I'm interviewing again. In walks Dave. He is out of work, and he seems to be grounded; he is making realistic promises, and he was in the army, which I suspect makes him a good team player. His first task when he joined Albion was to help us with our conference, "Russia: Practical Solutions", for the first time in the wonderful city of Newcastle.

Upon return, Dave hit the phones, selling our services. He used a whiteboard to track his progress, what we would call a "pipeline": wins, losses, near losses, near wins. We had not had this before, and his enthusiasm was infectious. I liked him.

Our business was complex, and it was generally an uphill struggle to find clients, because Russia was not a "walk in the park", but we had, by now, developed a rhythm, and we were pretty good at finding and retaining consultancy clients, by and large.

As I look now at our business calendar from those days, it is just astonishing how much was going on. There could be several meetings in different countries on the same day. It was great.

How we managed to find time to move house in 2012, I have no idea, but that is what we did and the house that I had moved into 15 years previously with a heavily pregnant Tatiana, was sold. That house had seen good times and bad. Overall, I was happy to leave it behind me. We moved into a lovely old "chocolate box cottage" built in the late 1700s, low beams and steep stairs. It was impractical and delightful at the same time.

It had a long garden at the back, which was not particularly well looked after when we moved in. I am on top of the old shed, laying felt and smearing it with tar, much of which was going on me, when my mobile phone rings.

My first thought: *Why can't people just send a message? I'm on a roof covered in tar!*

I ponder not answering it, but I am glad I did because it's Buckingham Palace.

Buckingham Palace invited me, plus one, to the palace next May, 2013, for a garden party hosted by Her Majesty, Queen Elizabeth II. Who would be my plus one? Without hesitation, I told them, my mother. She had always been a fan of the Queen; in fact, she practically was the Queen. It was the obvious choice, and I must say, with some relief, that my wife agreed with me entirely.

So, our business continued, and whilst hard work, it was also busy, enjoyable and challenging.

Our events continued, and from time to time had some memorable little quirk.

In Congleton, we stayed overnight in a delightful old hotel, the Lion & Swan, in preparation for the next morning's event. Over breakfast the following morning, some Japanese guests were chatting to a waiter and asking about the history of the hotel. Within his reply, he mentioned a legend that room five was haunted by the ghost of a lady of ill repute, who glided through the door to visit guests. I had just slept in that room. This lady from the seventeenth century did not think it worth bothering with me. I felt a little hurt! I would, however, thoroughly recommend the hotel, and I know it has had a massive refurbishment since I was there ten years ago.

I have no idea how many of these seminars we did over nearly 30 years. Lots! Across the UK, overseas, and online, they were happy days.

I remember getting a very strange phone call from somebody whom I will not name, but who worked for the Foreign and Commonwealth Office, the FCO. He was at that time based in the British embassy in Moscow. He called up and asked if he could speak at one of our events, because he wanted to sit some ambassador application exams and needed to find a reason to fly to the UK so that this could go on expenses. Yup, I was pretty surprised myself. However, having the embassy on a panel was usually quite a good draw for our events, so I agreed, and we slotted him into an event, which took place in Cambridgeshire. We funded and arranged these events, and my presentation was always longer than those of the other presenters, mainly because I had very practical topics to cover. I had 30 minutes, compared to other speakers' 15, and it worked very well, but not today.

He stood up, and his first words were, "I didn't fly all the way from

Moscow just to speak for 15 minutes!"

No, you flew all the way to do an exam, and we were your meal ticket. I was furious.

Off he went, 40 minutes in total. We could not find a way to stop him elegantly, and I did not then feel I should abuse people's time by keeping to my original timing. I crammed what I could into a few minutes, and gave them my number. In one fell swoop, he wrecked the event and charged the taxpayer.

2013-2014

It started well enough, 2013. We remained busy, and we had secured a good consultancy contract from my former boss, Boris, who was now VP of a large corporation.

Of course, at the end of May came the garden party in Buckingham Palace. Well, round the back of it!

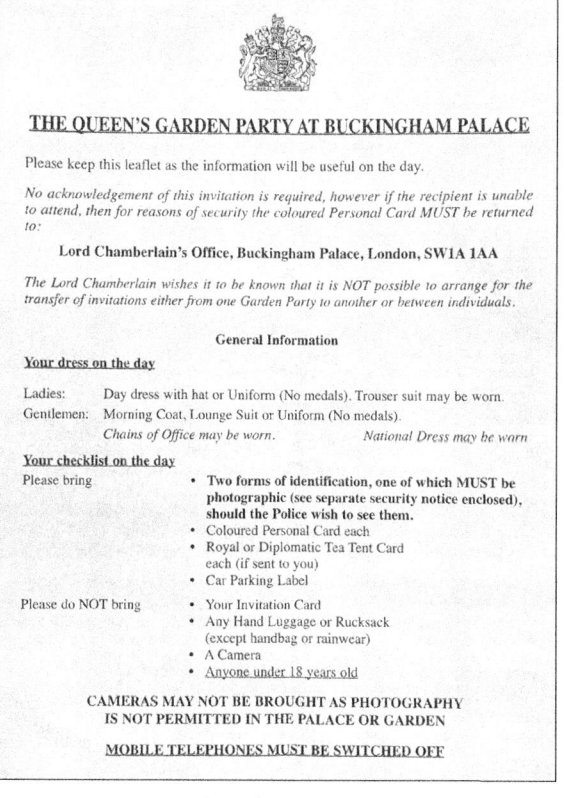

THE QUEEN'S GARDEN PARTY AT BUCKINGHAM PALACE

Please keep this leaflet as the information will be useful on the day.

No acknowledgement of this invitation is required, however if the recipient is unable to attend, then for reasons of security the coloured Personal Card MUST be returned to:

Lord Chamberlain's Office, Buckingham Palace, London, SW1A 1AA

The Lord Chamberlain wishes it to be known that it is NOT possible to arrange for the transfer of invitations either from one Garden Party to another or between individuals.

General Information

Your dress on the day

Ladies: Day dress with hat or Uniform (No medals). Trouser suit may be worn.
Gentlemen: Morning Coat, Lounge Suit or Uniform (No medals).
Chains of Office may be worn.   *National Dress may be worn*

Your checklist on the day

Please bring
- Two forms of identification, one of which MUST be photographic (see separate security notice enclosed), should the Police wish to see them.
- Coloured Personal Card each
- Royal or Diplomatic Tea Tent Card each (if sent to you)
- Car Parking Label

Please do NOT bring
- Your Invitation Card
- Any Hand Luggage or Rucksack (except handbag or rainwear)
- A Camera
- Anyone under 18 years old

CAMERAS MAY NOT BE BROUGHT AS PHOTOGRAPHY IS NOT PERMITTED IN THE PALACE OR GARDEN

MOBILE TELEPHONES MUST BE SWITCHED OFF

Royal garden party notice

It made for a wonderful afternoon, Mum and I taking the train to London, entering the palace through the front gates and across the quadrangle, through the palace and into the gardens behind. My mother did not meet the Queen that day, but there was something about it that I will never forget. Oddly enough, my most cherished memory is neither of the event, nor seeing the Queen from quite far away, nor the food and drink. It was after the event, a quiet walk through the spacious, manicured gardens, just strolling through this royal and very private space, Mum and I, away from the traffic, before emerging back into the London bustle of Piccadilly, and heading for the RAF Club.

Author and mother en route to Royal Garden Party

There was one difficult decision to make, and that concerned my old friend, Barry, whom you may recall named his company after a novel, just as I named my company after a pub in Clifton, Bristol. Barry had been at the original inception of our conference, and we considered him to be part and parcel of it, even although it was Albion who actually picked up the challenge and took on the task of organising it. It became our sole responsibility. Because he was a mate and because he had been there right at the start, we always gave Barry a preferential rate for being the exclusive travel sponsor. Well, as time passed, eight years in fact, and the rate had not changed, it was time for an increase. What we were doing was not sustainable and although mates' rates are a controversial topic, I simply could not do it any more and he refused to budge. We were forced to find another travel company and Barry refused to speak to us after that. After three years of this, however, I walked into his London office one day, gave him and Margaret a big bear hug, and we talked it through and reconciled. Even though we disagreed, we respected each other too much to fail to reconcile, after all, we were all adults. People fall out, it happens, but there is never a reason not to reconcile.

But 2013 it was not going to be a good year for more serious reasons, and it seems curious, as I write this, to think that this was to be the beginning of a cycle that would last ten years.

It all started with a spreadsheet. I scrutinised one spreadsheet more carefully one afternoon.

Misha and I used these to calculate who owed what to whom. We paid Moscow half of our consultancy revenue in return for the work and infrastructure they provided. Something was amiss with this document, and I began to question my friend, Misha. This was Misha with whom I had drunk beer, shared jokes and hotel rooms, travelled with and cried with, Misha who had helped me when I was fixing my house in Kent, whose family I knew.

The numbers did not add up, and Misha was not pleased with being asked about it. I went to the Russian bookkeeper and asked him about it. The conversation went thus:

"Where is that sum of money?"

"Misha needed it."

"Why?"

"I don't know. It's not my job to ask. If it were Ilya or Petr, I would ask, but I can't with Misha. He's the boss."

"That is not how this works."

I was upset, but I was also angry. When I spoke to our UK accountant, I soon became worried. Our finances had been damaged pretty badly. Not, I hasten to add, because of Misha, but because this business was tough. Nevertheless, in my heart, I knew that the business had to go forward without Misha, and that was difficult. He was a very close friend. I had known him almost 30 years. And this? Just money?

We had been paying the Moscow office but had been charged more than we should have. The accountant stated quite bleakly how long we could continue if we did not make changes. I recall meeting Misha in Edinburgh, where he was with a client, and we spoke. He had "found" another large sum of money that we should pay him. We had a row because my interpretation was the exact opposite, and he would not commit to explaining his argument.

At the same time, there were the first signs of unrest between Russia and eastern Ukraine. This did not get a lot of airtime in the press, but over the next few years, this would grow from annexation to something akin to a restricted civil war in the east. Of course, companies and clients pointed the finger at Russia.

We held our next annual conference in the conference suite at Newcastle United's football stadium. I recall Lorraine asking Misha to participate. He refused. Misha had consistently refused to answer questions on finance and was concerned by the nature of the discussion that would take place. He did not want this level of scrutiny. I had placed my trust entirely in him and had not felt the need to scrutinise. We conducted our flagship event without Misha, just as we had started it in 2005. It was clear that our business relationship of six years was over and, sadly, our friendship of some 30 years.

There followed a rather unpleasant period of uncertainty, as I was obliged to explain to clients that Albion was severing contacts with its Russian partner and I had to give the clients an option, to remain with Albion and transfer the activities to a new partner or to stay with Misha.

Business likes stability. A business can work with a regime it does not like so long as it is stable. Of course, part of the reason why my time in Russia has been more complex than, for example, my previous bosses' experience, Michael and Boris, is because Russia has, more or less the whole of my career, been both unpopular and unstable.

Two clients decided to remain working with Misha. They were apologetic, kind, but I understood their decision. They did not need change. In both cases, the decision to stay with Misha would prove not to be a long-term arrangement, but at the time, it was the right decision. This is business; it is never personal. We picked ourselves up, dusted ourselves down and carried on.

Business gets a bad rap in the press, in people's heads. We are portrayed as if money is our only concern, but to me, friendship is far more important. Misha and I had been the closest of friends. We always met up when we could, we chatted, we shared hotel rooms and train compartments, there was nothing we did not know about each other, and we truly fell out. He was not the happy student I had met and become friends with in 1986. That was 27 years of friendship, gone and for all the wrong reasons.

Years later, I wrote to him, suggesting we bury the hatchet, pick up our friendship but without the business. It was very similar to the situation with Barry when we fell out in 2014, but with Misha, even though we were far closer, it was not to be. He wrote back, wished my mother well, and said he did not need to rebuild the friendship, and that was that. I was later to learn that he had done this with a lot of people; I was not being singled out. It seemed unnecessary to me, but I accepted his decision.

The next time I was to see Misha was at his graveside following his sudden death early in 2019. Misha was at his house reading a book, then he stood up and died.

Though 2013 proved to be a tough year, despite falling out with Misha, we had to keep going.

2014

A Russian friend, Alexander, rented us office space in his premises out of town. Alexander found a young Nepalese chap by the name of Gopal. Gopal had a very professional appearance and became our general director. He recruited a couple of people, and off we went on our new journey together. Alexander was later to tell me that he had lost some money with Gopal on a tea deal that had gone wrong.

He laughed as he exclaimed, "Now I have a warehouse full of tea that Gopal sold me!"

Hmm, I see.

The following year, 2014, became the start of a serious decline in the West's relationship with Russia. Russia conducted a "referendum" and absorbed the Ukrainian peninsula of Crimea into the Russian Federation. Now, this may not have been as preposterous as it sounds. Crimea had always been part of Russia until Khrushchev, then general secretary, gave it to Ukraine, apparently "on a whim" as described by one Russia specialist. This referendum, however much the West seemed unconvinced, appeared to many merely to be a return to the status quo. There were complaints from the West, a lot of sabre-rattling, but not much else.

The shooting down of flight MH17 from Schiphol over Ukrainian airspace, that was another matter. Sanctions commenced, on a limited scale, but no longer was there talk of the expanding BRIC nations, Brazil, Russia, India and China. BRIC suddenly became BIC.

We had a Dutch client at that time, and I recall the conversation vividly.

"David," said the client, "we do not know if Russia is responsible for this, nobody can be sure, but we absolutely cannot be seen to have any involvement with Russia now, not as a Dutch company." And that was that.

A very memorable moment springs to mind from 2014. Sergei had

A screenshot of my TV showing Sergei, my erstwhile friend, in the main square facing the crowd following the tragedy. It is here that he famously sank to his knees and begged forgiveness.

called me and told me that he and some of his family were planning to visit the UK and could I help with their itinerary? We were just on the point of closing the Tonbridge office and relocating to Scotland and, by chance, I had arranged for us and the girls to see a small Simple Minds concert behind Alnwick Castle, Northumberland. This was a band we had all followed for years, and it was not difficult to get more tickets for our Russian friends because it was a field venue, not seated. And so it was that Sergei and his wife, also her brother along with his wife, walked into a Newcastle hotel and we all introduced each other. Sergei was accompanied by his wife and her brother along with his wife. I did not at the time recall that Sergei had married into the Firm. They seemed perfectly nice people and they had rented a little black hatchback, nothing flash. So off we drove, the two cars together, and arrived in Alnwick. We parked and made our way to the field in front of the stage. To the right was a booth, offering chairs to rent, which seemed better than standing or sitting on the grass.

"Quick!" I shout to my Russian colleagues. "We're Russian, let's annexe this part of the field, they'll understand!"

I hadn't really thought about it. The Russians smiled wryly. The concert was a washout, because it quickly started to rain, and it did not stop. None of us wanted to stay and we said our goodbyes, promising to meet up in Edinburgh a day or two later, which we did. Our Russian guests expressed interest in viewing antique furniture for their homes in Russia. It so happened that I have a good friend in the antiques world in Edinburgh, so over dinner, I made a call and we arranged to visit Leith the next morning.

This visit was fascinating to me. There were several floors of antiques, everything from Victorian sideboards to Roman swords. Our Russian guests were escorted by a young lady who scribbled down what they were interested in and what they needed prices for, and finally, when they were finished, we went to the office to arrange where to send a quote for all the selected items. It was only when Sergei's brother-in-law was giving his email address, which included the word "Putin", that I remembered the marital connection. Sergei had married the daughter of the president's cousin. He was part of the Firm. Only then, I recalled my annexing gag in Alnwick.

Years earlier, he had become quite a good friend. We were not very close, not like Misha, but we had great times. On one occasion, we rented a Porsche, driving from London to the Isle of Skye, and stayed one night on the island before returning next day from Skye to Tonbridge. He would generally stay in our family home, although now I come to think about it, I was not once invited to his in Saint Petersburg.

I recall showing him the tourist spot, Beachy Head. Incidentally, that was the scene of a death which a friend told me about, involving his girlfriend, her married lover (whom my friend knew nothing about) and her married lover's wife. The wife ended up at the foot of the cliff, whilst walking with her husband. He was not prosecuted. My friend told me how his girlfriend had constantly suggested a walk on Beachy Head, but fortunately for him he did not find the time – stranger than fiction, sometimes, the truth.

Anyway, Sergei and I were standing on Beachy Head and gazing over the sunlit waters of the English Channel. He mused that this was the first time he had seen the Channel from this angle.

I asked him what he meant, and he explained that he had previously been a submarine officer and that the Royal Navy and the Russian Navy would regularly follow each other in and around the North Sea and elsewhere. It was common, and everyone knew where everyone was, even if right in their slipstream where apparently the subs are more difficult to detect. It was regarded almost as a sport; everybody respected each other. Not like now. It has morphed into sabotage and espionage, often absurd and bungling, and sometimes with tragic consequences.

As friends, we helped each other. Some years previously, I was in the office one afternoon, sitting at my desk, and he rang with a problem. I was happy to help his daughter who had missed a flight from Moscow to London and was due to attend an English language course at Roedean Ladies' School. Would I please collect her on her rescheduled flight and take her to the school? Of course, I agreed. This was a father-daughter thing, tough sometimes, but unbreakable. So after work, I took the train from London Bridge back home, collected the car and met Julia at Heathrow later that evening. I did not think much of it. She was only fifteen, but it was getting late as we drove down the A23 towards Brighton – very late.

We arrived at the school around midnight, only to find it was firmly closed. Not surprising really, considering the time. I had an estate car at the time, and was remembering childhood holidays in France when, on Bastille Day, we had to sleep in the car. My mum and sister slept in a tent, whilst my brother and I were both on the back seat of the Ford Cortina and my poor father slept in the front seat, but this was a bit different.

No problem, I would put the seats down for her so she could stretch out and sleep in the back. I would recreate my father's Bastille night in France in 1971! Just as I resolved to do this, a light came on and a door opened. I was able to drive home to Kent, arriving around 02:00, for a short sleep, before taking the 07:22 from platform 2 next morning to the office. This had been some years before, of course. I only mention it because it would be about 12 years later that I would reach out to Sergei when my own daughter had a problem in the town of Sochi. I shall not go into details, but she needed support and I was several time zones away. She had not merely missed a flight, this was more serious, and I told him the nature of the problem. I asked him just to call her to make sure she was OK. To tell her she was not alone, and that everything will be all right.

He promised to do so.

But he did not.

Sometime later, I sent him a message. I could not understand it. Why would he not reach out to help her? But if you marry into the Firm that must be one of the consequences. I suspect his phone was now screened and I would not be on the approved list. After all, my mobile phone had been taken twice to be scrutinised by the Putin regime. It's what they do.

I found that difficult to understand, that the firm would take priority over the dad-daughter relationship. I like to think he was unable to help. The other way makes no sense.

I don't know if he is happy. He became governor of Kemerovo Region. That's an area roughly the same size as Ireland and Belgium combined. It is massive, but just one of many regions.

I switched on the television in a hotel room at Schiphol airport, Amsterdam and was astonished to see my erstwhile friend, Sergei on his knees on the town square, begging forgiveness. He had just said something stupid to a man who had lost five of his family in a shopping centre fire. The doors were locked shut and 60 people perished in the blaze. There would be an investigation as to why the fire doors were locked, but we all know why. It is not incompetence, it's greed.

In Moscow years before, the Russian Fire Safety Inspectorate had suggested that a one-off payment to a personal bank account would ensure that our office premises were "compliant". It may even have been the fire officer who would later crash into my car, I don't know. Either way, my friend was made to look like a fool and to look uncaring. He kept his job of course, for which his qualification was being married to the daughter of the president's cousin.

In fact, whilst writing this book, he has been promoted to Minister of Energy. Such is life in the Firm.

We chose Manchester as our next venue for our annual conference in November 2014, but we had a difficult time filling that room with delegates. Gone were the days when people called us about Russia. Gone were the sponsorship deals. This was now about just making it work. Companies were not interested in the annexing, trigger-happy, tampering and poisoning giant that Russia had apparently become.

There was one rather charming positive at this time. My mother had, almost in passing, mentioned that one of her neighbours was a veteran of the "Arctic Convoys". The Arctic Convoys were the lifeblood to Russia in WWII, supplying fuel, weapons, food and more. They are heroes and no more so than in Russia. I practically ran up to his flat, in the same block, and met Geoff. He had been born in Twickenham but had fallen in love with a Scottish girl and remained with her ever since. I loved listening to his tales of how, during World War II, he was on the merchant ships (his was HMS *Vindex*) which transported supplies to our ally, Russia. Yes, I know, it sounds odd, doesn't it? "Ally". Geoff Shelton had written a book, entitled *Masthead Lookout*, which related some of these tales. In this short publication were comic and tragic true stories of what Churchill had famously described as "the worst journey in the world". These guys had to deliver supplies from the northern tip of Scotland, round the top of Norway and down into the Kola Peninsula and Russia. They were faced with freezing temperatures, mountainous seas, aerial attack and Nazi submarines. If you inadvertently grabbed a handrail without your glove, your hand stuck to the ice. There was Geoff from Twickenham, up on the highest part of the ship, as lookout. Geoff was a thorough gentleman. He introduced me to other veterans, and we hatched a plan to incorporate these veterans into our Manchester conference.

Just opposite the conference venue, we found a Russian-owned restaurant, and we held a dinner for the veterans, along with some of those involved with the conference. The Russian owners were so proud to have Arctic vets, in their white berets with their medals, dining in their restaurant!

Perhaps even more interesting was how these veterans were received at our business conference. This conference was to take the same format as it had for ten years. It was popular, so we did not change the format, merely the presenters and the topics. Bridget was in the chair, and everything was in place: the stage, speakers, Q & A, roving mics, the presentations, breakout sessions, closing remarks and even the flowers and the choice of post-event pub!

Bridget Kendall, then of the BBC, hosting our annual conference

This year, we gave an extra slot to the proceedings: each of our three guest veterans speaking for a few minutes on stage. They told stories of lost friends, they related incidents, they reflected upon lessons learned, and in the room? Absolute silence from the audience; not a cough, not a chair scraping, nothing. The veterans stood down, and the audience rose to their feet and showed their appreciation for several minutes. They were moved, some company directors stood in tears as they clapped. We were pleased for these three war heroes.

As a postscript, Geoff later confided in me that they had all assumed the entire trip might be rather dull, but they had loved every second of it!

Again, the writing was on the wall, we could not continue with our annual conference as the business climate worsened. Russia denied involvement in MH17 and claimed it had conducted a fair referendum in Crimea, but the atmosphere had palpably changed. We would continue to promote Russia as a business destination until such time as these charges could be proven, but from here, the battle was uphill.

A lovely old English company approached us; I shall not say the name, but it is a very well-known brand, making a product which we all know and some people can afford. The idea was that we would purchase a containerload of this product, place it in Alexander's warehouse and sell in Russia. I recall the forecasts and spreadsheets, and Dave was very actively involved in this; I think he saw this as a way of making some good money on commissions, which indeed he would have, had we proceeded. For some reason, I did not feel the desire was there, not in Moscow, at any rate. With the international sales director moving roles at the factory in England, I pulled the project and we abandoned it. I think this came as a blow to Dave in particular. I recall a friend telling me that he was in the office and had been discussing with Dave this company, before the project fell apart.

There was a large spreadsheet with forecasts and commissions, and suddenly Dave said to this friend, "What am I getting out of this?"

My friend pointed out that he was on the payroll and this was his job, but I recall this as being an odd comment. Not one that I would have made to Michael or Boris, that's for sure.

This was also a year of change in other ways, as we moved to Scotland, and indeed Tatiana moved also, in a rather unusual show of strength from both parents, as the children moved schools. This all turned out to be less simple than envisaged, with some serious health issues for one of the girls. Our elder daughter was very poorly, and we felt a bit powerless. I have to say, our other daughter was an absolute pillar of strength at this time, a small, 14-year-old pillar but a real strong character. She had just put up with it all quietly, passing her exams, moving schools. She had a lot to put up with but did not complain once. They are bright girls, our daughters, kind and gentle. We brought them up well, we believe.

My brother really was a source of strength. He would call and just be there for her and for us. Our daughter made a full recovery, and we have always been grateful to my brother for his support.

My siblings and I were very different, and indeed, they are different to each other, but they were important to me. My brother was always ready to listen to the various things going on, and always ready with an empathetic word. In fact, he would regularly call and ask how things were, how were we doing, and I would give him snippets of the soap opera that was doing business in Russia! Alasdair and I, in some ways, were closer than my sister and I. There is no particular reason for this, except that perhaps my sister tends to focus on pragmatic things, and as she once put it to me, looking forwards, not back. Nostalgia was not really her thing, and whilst she was capable of being kind of course, her help often seemed to be mainly of a practical nature. We rarely called for a chat, without there being something to discuss. When we met up, it was usually at some family event or other.

Back in more mundane territory, we continued to muddle through.

Business was getting harder to find. I recall travelling to Birmingham to do a Russia business briefing, where only two companies showed up. Two companies from the entire West Midlands thought Russia might be of interest.

We did manage to win a tender with the government in Northern Ireland, which proved to be a boost to the business, but the environment had become tough.

What had Moscow office been up to this time? After the split from Misha, taking on Gopal and opening a newly staffed office early in 2014, we continued servicing the business. Gopal found Grigory, a good guy, but not good when faced with a challenge or working under pressure, but if you gave him a task and a deadline, he would do it. That is how we learnt to work with him. I noticed a slightly misogynistic streak in him, but that was not uncommon with people his age in Russia. He seemed a bit behind the times. They both travelled to the UK to meet our possible supplier, and they were introduced to Dave. Dave also travelled with me to Moscow, even though he did not speak Russian. To create a good team, each part needs to see how the other functions, where they work and so on. This would later backfire on us, as Dave and Gopal would form an unholy alliance when they decided there was a way to make money on the side.

One of the people whom Gopal brought in to the team was a thoroughly nice young man by the name of Artem. He was a different breed to most Russians. Artem spoke good English, but Artem had a broad smile and infectious personality. Russians are not known for their breezy, outgoing nature, but Artem had that charisma. This was a good team. Compliance became a big part of our activity, and Dave and Gopal worked well on this together.

We closed the UK office down south at the end of the year, and Dave decided to move to Leicestershire, where he worked from home. Dave had a lot of latitude at this point, more than was entirely comfortable, but we had little choice. Dave seemed like a regular enough bloke. He had needed a job when we took him on at the end of 2012, and we hoped that in return he would be loyal and able to work without any colleagues nearby.

We picked up a new client, and again, it was Lorraine who persisted in pursuing them. I was sceptical because the same people had approached us before, but when they were in a different company. This time, the outcome was different, and if it had not been for Lorraine, we would have missed this opportunity completely.

The year of 2014 had a tough start, a baptism by fire as it were, and a tough end with the conference, which would prove to be our last. In the middle of the year? Well, it was kind of tough. I had thought 2013 had been a challenge!

Gopal was not everybody's "cup of tea". He was very strict with those who worked for him, but this is the Russian way, and whilst he was not Russian, he seemed to have locked onto their way of doing things. Possibly better than I did. To me, it was slightly degrading to treat people as if they were incapable of making decisions. Surely, it was better to encourage them, to give them opportunities. Anyway, it was not his way, and it seemed to work.

Unfortunately, Russia is not a particularly tolerant country. Over the years, I have seen a lot of homophobia, racism and sexism, and it's ugly.

Anyway, Gopal's skin tone was enough to make him stand out, and one evening, walking to his apartment, he was set upon and beaten up. This was a beating for being olive-skinned. I gave him a sum of money so that he could get faster medical care. Many things can be sped up in Russia with a little cash, not just fire compliance documents. He was OK. It was a loan, but instead of asking for the money back, I simply gave him a pay rise and backdated it, so he did not feel embarrassed.

Of course, in addition to the complexities of doing business in Russia and the politics that seemed to dog the relationship between Russia and the West, the business also had the same pressures as any business, staff, overheads, finding and losing clients. One such client went bankrupt early 2015, taking several thousand pounds of our money with it as it went down. The liquidators came in and we were acknowledged as a creditor, so we had hoped to get our money back. We got nothing. After the banks, the bigger creditors, and of course the liquidators who were billing for their work for several years, we were just a small company. The bulk of the UK's economy is powered by small companies. Something is not right there.

We resolved not to try to continue with our annual conference, not after the difficulties of putting it together the last time. Ten years was a good run, and we just ran out of companies interested in Russia.

2015-2018

Geoff Shelton informed me that he and others had been invited to Moscow as guests of the Russian government. The invitation was in recognition of the 70th anniversary of the end of World War II, and was to take place in May, 2015. Geoff kindly invited me to be his chaperone and interpreter, to which I readily agreed.

It was a turbulent time and, on top of that, there was a general election. Towards the end of the year, Russia would be accused of Brexit tampering, and our situation would become pretty torrid, as we were defrauded, but of course, as I packed my suitcase to take Geoff to Moscow for the VE Day celebrations, I knew none of this. It was in hindsight that I would look upon this trip as a kind of moment of calm in an increasingly mad world.

We were dropped off at Glasgow Airport and had a quiet dinner before flying the next day down to London to connect to Moscow. Each vet had a chaperone, just like me, and one of these was a charming man in his early eighties, still very sprightly. We had to resolve some problems at Heathrow, but were upgraded by Aeroflot and flew to Moscow. Arriving in Moscow was a very different experience. We were escorted to the VIP lounge, so there was no waiting in queues for these gents in their nineties. Our passports were stamped and returned, and our luggage placed in three separate limousines, one car for each vet. The limousines whisked us past roads blocked for us by saluting police traffic officers, and within no time, we appeared at the Golden Ring Hotel in central Moscow.

The following morning, buses took us to Red Square, and we were shown to our seats by the parade ground. Now, these were no ordinary seats. We were on the permanent podium outside Lenin's Mausoleum, the exact spot where Soviet leaders have stood for decades for march-pasts, speeches and state processions. Beside us were senior members of the armed forces and dignitaries.

Red Square 2015

The then President Mugabe was there, and just in front of the vets, and not at all far from me, sat the president of China, and slightly closer, Vladimir Putin, president of the Russian Federation. I had no idea if I could take photographs, but I thought somebody would soon tell me if it was not allowed. Above us were cables with TV cameras zooming over the proceedings, and in front of us was Red Square. We witnessed the most spectacular show that afternoon. Army, navy and air force paraded past, tanks and rocket launchers trundled by, and a fly-past of Russian fighter jets screamed overhead.

The smell of diesel and the trail of smoke brought a reality to this event that was very different to watching on television.

Putin made a speech and gave awards, and finally, the show was complete. The crowds would soon disperse, but before they were allowed to do so, the VIPs were led down from the podium to a fleet of golf buggies and invited to take our seats. As I sat there with Geoff and one other veteran, Russian naval cadets in blue-and-white-striped crew shirts came up to the golf buggies and cried "Spasibo" to the veterans, "Thank you!" The veterans were seated there in their blazers, white berets and their medals displayed on their chests, and they were visibly moved. Geoff once described the link between the Arctic veterans and Russia as "a golden thread that will never be cut". Oh Geoff, I so wish you had been right on that because I think you would agree it has been severed now. Perhaps it is for the best that you have not stayed to witness that.

Author on Red Square 2015 (top of pic, near centre)

Geoff on Red Square (on the right, middle row, white beret)

The buggies start to move towards the Kremlin's Nikolsky Tower, an ornate fifteenth century construction, with a gate, through which the entourage of cars and golf buggies drove, and on into the Kremlin's magnificence. It is actually a beautiful and serene place, and of course, the Moscow Kremlin is home to the Grand Kremlin Palace.

I had been in the Kremlin before, but as a tourist, not as a luncheon guest of the president. High ceilings, paintings, thick carpeting and gold everywhere, this was the heart of Russian power, opulent, almost ostentatious, a palace, of course. I had been in a few but this was on a different scale. We are ushered into a banqueting hall and seated at round tables. To my left is Geoff, and to my right, a Russian air officer in full uniform by the name of Anatoly.

Kremlin banquet

Luncheon was a formal affair, again, accompanied by speeches. Quails' eggs and sturgeon caviar to start, a delicious stolichny salad followed, and then a melt-in-the-mouth confit of duck with orange jus; hand-rolled truffles to finish off. Geoff turns to me, because he notices that I have been chatting to Sergei.

"David," he prods me in the ribs. "David, ask Anatoly if I can have a quick chat with President Putin."

Right, a quick chat with the Russian president. I tell Geoff that in my limited experience this is against every protocol ever imagined across the globe, and that the chances of meeting the president are slightly less than zero, but Geoff just twinkles at me and tells me to get on with it.

"Anatoly Mikhailovich," I venture. "My colleague, Arctic veteran, Geoff, was wondering if it may be possible to meet the president for a quick chat?"

I expect silence, protest or a flat refusal, but Anatoly actually starts choking on his duck. Now I feel bad.

"Geoff, I reckon it's a no."

The luncheon continues, I talk to Anatoly and Geoff, and they chat to their neighbours also. It's very civilised. The speeches are made and finally, the chairs are heard scraping back at the top table, and everybody rises to their feet, including the veterans, infirm as they may be.

Infirm? Geoff? Apparently not. Grabbing his walking stick, he makes a dash for it, to the left, in the direction, not of the entourage, but a kind of pincer movement halfway towards the door. Anatoly has been unable to react in time to see me rushing behind Geoff, trying to avert a major incident with the president's security brief.

The president's entourage is to our left, Geoff is ahead of me, the exit, to my right. Geoff is using his stick to remarkable effect. I do not recall seeing him moving at this speed across a room. Sure enough, Geoff intercepts the president. Putin notices the white beret of an Arctic Convoy veteran and this beret has the same effect as it had upon Governor Efremov when I had that dinner in London. Everything else became unimportant. The president greets Geoff in English and a brief conversation ensues, in which the Russian government thanks the veterans for their pivotal role in assisting Russia during the war, and Geoff expresses his good wishes to the Russian people.

Then it's over. The president moves on, probably to have his security detail punished for letting somebody get so close.

Geoff beams at me: "Right; shall we go now?"

Back at the hotel, I make sure Geoff is comfortable and pop out to see my friend Luke in a bar. I tell him all the day's events, and Luke grins at me as if I am a child.

I used to know dozens and dozens of people in Moscow. Back when I lived there, even more, but as the years went by, obviously, people moved on and moved out. I knew fewer people in Moscow these days, but Luke was a really good guy, an English lawyer from Derbyshire, with a very dry sense of humour and bundles of talent. We first met at the British embassy years earlier when I was trying to find a legal sponsor for our conference. He was introduced to me by another friend and lawyer there, and he was like a breath of fresh air. He asked for details and we swapped contact numbers. He was businesslike, no frills, no nuances and no games. I liked that.

We started as colleagues and became firm friends. I cannot even say how many events we did together, how many meetings and how many times we would meet up over a few beers. I recall playing golf with him at the Agalarov Club, and it seemed like he knew everybody. Luke was enjoying life, enjoying Moscow and participating actively. By coincidence, I realised, when I visited him on business, that his office was the same block that I had worked in when I lived in Moscow in the early nineties. Now it seemed a bit more upmarket.

Luke was very clear on what he believed. You may not always agree, but you don't have to. That's not what friendship is about. If you feel bruised or uncomfortable, that is on you. I have come to understand this over the years. I don't need air-kissing, cycling buddies or book clubs. Friends are a lot deeper than that, and you get to choose your friends…

Luke became a firm mate. He would have my back and I would have his. On one occasion in Moscow, we were having a beer and a chat, and when we parted company, and I had time to reflect, I suddenly felt a bit down. I cannot really explain it; it happened in an instant. From time to time, in our business, we felt like that. This was no longer the nineties, but there was something constantly oppressive about doing business with Russia. Almost like, you had to look over your shoulder the whole time, or you thought you did, which is effectively the same thing. Anyway, for reasons I will never know, a few minutes later, Luke came back in and asked if I was OK. I said I was, and he shook my hand. "You're OK, mate," and he left.

Luke

Here I am with Luke, the day of the Red Square parade, May 2015, and Luke is laughing away at my enthusiasm about the day. I could not stay long, because the Russian hosts had laid on a dinner and then a bus back to Red Square for fireworks.

Well, we had the dinner, but nobody had the desire or even the energy to board a bus to watch the fireworks, so we watched them from the top floor of the Golden Ring Hotel.

Anatoly, the Russian air force officer from lunch, comes up and asks if I have any photographs of the day's events, because he had not been on Red Square. Could he please see my photos of the day? Without thinking, I said "of course" and handed him my phone. Immediately, he was gone, and only an hour later, he reappeared. I have not trusted my phone since that day.

All in all, this visit was one to remember. The entire trip was three days, and we were treated like royalty. Finally, it was time to go. Limousines took us out to the airport, we were ushered into the VIP lounge and our luggage and our passports were dealt with whilst we enjoyed a glass of champagne and started our farewells to our hosts. On boarding the Aeroflot jet, I was delighted for a change to be able to turn left onto the plane and head for first class, where the veterans and their chaperones were again treated with the utmost dignity and kindness.

Geoff making friends

Then we landed at Heathrow, and we were back to reality. For the connecting domestic flight, and despite his age and his white beret, Geoff was told to remove his shoes at security, a tough thing for a man to do, with nothing to lean upon except me. This man, who had for several years suffered torment and constant threat of death, who had fought to ensure the freedom of the Western world from fascism, was now trying hard not to test the patience of a youngster at security, who had the demeanour and charm of somebody who had been bullied at school.

I shall always be grateful to Geoff for allowing me into his world. Knowing him was an absolute privilege. Despite his humour, his enormous dignity and his charm, Geoff was an elderly man, and sometime later, his health started to fail him. Finally, he had to go into hospital, first the New Victoria, then the Queen Elizabeth. We visited him in both, and whilst he was in the latter, Lorraine and I took our daughters to see him. We sat and chatted, Geoff shared some stories and jokes.

I said to the girls, "Of course, you know, we met President Putin?"

"My dear David," chuckled Geoff quietly, "We did not meet Mr. Putin. Mr. Putin met us."

After some difficult weeks, he was fit enough to go into a different, smaller hospital. We visited him there of course. Geoff was his usual, joyful self, but he was not pleased to be in this place. He said it was as if the other patients were all either asleep or just unable to hold a conversation. He just had nobody to talk to.

I asked if Geoff would like anything, and quick as a flash, he said, "I would love a beer!"

I returned with a couple of beers, which we shared whilst chatting with Lorraine. Geoff wanted to be placed into the Erskine Veterans' Care Home, and he almost got there, but for a slight health scare, which delayed his plans. I think this got him down more than perhaps even he realised, and Geoff passed away in April, 2018. I was asked to conduct the eulogy, which was a privilege I shall not forget. The Russian Consul and colleagues placed a wreath upon the coffin beside Geoff's white naval beret. As I read my eulogy, candles were lit in various churches across Russia by some good friends of mine, and we bade farewell to Geoff, Englishman, gentleman, sailor, war hero and true friend. May he rest in peace.

In September of 2015, I received a letter from Dave, offering me his resignation, which I of course accepted. Dave had been with us three years, and although he had not achieved the great success he had hoped, he had been a useful part of the team, and we got along OK. He had met our family, and we had invited him to our home. One of his passions was collecting coins and banknotes. He had received an offer to conduct talks on cruise ships on this topic, and it did sound like a nice gig. Lorraine and I went to Leicestershire to say our goodbyes and thank yous. We gave him a little cash and a lovely watch, and we collected his company car, a silver

Mercedes, which we then drove north to Scotland. I noticed that the car was not in great condition, which surprised me, because I thought he would have had it fixed.

Towards the end of the year, I was sitting in the office and received an email which puzzled me. It was from a company CEO whom I had met at an event, and who would later become a friend. In the email, this gentleman thanked Dave and Gopal for their visit, and promised to follow up. There had been no meeting, or so I thought, but of course, when I was able to speak to Peter and learnt what had happened, it turned out that there had been a meeting. So disingenuous were these two employees, as I would later discover, that Gopal had actually opened a new company in Moscow with the same name as the company I had founded. This of course would prove unwise, because it would be regarded as an attempt to create confusion, and it did. Peter genuinely thought before, during and after the meeting that he was talking to Albion and its Russian equivalent. If Peter had not copied me in, quite unaware that Dave and Gopal were operating against our company, we may never have found out. This act, of course, encouraged us to dig deeper. I had a lunch meeting in Newcastle with a client, who confirmed that he had been giving leads to Dave for some time, but those leads were not passed through the company, despite Dave being at the time on our payroll. Then a company in Middlesbrough also confirmed that they had been under the impression that they had been clients of our company, Albion, when in fact, they had been working with two people operating independently. This Middlesbrough company told me they had sent quite a few enquiries our way. Not one of them had made it to Albion. They were intercepted by these two individuals. The business that we knew about, that had been diverted, amounted to some £32,000, but we will never know the true total of business taken from us. It was time to call the police.

This was to be the beginning of a rather unpleasant journey, as we began to unearth more instances of business which was diverted from Albion to these two individuals. I wrote to Dave, and what I received in response was as if from a different person. Arrogant and in denial, he said he had done nothing wrong and that he would "defend himself vigorously".

Police Scotland interviewed us, and handed the files to Leicestershire Police, who pursued the case relentlessly. We discovered emails where Dave had used the Albion server, not very clever on his part, but substituted his bank details for Albion's. Dave was arrested at his home in Leicestershire and charged with fraud. Unsurprisingly, we spent a lot of time on this case.

There are two things that I find very difficult to deal with, and I will fight them as a matter of principle. One is bullying, and the other is dishonesty. This was dishonesty with betrayal, and we were not letting this go. Actually, ignorance is another thing I struggle with, and hypocrisy. OK, I seem to have a longer list than I realised!

We had one very good new team member, and he was to be a big help at this time. If you asked Sasha where he was from, he would either say that he was Ukrainian, Jewish or Moldovan. I really do not know what it depended upon, but he lived in Ukraine, and relocated to Scotland at the start of 2016. Sasha was one of the good guys, and that has remained so, as long as I have known him, and is still the case today.

Dave, however, was a very different matter. We went to the Crown Court, but the case was not initially heard, simply because of the sheer backlog in cases. This was to mean that we would lose one of our witnesses because frankly, he had a business to run and could not spend another day in a small room in Leicester, hoping they would get to our case. No matter, said our barrister, we have more than enough evidence to convict Dave. We finally had our day in Leicester Crown Court, roughly the same time as the American election and Russia being accused of US election tampering. There's never a dull moment with Russia.

This of course was a criminal court and there were all sorts of folk in there. Dave was in the dock with a police officer and the jury heard the evidence. I took the stand, as did Lorraine and our client, and we all basically said the same thing. Dave demonstrated such body language, laughing and sprawled on his seat, that the judge warned him that his behaviour would be noted by judge and jury. It did not seem to enter Dave's head that a little humility might be more appropriate, given that he was facing a possible custodial sentence. We had an excellent barrister, who was adamant that we should win this case. Dave had a barrister, whom I was able to take on reasonably easily. I wonder now if his heart was really in it. I recall him suggesting that Dave alone was responsible for our database of companies, to which I replied simply "that's absurd". I did not even have to explain that Dave joined 16 years after the company was founded, and we had not somehow hobbled along without a database until he turned up! How could we have run our business? His barrister seemed to agree, because he did not pursue his own line of enquiry.

Anyway, we won the case, and sentencing was adjourned.

We invited Dave's former colleagues to the sentencing, because he had to see the people whom he had let down. Lorraine and I, Artem, Sasha, Grigory, Andrew, my good friend Gary, and a client, were all seated in the public gallery, whilst the defendant, our erstwhile colleague, sat a few feet away in the dock, and our barrister, a couple of rows in front of him. It was important to us that Dave should know that he was being judged not only by a jury in the criminal court, but also by the people whom he had worked with and who had thought he was a colleague, as opposed to a thief.

His sentence included a suspended sentence, a fine, community service and of course, a criminal record. Most importantly, the acknowledgement that he was a criminal.

I recall thinking, at this time, that it was ironic that I had taken on Dave partly because he had been in the British Army. I thought that would be some kind of guarantee of integrity. He was a cook in the army, as it turned out, so not exactly front-line calibre, I suppose. No offence to British Army cooks.

Dave was handed his sentence, and escorted out of the court. However, it was not so simple as it should have been. On his way out, Dave had to walk past his colleagues. Lorraine and I, being the closest, were subjected to what appeared to be a threat.

"Now it starts," he muttered darkly as he passed us.

I laughed to myself and thought, *What an idiot.*

However, Lorraine scribbled a note and handed it to our barrister, who stood up and addressed the judge. When the judge heard what Dave had said, he called for the defendant to be brought back into the court and placed upon the stand. He told Dave that he had the power to place him behind bars right now, but that Dave could avoid this by explaining what "Now it starts" meant. The judge suggested it had been a threat. Dave spluttered and said he was referring to his community service, which will start… I do not recall if the judge laughed at Dave, but he certainly did not believe him. Instead, the judge suggested to Dave that a public apology to Albion might be appropriate, and that is what happened, Dave turned to his colleagues, bowed low and apologised before being led away once again.

Justice was definitely served that day.

Of course, the business continued while the court case was ongoing. Business does not stop for a merc fraud case. We continued our events, our sponsorships, our prospecting and our client support.

> Генеральный консул
> Российской Федерации
> в Эдинбурге,
> Великобритания
>
> Consul General
> of the Russian Federation
> in Edinburgh,
> the United Kingdom
>
> 58 Melville Street, Edinburgh EH3 7HF
> Tel: 0131 220 69 75   Fax: 0131 225 95 87
> edinburgh@mid.ru   www.edinburgh.mid.ru
>
> Mr David Cant
> Managing Director
> Albion (Overseas) ltd
> Riverside House
> River Lawn Road
> Tonbridge Kent
> TN9 1EP
>
> Dear David,
>
> 05 September 2016
>
> I would like to thank you for your generous contribution to the reception on the occasion of the 75th Anniversary of the First Arctic Convoy codenamed Dervish.
>
> It is with your help the Veterans and other guests enjoyed this magnificent evening on board the Royal Yacht Britannia and received exclusive commemorative gifts.
>
> We also believe that it is a real step forward in building up the lasting legacy of the Arctic Convoys.
>
> Your support to this project is sincerely appreciated.
>
> Looking forward to meeting you soon,
>
> Best wishes,
>
> Andrey A. Pritsepov

Consul letter

Sometime towards the end of the year 2016, we realised that we were about to celebrate our 20th anniversary. This had been a difficult period, and we were not as organised as we had been for our 15th at Bolebroke Castle. It ended up just being a dinner in Soho with friends and clients. I shall not give the restaurant a shout-out, because we felt we were thoroughly ripped off! We had far too much vodka for a group of our size, which in itself was not a problem. Apart from me having to be put to bed by the long-suffering

Lorraine, I later discovered that one guest was found by his friend in the flower bed at a Surrey train station and taken home, whilst another fell asleep and woke up in Margate. The real problem was that the vodka was charged by the shot, and not by the bottle, and that's a lot of shots between a dozen people over an evening…

Barry and Margaret met us and donated two saplings, an oak and a silver birch, representing our 20 years of work between Britain and Russia. This was a meaningful gift not only because it was so original, but of course because it was Barry that I had reconciled with after we had fallen out a few years previously.

So it was quite sad, when I had planted them later, that they were dug up in the night and destroyed. We rented property at that time, owned by the Church, and one of the Church officials was convinced that he had the right to walk onto the property any time he wanted. We apparently lived in his fiefdom. He denied it of course, but those saplings were destined to be planted permanently on the Black Isle, where my mother was born, in her garden. It was sad to me that they did not make it, but it was not the first time, nor the last, that somebody claiming to be "of the Church" would behave badly.

We were not done with Dave. We had only actually brought in one case to the Crown Court, and it was all they needed to convict. There were others, however, and so we took him to the High Court on a civil suit, which we also won. It was mid December when the judge ordered Dave to hand us back £10,000, and when he asked me when I would require this to be paid back, I recall saying that we could wait till after Christmas. I kicked myself for this afterwards, because Dave had shown us zero compassion as he stole and stole. In the end, it was irrelevant. He did not pay and the High Court seemed to accept, on a subsequent appearance, that he was broke, but we had our win, and perhaps he needed the stolen money more than we did.

In Moscow, we had decided to move out of Alexander's warehouse area and take an office nearby. The current team of Artem, Darya and Grigory moved to the new premises.

Gopal of course, complicit in Dave's fraud, was fired. I did not pursue him legally. Looking back, I wonder if I should have detected a trait in Gopal's character that would suggest there was something about him, something to feathering his nest. There was the debt he had dumped on Alexander by selling him tea that was clearly a disastrous deal, but even when Gopal travelled to the UK for example, he was the only person who ever exercised a rather archaic rule that suggests a per diem allowance should be paid to the visitor by the inviting host company. It is illogical, as all costs are paid anyway, and he was the only one ever to request it.

It was beginning to feel like there were a lot of people around us who were more interested in short-term looting than a long-term career. I tired of it, and asked Artem to find a new general director. He suggested Elena Nikolaevna. They had worked together in the Russian Railways company. She seemed competent, so we took her on. Very quickly after this, we won a contract for a large automotive company, and that required separate "class A" offices. This worked well. They found premises, Elena worked from their office, as our general director, and the client's activities were overseen under our stewardship. Meantime, our team could carry on, with Artem being the obvious choice to be the team leader.

The big issue in 2016 was the fraud problem, just as the big issue in 2013 was Misha's departure, and 2014 was annexing Crimea. There could rarely just be a time of calm. Well, business itself ran actually quite smoothly now. The new arrangement seemed better.

It was, but for one thing. Artem was great, very personable, nothing here had changed, but I started to notice that he spent a huge amount of time on the phone to his family. He also seemed to change cars a lot, and drove absolutely everywhere. Artem was very helpful when we were in Moscow, and particularly on one occasion when Lorraine found herself out there on a business trip alone. By the way, here is an interesting thing about my wife: Lorraine did not ask for a career in Russia, that was down to me. She had a prestigious career. Our world was alien to her without the language, experience and knowledge of the country. Flying out there alone must have been scary for her. Did she show it? Not a bit. She stayed in an apartment and did a FaceTime video tour of it for me, showing me everything it had and smiling and laughing all the way through. Lorraine does not make people feel uncomfortable if she can help it. Artem made her stay much easier, driving her around and generally being there for her, but Artem seemed distracted when it came to work.

I am deliberately not talking much about the work, the business, itself, mainly because it is mostly quite dull. The interesting bits were those involving people, travel, incidents.

Many years previously, I had been at a party hosted by my friend Richard. We were all homeowners now, so there was no cigarette smoke, no flinging weighted socks down to friends to get them in and no unexpected people beside you when you woke up next morning. No, this was a party in a living room, with actual wine. I am standing, and chatting to various people, some of whom I know, some not. I get chatting to a young man, and ask him what he does for a living, just normal, polite conversation.

"I fly Tornado jets," came the response.

I wait for the punchline, or a snigger, but it does not come. I expected him to be an accountant or a lawyer or something more usual.

"Very good. No seriously, what do you do?"

"Really, I fly Tornadoes."

This guy is either very good, or he's an idiot. I notice Richard is standing not far from me.

"Rich, what does this fellow do, because I'm not sure I believe him."

"He's in the Royal Air Force, mate, based at Leuchars."

I'm the idiot as it turns out. He really flew Tornadoes, and was a thoroughly nice guy.

Now roll forwards many years. I am sitting in the library at the RAF Club on Piccadilly, London, and I am chatting to a potential client. I am not sure whether we are meant to be there, but it is the only quiet place in the club.

The gentleman seated with me is a factory director and wants to learn what we might do for his company to enter the Russian market, all bread-and-butter stuff to us. Just as we were about to have this conversation, he asked how it was that I came to be a member of the RAF Club.

"My father was in the Royal Air Force, and I was offered affiliate membership because of that."

Is what I should have said.

Because that would have been true, but no, I hear myself telling him:

"I flew Tornadoes."

No sooner do I say this, than I think that was a really bad idea, and it was. This chap immediately opens his briefcase and fishes out a book about fighter jets. My heart sinks as I consider how to conduct a conversation about flying a jet. Do they have pedals? Do they take petrol? My knowledge is scant. Where's Richard's mate?

I am in the library and about to be revealed as a total fraud by a potential client. He is starting to chat about jets; it is almost as if he is limbering up. I am panicking so I say, as calmly as I can:

"To be honest, Steve, we're not really meant to be having a business meeting in this room, and so we don't have much time. Much as I would love to talk about my flying career, I think we should get on with the business."

We got on with the business, thank the Lord.

I was not off the hook though.

A couple of weeks later, my friend Gary, who is in Russian business also, is with me at Steve's factory to discuss things in more detail. Before the meeting starts, we are offered a brief factory tour, and Gary is a few steps in front of me and the client.

"So, tell me more about your flying days then, where were you stationed?"

I so nearly told him, Leuchars, but I bit my lip and pulled out my last card before being revealed.

"To be honest, Steve, I really don't talk about that part of my life now, because of my career with Russia."

"Ah, of course. Forgive me."

And that was that. Sorry Steve.

Around this time, I had a call from a lady called Xenia. Xenia had had a bad experience with Gopal, I do not really know the details, and technically, Xenia was a competitor, because her business was also (and solely) in compliance, but we had lunch at the Pushkin Café. We seemed to share some experience and values, and we remained in contact.

Things politically had settled down with Russia, so by 2016 and 2017, there was a flow of consultancy work again, and of course, certification work.

Of course, the Russians continued their campaign of bizarre activity, with the Skripals being poisoned early in 2018 by two people who could not apparently find the cathedral. The two morons were clearly as bad at poisoning as they were with geography, because both their intended victims survived, whilst an innocent woman lost her life because she came upon the substance by chance.

However, by early 2018, it had become clear to me that there was something not right in the Moscow office again. Things just seemed to be too dormant, ticking rather than thrusting. Grigory was reactive not proactive, Darya was just young, not really that committed to a career in business (nor had she claimed to be), and Artem seemed to be out and about a lot helping his family. In the early months of 2018, I asked a Canadian friend of mine, who lived in Saint Petersburg with his family, to help me out. You see, I couldn't manage everybody from three time zones away. They had to learn to manage themselves, but if Misha, Gopal, now Artem, were not leading in a fair and honest manner, then what chance did we have? Elena was physically now well ensconced in the client office, and I needed a better idea of what exactly was going on. My friend agreed to find out.

Albion event advertisement

My worst fears were confirmed. He told me that things were not being handled in the way they should and that Artem was not leading by example.

I was on a family holiday on the island of Crete in May of 2018, and by sheer coincidence, so were Xenia and her partner. It was not planned that way, and we were not in the same resort, but they were on the island part of the time we were there. By this time, Xenia and I had become quite good friends. So there I was, standing by the pool, on the phone to my friend, currently in Moscow, who was telling me that the set-up was not working. It dawned upon me that I needed to make a fresh start, just like we had to do in 2014 after Misha, and just like we had to do after the Dave and Gopal fraud.

How did this make me feel? Exhausted. Misha's behaviour had taken a lot out of me. Then there was the fraud, the criminal case, the civil case. Now another change, and more hassle. Why is it so difficult for people just to work?

I had not elected to discuss any of this with Xenia, but it seemed an obvious solution.

Back home, I set about firing Artem, and it was not pleasant, but we got it done, with Elena's help. It was ironic in a way; Artem helped Elena to get her job, and Elena helped me to get rid of him. As is so often the case in Russia, Artem issued threats, and as always, we ignored them. I let Darya go, and gave her a good parting severance; she wanted to spend more time with family, so it worked for her. Finally, I took Grigory with me into the new set-up.

Based on the Frunzenskaya Embankment, Xenia's office seemed to be full of Ukrainian women, and she ruled over them with an iron fist, as had Gopal, as was the Russian way. It was just not my way.

She had set this office up after a falling out with her previous business partner (notice a pattern here?), and she was running a small but successful compliance practice. It would not be too difficult for us to keep our compliance work separate, because most of it was done via the UK and Elena just put a stamp and signature on documents from her other office. Actually, getting Elena to sign anything was becoming increasingly difficult, as she became increasingly comfortable in her position. Elena was on a very high salary indeed, and this was because it was set by the client. Anyway, off we went and took some space in Xenia's premises. Without Artem and Darya, we only had Grigory and a client who was inhabiting our premises.

As a brief aside, I have mentioned travel. I enjoy travel, but I am not very good at finding the best deals. That would be Lorraine. She can find the best places at the best prices, whilst I will find the most expensive hovels and the worst possible flight connections. I don't know why this is, but it is.

Rather, it usually is, until this trip. Lorraine had found a hotel room for me, which seemed reasonably priced and was right in the centre of town. I recall it very well. I had to lug my suitcase out of the boot of the taxi, because he could not get past the barrier. I trudged through the snow, searching for a sign for a hotel. All I found was a metal door and a small nameplate beside it. I rang the bell and the door clicked open.

At the end of the dark corridor was a small reception, more like a window. I checked in and paid for my accommodation, then went to the room, looking forward to a hot shower and an early night.

The first thing I noticed was that the bed was round, and located in the centre of the room. The ceiling was entirely made of mirrored glass.

In the corner was a Jacuzzi bath, also round, and two champagne flutes on the side. But wait.

There were no wardrobes, no shelves and no windows.

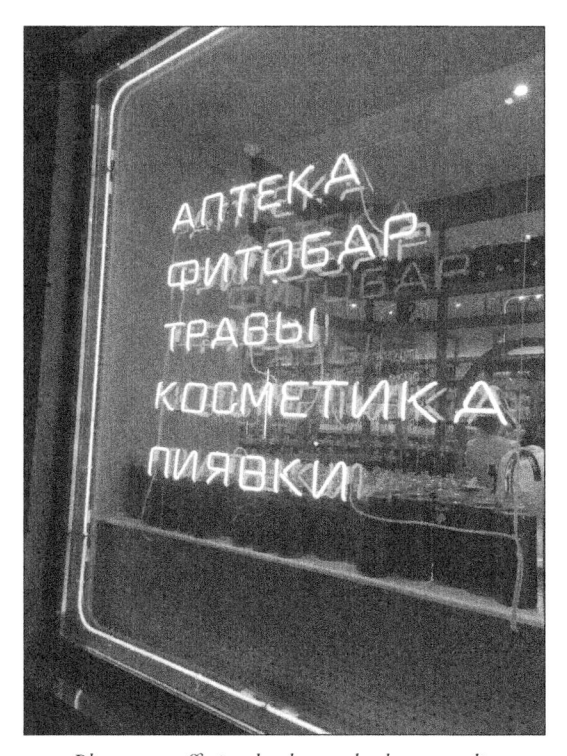

Pharmacy offering leeches and other remedies

I returned to reception and enquired if, by any chance, they also rented these rooms by the hour?

"Yes, most of our guests pay that way," she replied.

I stayed just one night. That also proves that even Lorraine can very occasionally get it wrong.

This particular trip, I had one main objective.

We needed additional resource, as I explained the following day. Xenia produced a young lady, just approaching her 22nd birthday. Half Ukrainian and half Russian, she seemed very quiet, though I think this was true of all Xenia's staff, possibly because that was the management's preference. Katya spoke some English, so she fitted the bill.

It did not take long until Xenia started behaving oddly.

To start with, she was charging a ridiculous amount for her services, so we swiftly placed Katya directly onto our payroll.

Then Xenia made some odd comments about how easy it would be to terminate our office space contract. It was not so much that we had put ourselves into a position of vulnerability by taking office space in Xenia's office, it was more that the arrangement suited both parties and should have been allowed to work. So often in Russia, if something is working, their thinking then takes them to "what else can I get out of this?".

On my next trip to Moscow, I met Xenia and I asked her to explain the threat. It's not OK, particularly as we were meant to be friends. Xenia did not apologise. Nor did I expect an apology, because Russians don't say sorry. I had the impression she did not even understand what bothered me. I have read an article about how the Russians generally do not apologise, and I have to say, that is my experience. They consider an apology to be a sign of weakness, where I consider it to be a sign of strength. It has to be justified and sincere of course, but a strong person will apologise. She did not.

Either way, I won't be threatened, with or without an apology, so we moved out and opened our office in the same complex.

I am now in a dreamlike state. Within less than five years, we have had four changes in Moscow: Misha, Gopal, Artem and Xenia. Why is this happening? Because Russians need to be managed, and the problem is, when you find a good manager, you just have to hope, from three time zones away, that they will not become distracted, play games or try to create opportunities for themselves. This had happened to Michael and Boris too; this was not just me. Indeed, that is why Michael put us into their Moscow operation, Matthew, me, Tom, and when he put Misha in? We know how that ended.

Anyway, we open the office, and we have no Moscow management. I rely on two members of staff to just get on with the job.

You may wonder why I did not simply install a Russian Harvard graduate to manage the business. Simple answer: it was unaffordable. We would have spent all our consultancy income on a manager who would manage a business that had become unsustainable because of the manager. There was another reason: Michael had always been able to keep staff with the simplest of gestures, a smile, a copy of a magazine, a small gift, but that was in Soviet Russia when even food seemed to be a luxury. Now Moscow was a very different place, fast-moving, never sleeping, deal-making. Everybody now was looking after number one, with a few exceptions, and to manage and control this, you had to control everything they did, ensuring that they were busy, giving detailed instructions with deadlines, basically, subjugating them. That was not my style and it has taken me a lifetime to understand that this is what *they themselves want*. There are those who make decisions, and then there is the bulk of the population. They dislike democracy that comes with responsibility.

This time, I was going to try something different. Grigory had no desire to shine, to rise in the company, to learn English or come up with ideas. He was a Soviet figure, set in his ways, and that was that. His colleague seemed more ambitious, with her English language and her interest in travel. I invested in her. I did so, for example, by asking her advice, by consulting with her on a new possible employee, and by taking him onto the team. I equipped her with a visa. I had learned these things from Michael.

There are some with little or no ambition, and it is a difficult, probably pointless task to invest in such people. They have a role, but not a leading part. You encourage the ones with more drive, more "fire in the belly", as Boris would have said. As with all employees ever, I assured her that if she tried her best, used her initiative and worked hard, she would get all the opportunity she needed to earn, to travel, to be promoted and even to be part of the management, in time. All this did not happen overnight, of course, it was a gradual process. More than 30 years my junior, I looked upon her as a business protégée. I thought she and Sasha were two people, to whom I could entrust the business in years to come. I would even have those conversations with both of them. That was my thinking.

At the start, everything was fine. Katya liaised with colleagues who spoke no English and clients who spoke no Russian. On trips to Russia, she would accompany me to meetings because she needed to learn. Initially she did not participate, but that was OK, because in my early meetings I was the same. She would gradually learn, just as I did. My job was to encourage and assist.

2019

It was a new year and a new start. It was also time to galvanise things a bit, to create opportunity. We arranged a long, varied and intricately planned trip. This would include Timur and Nikolai, former employees of Michael's, who were doing some consultancy for us on oil/gas. Five people in total squeezed into one car. There were lots of logistics and a huge number of meetings from the Isle of Wight to Thurso. We were synchronised and on fire!

Katya and Grigory in factory

Andrew helped immensely. Not formally on our payroll, with commitments elsewhere, he has been a team member for some 15 years and is somebody we do not want to lose. Always cheerful, with a wicked sense of humour, Andrew did a lot of work years previously with our events but would also later be pivotal in helping our resurgence. Without a couple of beers from time to time with Andrew and hearing his stories as a pilot or as a guitar player in a band, we would be a poor company indeed!

I recall how my knowledge of Russia came in handy on this trip, and I surprised even myself. We were in the town of Stoke, having breakfast in the hotel, myself, Katya, Grigory and also Mike and his wife. You may remember Mike as being the one who filled my jacket with ladies' underwear in Siberia. Well, we were now doing a little business together, despite his sense of humour. I mentioned to Mike that Grigory would open his banana in the Russian way, not as we would open it. Katya heard this and was intrigued. Sure enough, Grigory finally reached for the fruit, and proceeded to open it before eating it. He did not disappoint, oblivious as he was to the fact that the entire table was silent and watching him intently. You shall have to google Russians eating bananas if you want to know how they do it, but goodness knows what you will find, for which I am not responsible!

There would be more opportunities to travel, as we needed to be in Cologne for a food fair. By now, we were very actively involved in promoting the food sector in Russia. In Cologne, instead of a joint dinner at the end of the day, as is customary for colleagues on business trips, Katya would vanish, wandering around town with her phone, taking photographs and seeing more of where she was staying. There was nothing wrong with this; she just loved to travel and to understand the city she was in.

Of all the colleagues I ever had, Katya was the most inscrutable. She could be charming when she wanted to be, but most of the time, didn't want to be. She reserved that for her friends. I tried and tried to get her to just be a bit more relaxed in front of clients, but she remained frosty in meetings, and it was unnerving to people. Some of them commented on it.

I recall one UK trip, where we were to stay in some place where we needed to collect a key from an office. I could not park, so asked her to collect the key. I added that the password is "The geese fly backwards over the Kremlin". This was of course not true; I just thought she would laugh, but as I saw her return to the car on the busy street, I could kind of tell from the look on her face that she had taken me seriously. Anyway, it made me laugh.

It was now November and we were in Abu Dhabi, this time, for an oil and gas exhibition. We worked that show every day, talking to some two hundred companies. Katya had arrived a day early to look around; it had become a kind of tradition, cost us very little, but was a sign of our commitment to her in return for her work for us. She would take herself off at the end of the day to go sightseeing.

There was nothing sinister in this, but I sometimes wondered if she knew she was on these trips first and foremost to do business. In addition, there was a little concern for her safety. I recall her going out into Abu Dhabi's evening darkness, and I stood there, asking her to cover her hair because of the town we were in. A blonde girl in her early twenties would be conspicuous at eleven o'clock at night in this town. What was she doing? Nothing untoward, just taking photographs, which she would then put on her socials. It was all very innocent. But I recall worrying that night, and calling Lorraine. I envisaged all sorts of scenarios, and it was as if she was my own daughter, I was that anxious. She, of course, returned safe and sound around one o'clock in the morning. I recall being quite angry with her, not only because she could have been in danger, but because I was starting to question her priorities. Travel was more interesting than work. I realised that I had conducted every meeting at the show. There was no fire in the belly. The difference was, when I said this, she just rolled her eyes, not the same reaction as I'd had when my boss challenged me years before.

Author and Katya, British Embassy Residence, Moscow

Only my brother would suggest to me that there was something between me and her. I probably should have understood then how little he knows me. Katya was like a business daughter to me, and that was my mistake.

Towards the end of 2019, I was in Moscow and I challenged her on her travel habits and her priorities. She responded that after 18:00 she was free to do as she liked.

Did I see the warning signs? No, I did not. I had already invested in this person and I wanted my idea to work. My determination to ensure her success was my mistake. She did not ask to be helped. She was not as interested in business, as I needed her to be.

So, I invested more. I must have been blind not to see it. I was trying to bring out the good business qualities in this person. She could be diligent, empathetic, imaginative and industrious. I had seen it, but in hindsight, she probably needed a few more years before she would be ready to focus on career and make business decisions. I was too early, and that is my fault.

On her recommendation, and my deluded notion that this would encourage her to feel valued, I had employed her friend, Dima. He was a nice, young guy, shy, quiet and the same age as her. He was gay, and being gay in Russia is a bit like being Nepalese. Gopal was beaten up only because of his colour.

Sure enough, Dima would get beaten up, just like Gopal, this time, for his sexuality. I saw him after it happened. His face was a mess, and as with Gopal, I helped Dima, because it was the right thing to do. Cash and a mobile phone would help him but also they would make him feel like somebody actually cared. One thing I learned, as a Samaritan, is that the feeling that somebody does not care is the worst feeling in the world.

Christmas and New Year, 2019 were to be a dream holiday in Cuba, myself, wife and daughters. For a number of reasons, it did not go to plan.

This holiday was meant to be so joyful. There had been some issues between one of our daughters and my wife. It was really not anybody's fault. But it had got me down, because I always found myself stuck in the middle. It was unfortunate, but it happens. We all got through Cuba, and spoke about it. But at the time, it meant my wife leaving early, which left me feeling upset and angry, so angry indeed that I blurted out a comment to the family about disinheriting them. It was not meant of course, nor did I even say it to the girls; it was mere heat of the moment. I foolishly mentioned that troubled daughter/wife relationship to my brother and sister in the aftermath of this holiday, on a rare occasion when I got to see them. I was still upset about Cuba and told them of difficulties and misunderstandings where I was constantly in the middle.

Cuba on horseback

Lorraine departing Havana

The Silo would not understand that. The Silo withdraws, protects its own and excludes others.

The Silo is the cornerstone of why we fell out. Reaching out must have been alien to them. Seek assistance? Absolutely not. Do not admit to problems. Everything I heard came from our mother. Everything must be seen to be OK, but we did not operate as a Silo. We shared, asked for and offered help.

Cuba turned out to be a short-term blip. I blame nobody for it, not the girls, not myself and not Lorraine. Moreover, I was there.

2020: COVID THUNDERCLOUDS

Nobody had any idea what was about to hit. People were only just beginning to notice the news about a Chinese virus, but nobody was paying it much attention in January. At the end of the month, Albion took part in what would turn out to be its last UK event ever. This was at the kind invitation of the Ministry of Trade, the DIT, and the event, which went well, was held in the Midland Hotel in central Manchester. The Midland is allegedly the place where Mr. Rolls and Mr. Royce met for lunch before deciding to collaborate on producing a car. Rolls-Royce effectively bookended Albion's UK activity, with our first client having been a RR group company and our last event being at this venue. It was to be a series of events across the UK, but unfortunately, the virus was going to end all of that.

I continued to invest in Katya. By now, I had misgivings, but no alternative. We attended another trade exhibition in Frankfurt, February 2020, but the show this year was poorly attended. There were very few people, compared to Cologne or Abu Dhabi.

People were talking more now about the China virus. By the beginning of 2020, it had spread to Western Europe and people were comparing it to Spanish flu of one hundred years before, but still, we did not know the extent of the disruption to come.

We had several projects going on at the time but constantly ran into companies that wanted us to conduct work for free; big companies. Albion was always clear; we do nothing for nothing.

Several projects finally died at this point, after lots of trying.

The previous year had not ended the way it had started, and in 2020, we had some serious catching up to do!

It became increasingly apparent that Katya did not enjoy work. The work had of course been tough, not to mention that after the falling out with Xenia and our office move, we were immediately burgled.

The more I tried to encourage her, bonuses, travel or possible promotion, the more she seemed to resent attempts to improve her performance.

Deadlines, reminders, discussion, everything was met with a sigh and another roll of the eyes, which I was not meant to see.

Whilst I was coming to the conclusion that she was just not ready for it, she was the only option.

In the middle of March, Katya was due to fly to the UK for a series of meetings with potential and existing clients. We were trying to create an impetus, but as Covid seemed increasingly in the news, Katya, who was in Kyiv at this time, decided not to fly to London and instead to return to Moscow. I was certainly not going to try to change her plans, so I simply conducted all the meetings without her. The presence of a Russian manager in meetings tended to give companies some confidence, but it was fine. I did not need her to progress the discussions, and she would be briefed later.

I had learnt to understand much of the Russian culture, and much of it I loved; the arts and heritage, the history, the warmth of the people (no really, when you get to know them).

There is also a lot that I found difficult. One of these was an apparent ability of many Russians to confuse kindness for weakness. Time and time again, I have helped Russians and been repaid with bizarre behaviour. I tried to encourage people to think, allowed mistakes, but kindness and understanding had left me damaged, (and poorer). I had not factored in the "every man for himself" mentality that gripped the country when freedoms were introduced. No sooner had Yeltsin's government relaxed the rules, than chaos ensued. Putin became popular *because he told everybody what to do*, far more comforting than the Russian form of democracy. In this new world, you offer somebody a bit of freedom to run things their way, and it will blow up in your face, which of course explains a lot when it comes to Putin's invasion of Ukraine, that and their love of having a "strong" leader.

There were other things about the Russian people that were exhausting. A serious problem with communication, which is common knowledge and well documented, a "closed culture", where information is power and is not to be released.

In business, you only receive information if you specifically ask. Nobody will give the background and information comes in fragments. It made no sense to me, but no amount of training made a difference. We tried. I spent days with staff and a flip chart, encouraging them to talk. Even the younger generations seemed to consider this beneath them, so they just kept making the same mistakes.

"Only a fool smiles for no reason" goes the Russian saying. What a sad state of affairs, and of course, imagine how that goes down with clients.

After decades of working with Russians, I could not effect real change in this thinking. They always went back to their old ways.

I once asked why it was that most new commercial banks were run by women, and the response was that "It's not real work". Was he joking? I don't know, but he wasn't smiling. Certainly, the Russia that I worked in was sexist, racist and homophobic, and to a large extent, still is.

I got into a taxi in Moscow some years ago and struck up a conversation. We got onto the topic of Russian culture, communication, values and assumptions, and of course, the notion of planning, or even the desire to plan. I don't know how many people have waited how many hours or lost how much money over the years unnecessarily. The taxi driver explained it:

"Russians do not plan because we never know what is around the corner," she exclaimed with conviction.

"Could it be that you never know what is around the corner because you don't plan?" I responded.

Whilst I was often left frustrated by Russians' desire to be told what to do, my comment earlier about the jungle still holds true; they are very practical. Faced with daily difficulties, a Russian will get through everything. Most Russians I know can strip an engine, build a brick wall and dig a well. Russian women are famously resourceful and, in my experience, better organised than the men, better planners for sure, though the bar is not high, and pragmatism is not the same as planning.

This ability to muddle through with the help of family and friends, to put up with hardship, in addition to making them resilient, possibly also makes them too willing to tolerate what other cultures would not.

There is a lack of initiative, I mean on a general level. If somebody goes to a meeting, and the other person does not turn up, they will either wait forlornly for something to happen, or call their boss and ask what to do next. You may recall part of the reason I left Russia in 1993 was when the cook asked me how many potatoes she should buy at the market. And there was the thing about driving down staircases, which was possibly not ideal…

I spent a lot of time teaching cultural differences to company executives relocating on business to Russia. Russians can be very formal, whereas in business, we tend to be less so. That does not mean we are right.

They can be very direct; so, for example, asking how much you earn is considered normal in Russia, not at all intrusive. They even have an expression for when you come back from the toilet, which roughly translates as "happy relief"!

I had come to take the good with the bad, the positive with the negative, but there is no doubt that I was tired. I was still waiting for the big break that was so eluding us.

Yet I doggedly stuck with Russia, despite its difficulties, and I stuck with consultancy.

The export business that we had started, created by that fraud case, failed when our stock was stolen by our Russian partner. So having discovered the fraud and dealt with it, our attempt to recreate part of the business fell flat. The partner's name was Igor. He was former Russian special forces, with a massive frame; as broad as he was tall. We developed a good relationship with Igor. I suspect he was a nice guy, but his wife had had a baby and something went wrong in the hospital where the baby was delivered. The baby would not survive, and the marriage failed as a result. At some point in this awful situation, it seems Igor took our stock. To this day, I believe that he was desperate. I wish only that he had told us. We would have tried to help.

As I mentioned before, the world was beginning to report on a sickness emanating from China. My daughter, at this time, was studying Russian language in Siberia. The Chinese infection spread, and the news became focussed on what was to become a pandemic.

Lockdown was about to start, it seemed.

THE PHONE CALLS THAT CHANGED MY LIFE

I am sitting in a café with my wife when my phone rings.

My daughter had been in Russia studying, but the students had to leave because of Covid. She headed for her mother's property in Turkey, but was denied entry at the airport because of new rules. Travel was complex at this time, and the rules were unclear and changing constantly.

It was no great problem. My ex-wife called me and together, we arranged for her to fly to London to stay with her friend for a couple of days whilst we decided what to do next. I sent a little money to this friend, thanking her for agreeing to help.

Whilst we may have gone our separate ways years before, Tatiana remained her mother, and I, her father. We planned together.

Then, as sometimes happens, Tatiana changed her mind.

I asked her to stick to the plan, but instead, she called my brother to get him involved.

My brother called me. I asked him also to leave things as they were, just as I had asked Tatiana.

My brother then gets my sister involved, and with Tatiana, they change the plan, overruling what had been agreed, and favouring the new, sudden change made by one parent over that made by both.

That evening, my wife and I discussed options. London was only good for a couple of days because the friend's accommodation was small. Was Mum's flat an option? Too lonely without Mum. Our flat? It was too small and could lead to tensions. That left my brother's house or my sister's. The latter seemed perfect. My mother was there, and the house was large so isolating would be easy. We resolved to call my sister the next day to ask if our daughter might spend lockdown there.

We did not get to make that call.

We found out on social media next morning that our daughter was already at my sister's house.

My siblings did not tell us what they had done.

They did not tell the friend what they had done.

Had they listened, slowed down, allowed the situation to be handled properly, calmly, it would all have been dealt with, together, but instead, there was this brutal, chaotic and unthinking lurch.

My brother would later say it was an "emergency", everyone was in danger, and infections were spreading. Really? So, why collect someone from the airport, who was considered a health risk by the Turkish government, then return to family?

The logic was flawed, and the manner of its execution was a disgrace.

All that is history now, but it created immense damage. Not just because of what they did and how they did it, but because of their behaviour afterwards, which was downright cruel.

The relationship with my siblings has not recovered.

Things could have been so different.

LOCKDOWN SCOTLAND

There followed calls, messages. They seemed to be surprised that we were upset. There were some very unpleasant exchanges. Anger turned to frustration, then a sense of injustice.

Then silence descended.

There were Lorraine and I, like so many others, in lockdown in a small flat. At least we had each other.

There was loneliness and a particularly cruel urban Scotland lockdown, a "demonstration" perhaps of independent thinking from Westminster. Days were long. The silence was worst of all.

We had an office. Work offered respite even with its problems.

I started jogging, but within ten days had torn a ligament. I was using an app called Couch to 5k, and chose the wonderful BBC's Jo Whiley as my app voice. I limped back, in agony, listening to the app congratulating me, which provided me with some amusement.

I was aware that my colleagues in Moscow were also not having much fun, despite the relatively easy lockdown they had compared to us. I arranged several dinner deliveries for these colleagues, which were appreciated because they were not remotely expected.

We began volunteering, anything to allow us out. We would pick up meals and deliver them to people all over town who needed them.

We would take walks in the park. I look back upon these walks now as a really special time. It was as though the world was somewhere but through an impenetrable fog. I am sure everybody felt something like this. I loved those walks on dull, chilly afternoons, arm in arm with my wife, chatting about this and that, avoiding the elephant in the room.

Lorraine was suffering, and I could not bear it. Why should others' dysfunctionality torment her, when she had done nothing wrong? I was heartbroken at my wife's agony and their nonchalance.

Covid charity work

The ensuing silence from my siblings was unbearable. I continued to try to explain my hurt, but they had evidently said what they'd wanted to say, and it seemed we were an irritation. So, silence it was.

There is a saying that the opposite of love is not hate, but indifference. I have thought about it a lot. The worst thing was the silence. Having no interaction was tough – being denied a voice – we only wanted to talk.

I found myself writing to them about divorced parenting, suicidal thoughts, mental health, topics I knew as a divorced father, a trained Samaritan, and as the husband of a bipolar wife.

My siblings shared none of this experience, so far as I am aware, and they did not ask me about mine.

Now, years later, they have still not asked how we felt then or afterwards.

We were discarded.

It hurt – really badly.

I was unable to speak about this for several years. I wanted to protect my wife from my hurt, my sense of being left at the roadside by people whom I had loved.

After four months, having drafted many letters to siblings, to my daughters and to my wife, which I printed and shredded, I sent a message to the eldest of the group, the husband of my sister, in the hope that sage experience might finally help.

This was a massive mistake.

My message had touched upon the topic of suicide (not mine). Could he help us all to move to dialogue?

His response was beyond belief; ignorant, unkind, not one part of it based upon actual knowledge, just his assumptions. Because I had asked my siblings for help with the relationship between my daughter and my wife? How ignorant was this man? I resolved not to reach out to my siblings for help again. He had crossed a line, his ignorance, matched only by his arrogance. Worst of all? My message was about suicide. He responded with *a smiley emoji.* That was a new low.

He later sent me a good luck message to do with sailing, as if he was aware that he had behaved in a despicable manner, but I had nothing more to say to this unpleasant man.

In terms of business, we were having to work very hard just to maintain status quo.

Lockdown was not really lockdown in Russia. They had a rather bizarre system of placing a QR code on your mobile device if you tested positive, so the government could track your movements. This seemed to be more about control of people than control of the pandemic. The Russian people were sceptical of Covid vaccines for example, convinced that their biometrics were being harvested or that there would be a chip in the vaccine to monitor their movements. Somewhat oddly, this cynicism is matched by a reliance on their government to be right on the big issues. They get on with "ducking and diving", but the government "will be right" when it comes to foreign policy.

This would have a disastrous result just two years later.

Back to Covid, the UK's response was incompetent as is now well known. Ordering non-compliant protective gear from Turkey, swinging back and forth, the health minister resigning having been caught having an affair, parties at No. 10. It was all very "dumbed-down Britain".

Countries on full lockdown, such as the UK, had fatalities. Countries with a brief lockdown, such as Russia, had a similar outcome. The Scottish government seemed intent upon beating Westminster on incompetence.

Months later, we were allowed out, the Scottish economy battered. Of course, we would just pay it in tax. If this was Sturgeon's determination to make a name for herself, I suspect it backfired when she was arrested in 2023.

Albion Russia was without a person at the wheel. Grigory was first to panic; Dima remained silent. Katya agreed to become more involved with management in my absence, but only upon her terms, no scrutiny, no questions, no reporting and no deadlines. It took a while for this to become apparent, and for our collision course to become inevitable.

The news showed the same story every day, as if the press' mission was to deliver the same bad news in as many different possible ways. It was not a full, objective reflection of what was happening. People were dealing with it; the vaccination was underway.

For months, this went on.

One thing Katya did for the company was to tell me what a vile colleague Elena was, with her shouting, bullying and slamming the phone down. Elena did not show her true colours to me; no, with me she was sweetness and light. I consulted with my colleague, Kristina, who confirmed that Elena was Elena's sole supporter. She gave all her work to her colleagues whilst pretending it was hers. This suddenly made sense. When I had needed her assistance, she took time to respond, clearly consulting with people who knew. When I asked her for something that involved taking responsibility or risk, she would suddenly become a "mere employee, without the right to make decisions".

It had apparently been this way for some time. Everybody had just put up with it. In Russia, there is an assumption that management will not listen, and there may be repercussions. So, until Katya disclosed and Kristina confirmed, nobody had said anything about this loathsome woman.

I resolved to fire her at the earliest opportunity.

Whilst all this was going on, the situation with siblings remained the same. Silence seemed to me to be a cruel type of bullying.

Lorraine and I decided to close the office. We packed up, gave away what we did not need, and set up at home.

Early August 2020 offered a chance with the family issue.

I met my brother, dreaming of discussion, reconciliation and meaningful hugs.

It did not go that way.

I had to listen but had no chance to tell him how we felt undermined, ignored. Even, as time went on, abused. A big word, I know.

Abused.

Then he left.

It got worse.

We were to meet for lunch, with his wife. He arrived alone, she apparently feeling "too bruised". We had not even spoken.

Lorraine stood up in tears and left. Bruised? My wife and I were black and blue.

I stayed to talk to my brother. It was like trying to nail jelly to a wall. He would not have the discussion that we so clearly needed to have. He refused to talk about what had happened, about how everybody felt, about how we might fix this. He offered a selection of opinions, of course, the main one seemingly centred around the notion that he had saved the day.

I should have left with Lorraine.

THE LOSS OF THE FAMILY STANDARD

My mother had moved, around the time of the outbreak of Covid, to my sister's home and was well looked after. I shall always be grateful to the family for looking after her so well, which I wrote to them about. Her health was failing her, and Covid separated us.

Finally, in early September, 2020, our mother passed. She had known about this family rift and after Covid wanted to preside over a meeting, where she would be arbiter. She said this had happened before. But it was not to be. Without her, we went our separate ways. She was so kind and generous to us all when she was alive.

She disbursed her estate to us all, and nobody complained.

We did not repay that kindness to her by reconciling. God knows I tried.

Lorraine organised the funeral service card, the wake, the venue, catering and so on, but felt unable to go to the funeral. Mum was such a good friend to her. It was Lorraine who would take Mum out, buy her things and go away with her, so to feel unable to attend her funeral was a cruel blow. But, how could she? She felt frozen out.

At the funeral, I hid the shame I felt at my siblings and their spouses. I went to the funeral with the girls, carried the coffin. I was unable to speak. As the service continued, and I sat on the front row with our girls, my daughter quietly took my hand and I took comfort from that beautiful, strong gesture.

I wondered if the unpleasant man noticed that? The man who had, weeks previously, written vitriol, convinced that he knew everything, when in reality, he knew nothing.

And his smiling emoji…

As the coffin descended, a benign goodness was syphoned away.

Decency, common sense, real Christian values were lost. Not somebody who tells anybody who will listen that she is "a Christian", but an actual *Christian*, with love, empathy, compassion, forgiveness and devoid of unkindness.

Love should conquer everything.

In a normal family, it would.

CIRCLING OVER EUROPE

Meanwhile, with the other chain of events…

Finally, November, 2020, I was able to travel to Moscow office, which had been left without a rudder since February.

It was difficult and, like so many things during Covid, faintly comical.

I routed via the Baltics, as I had done so often over the years. Upon arrival, I had a lengthy wait but finally came the time to board, so I made my way to the gate.

That's when things got complicated. I was not allowed to board. I showed them my passport, my visa, my Covid test, but no. The problem, as they explained, is that Russia always had a problem with the Baltic nations, and so they make things awkward for passengers routing to Moscow via those countries. In other words, Russia was using Covid as an excuse to make some mischief. They suggested I fly to Vienna and continue my journey to Moscow from there.

I flew to Vienna. It turned out that the man in Riga had been incorrect in his assumption that this was anti-Baltic mischief-making, because I was not allowed to board in Vienna either.

I flew to London, did a new Covid test and took a direct flight to Moscow.

The actual reason for this was that new rules dictated that you could only arrive into certain jurisdictions directly, but nobody had told anybody, so nobody could explain it in any airport. Such was the chaos of Covid.

I finally land in the right country, and I have the meetings I need to have with Katya, Grigory and the lawyers. I return to the UK.

One meeting would change things. Elena declined to meet me, saying she was ill. I finally met her deputy, Kristina, who turned out to be delightful, with a sense of humour and an ability to engage that can be difficult to find in Russia.

MY PERSONAL RUSSIAN LOCKDOWN

December 2020, I decide to conduct one final trip to Moscow before Christmas. That proved to be an error of judgement.

Day one, the Marriott, Katya glances at her phone and tells me that all UK flights are to be grounded. I have one day to get out. This reminds me of Sasha's advice in August, 1991; get out of Russia because of the coup.

I did not follow Sasha's advice in 1991, or hers in 2020, and that was why I was in Moscow until mid January, 2021.

Christmas Day was spent with colleagues, whilst Lorraine spent Christmas alone in the flat in Glasgow.

Days came and went. Luke kindly invited me to his home, but I declined because Christmas is family time. Perhaps it is just as well that they had that Christmas as a family.

New Year was quiet; I moved from the Marriott to a hotel slightly west of the centre, the one Geoff and I had stayed in some five years earlier. It was slightly cheaper, but the main reason I moved was to get a different view from my room.

The highlight of my stay was when I seemed to switch on our "Alexa" from my hotel room in Moscow, and played a track in our home in the UK, which scared the wits out of my wife, and to some extent, myself.

I did have time to wander around Moscow, and that is mainly how I passed my time. The Marriott is right in the centre; turn left and you can walk down to Red Square and the Kremlin, with the massive red stone department store on the left, "GUM". When I was a student, this had been more museum than store, but after the political upheaval, everything changed, and it became the single most prestigious store in Russia. It had a fountain at the centre, three beautiful rows, ornately decorated, with the most expensive world brands on display over several floors. It was, really, Harrods in Moscow. My guess is that it is gradually filling up with Chinese goods now.

Moving out of GUM and across the square to the Lenin Mausoleum, this was a now rather controversial place because Vladimir Lenin remains on display to this day despite being dead for a hundred years. I have not gone to see this macabre sight, but I recall, as a student, seeing a queue of people snaking around and out of the square to pay their respects. I think they were bussed in from the regions and schools. It was definitely not for me.

More to my style was the Alexander Garden, which extends the length of the Kremlin. You can see the Eternal Flame in its marble glory, with the names of the "hero" cities of the Second World War. Walk far enough, through this green space, and you can cross over to see the Lenin Library which is massive, but that's all it is.

Then you can walk back north up what used to be Gorky Street, where I had my run-in with that rush hour taxi years before.

I suppose Pushkin Square is the absolute centre of Moscow, commemorating the poet whose life was cut short when he was shot in a duel in 1834. The square is pleasant enough, but it's almost too central. Nobody stays for long. Walk further north past Mayakovsky Square, commemorating a rather different kind of poet, rather more Soviet, but then you get to my real part of Moscow, the part I knew best, Belorussky Square. It is a sprawling place but full of little cafes and bars, kiosks and streets, a curious blend of modern and traditional. The station is where I would arrive from the airport for many, many business trips. I would take a small apartment somewhere around this area and conduct most of my meetings in the same place where possible. Plus, usually, a few beers with friends after work followed. I liked this area of Moscow. It was no better or worse than other areas and, as a student, I knew other parts of town better, but if you travel to a place on a frequent basis, and you are not keen on hotels, you really have to make one part of town your own. This was my part of town.

When I moved hotels during Covid, I went to another part of the centre of this vast city, Smolensky Square. We once had offices nearby, and whilst it was on the very busy "Garden Ring", an eight-lane road circling the city, it also had plenty of smaller streets around it. Perhaps most interestingly, it was near the so-called "Arbat", a pedestrianised street taking you towards the Kremlin. It seemed mainly for tourists now, market stalls with multicoloured Russian hats, pseudo, acrylic, mass-produced "art" and kitsch, but it was pleasant enough. The Hard Rock Café now stood where previously there had been a great Mexican place. I recall having dinner there with a friend from the BBC and then going to the bar area, where we chatted until we noticed that the sun had come up outside. I had little interest in the Hard Rock, which I notice is now "permanently closed" according to Google, perhaps unsurprising for an American brand. I did find an Irish pub called the Ulysses, which provided respite on the occasional evening away from the hotel room.

Ulysses pub in Moscow a sanctuary during Covid in Russia

But of course, what I was really doing was waiting until the flights resumed to London, which eventually, after checking on a more or less daily basis, they did.

I returned, a month later, to the UK.

2021

Sometime around Easter 2021, Dima finally left. He told me he was going on holiday and would get on with projects upon his return. That was a lie, of course. We did not see him again.

Spring 2021, one client announced a global restructuring, so we would lose that piece of business anyway. We had had a good run, Elena in particular, but there was no place for her, now that I had been told what she was really like.

I was becoming pretty good at firing in Russia by now.

Firing people in Russia is not easy. There is a lot of blurry ruling. Usually, if you want to get rid of somebody, the parties agree to a severance pay equivalent to three months' salary. With a director, it may be a little more complicated, so I enlisted the help of Luke and his legal colleague, Ruslan. I did not want just any lawyer for this; I needed somebody upon whom I could rely completely. After firing Elena, I would need to ensure a smooth continuation of the business, with Kristina as her replacement.

Luke and I had many calls, along with Ruslan, over several few weeks. It was clear that Elena did not expect to be removed from her throne and did not plan to go gracefully. This was going to be a battle, but I was determined to get rid of this cancer in the company.

In the meantime, whilst my mother's estate was being allocated, Lorraine and I bought Mum's property from the estate. The property had been in the family some 30 years.

Emptying a property when somebody passes is unsettling.

Whilst Mum was still alive, she asked us to sell her car, and she wanted to find a new home for her grand piano. Mum was practical and sentimental in equal measure. We had dealt with this already, so she had made this particular task easier for us. The piano, I am pleased to say, now resides in a five-star hotel in central Glasgow, together with an inscription, its new location and the dedication message having been arranged by my wife, Lorraine. The hotel were so grateful for this gift, and they laid on a wonderful afternoon tea, which unfortunately, neither Lorraine nor I were able to attend. Though other members of my family found time to go of course.

Every Item told a Story

The Piano

Some items in the property were precious, not valuable but worth keeping. One of these was my father's school desk. He had held onto it and added to it over the years. He had pinned under the lid, one of his last school timetables from 1948, showing extra Latin, and a list of hospital tutors for his first year at university. There were letters, interesting papers, all sorts. I recall laying all these out: letters, ties, gloves, hats, Bibles, jewellery, just things that I felt we should decide upon jointly, and of course, the desk.

Desk showing timetable and letters

I do not know what happened to that desk, but one day, it was no longer there.

That had happened before. In our grandparents' home was a precious item that reminded us of our childhood. We decided to share it between our homes. That was 2018, and I have not seen it since.

My wife's family are the salt of the earth. At the epicentre of that family is Lorraine's second cousin Izzy. She is brave, funny, smart, energetic, patient, a medical professional, strong-willed, not judgmental and totally trustworthy. I could go on. I had met her some time previously and I warmed to her immediately. She was an absolute stalwart at this difficult time, and later she was a huge support to me and to Lorraine. She was there when some in my family had vanished. I cannot imagine her family having the same issues as ours appear to have. They have words, sort it out and move on; so far as I am aware, like every normal family.

There was too much going on at this time.

LUKE'S DEPARTURE

May 2021, I call Luke and Ruslan. Luke does not pick up. Ruslan answers and delivers the chilling news that Luke is in a coma.

We had only been chatting a couple of days ago.

He had been run down on the street on his way home, and, to the best of my knowledge, they did not catch the driver.

I was in shock. Luke spent his 40th birthday in a coma, and over the passing weeks, it became clear that Luke was not coming out of it. To my immense sorrow, on the day of my birthday, 10th July, he passed away.

Luke's funeral service

His funeral would be on 14th July. I flew out to Moscow.

It was a hot day as we stood outside the Anglican Church of St Andrew's, Moscow, and I chatted to Ruslan. Dressed in dark suits, we took our places inside. We were allowed to approach the open coffin to say our farewells to Luke, but I chose to remain seated, paying my respects from where I was. My dear, funny, strong friend Luke. I had drunk beer with him, played golf with him, argued with him, confided in him, done business with him. This should not be. Several people stood up to say a few words, another friend, Luc, and Trevor from the British embassy. I wanted to get up. I wanted to talk about how Luke had come back into the bar that evening to make sure I was OK, but I was choked. To hear his wife speaking, through tears, wishing Luke well wherever he was and promising to look after the two girls, that broke my heart. It was such a young family torn apart, and my real thinking was that Luke had not been run over by accident. Strange things happen in Russia, but that was not for now. I attended the wake later, and flew back to London.

DIGGING OUT THE CANCER

At this time, Katya was heading for departure, if not in the way she intended. She had told me that she needed to stay to look after a friend's house; she would take her laptop and continue to work. In fact, when she asked me, she had already left. I asked her if she would be at Luke's funeral because he had been kind to her. That's when I discovered that she had actually already left the country for an extended holiday in Ukraine, visiting friends. She should have been in Moscow. She should have been at Luke's funeral. It was so disrespectful. I had had enough. We were finished, and I asked Kristina to fire her.

It had been exhausting, trying to help this girl, trying to give her a career. I was relieved when we got rid of her.

The tougher task, getting rid of Elena, was still ahead. I returned to Moscow for this main event. I would do this myself.

Firing Elena turned out to be a rather amusing affair, mainly because she was evidently not a deep thinker.

This is how the discussion with Elena had been going over the past few weeks. She knew she was being fired, and was defending her corner, trying to get the least bad deal she could. I shall give a summary of the conversation we had over several weeks, by telephone, then with lawyers and finally in person:

David: I am firing you.
Elena: I will have seven months' salary if you want me to leave.
David: You can have one.
Elena: Six.
David: Two.
Elena: Five.
David: Two.
Elena: Four.

David: Three.

Elena: Four.

David: Three.

Elena: Then I will alert the authorities that the company has not been paying tax.

David: You told me tax is up to date, and you are the general director, so I would say that would be your problem, not mine. Probably unwise.

Elena: OK. Three.

This was never going to end differently.

Somewhat foolishly, she also said that she had ten thousand dollars of company money at home. When I asked why, she told me it was insurance in case she did not get the deal she wanted. I explained that I would call the police if the money was not returned within 24 hours.

OCTOBER 2021.
THE MARRIOTT GRAND,
CENTRAL MOSCOW.

I sit to Elena's right, Kristina opposite, and the new lawyer to my right. Elena's knee shakes the entire time. She does not like having been found out, losing her throne and being replaced by her deputy. She does not like it one bit, but she had a good run with us, earning a lot of money whilst delegating her work to Kristina and various other people before, who left because they could not stand her, as I later found out.

The cash was counted in full view of the guests drinking coffee in the bar area. Ludicrous I know, but it was a risk I was going to have to take. I would then need to take this sum from the hotel, and that can get nasty if you are followed, but I was not followed.

When we signed the documents confirming that she would be replaced as general director by Kristina, she burst out laughing, but I saw through this for what it was.

She did not have the grace to say thank you for the career, for the generous income, or for the Thai holiday for her and her son, for which I had paid.

Nor even the tea. She did not even part company with us graciously. She shook the lawyer's hand, span upon her heels, ignoring me and Kristina, and left. I think it might have been some kind of display of pride or defiance, but what it looked like to us, as we ordered some fizz, was a display of childishness.

That was the last we saw of her.

Kristina and I got on with the job ourselves. What a breath of fresh air she was. Suddenly I received figures on time and without dissembling, without trying to hide parts of the accounts. Suddenly, I had an honest and hard-working colleague.

There had been a sea change in the business, and changes had to take place. With Kristina, this became easier. We let one person more go, and they went in a most odd fashion, with the usual threats.

There was a minor dispute about severance pay, so this girl got her mother involved. The mother and daughter came to the office to confront Kristina, making wild accusations, none of which was true or backed up by evidence. Grigory sat in the corner, offering no support to Kristina whatsoever, choosing not to get involved.

Later in the same day, I received a message on my phone from this girl, but clearly written by the mother, basically saying that the mother had been in the police force and that they would ensure there would be problems if we did not pay the severance in full.

I responded that the mother was probably a porter or a cleaner, because a police officer would know that blackmail is illegal.

The messages stopped.

Moscow had become a city inhabited by swarms of people making sure they were OK, irrespective of the cost to others. I don't think it's because they are Russian, I think it is because of tumultuous events. I was just unlucky that I had to be there during these events.

Towards the end of the year, I sensed trouble between Kristina and Grigory. He had always been good at carrying out instructions, and I had always got along fine with him. He was not good in a crisis, as I had discovered a couple of times, most noticeably at the beginning of Covid, but now I could sense that he was resentful of Kristina's promotion; perhaps he thought it would be his. This manifested itself mainly in a lack of respect for her. He began using the familiar version of "you" in Russian, similar to that found in French and German.

We arranged a call. I asked him if anything was wrong, if I could help in some way. He answered no. I asked them to explain their issues to me. She said he seemed reluctant to conduct tasks and that since Elena's firing his demeanour had changed. Grigory gave one-word answers, and I asked if he could treat Kristina with the same respect that he treated others including myself.

He declined. I fired him. It was simple. I did not like his tone, and to be honest, he would not be missed. As always, we did everything by the book, gave him the severance despite my better judgement. That was the law.

Kristina and I continued working, ensuring that clients' needs were dealt with, and ensuring, for example, that our remaining staff were OK. Business continued. Life went on. We had plenty of business to build upon; we just needed to replace the staff members with more competent people, which should not take long. In fact, we took on the first replacement, a young man who was a friend of one of our staff. But further tumultuous events would not allow this hiring to last for very long. He was in our employ for just a few weeks.

2022

Christmas came and went, and in January, a Moscow colleague arrived in the UK for client visits over the course of ten days.

We had a lot to look forward to, particularly after a gruesome two years. My colleague flew from Heathrow back to Moscow, and I drove home.

My mum used to joke: "Don't be glum; the worst is still to come."

Up until now, I don't suppose you could describe things as a walk in the park, but one morning in late February 2022, Russia invaded Ukraine.

I had been in Moscow just two weeks before this took place.

INVASION

First to go were the clients, understandably, with one exception. The clients were for the most part very nice to us about it, but it was very quick. There was no attempt to keep the business relationship going; this was force majeure, it was finished. We were finished. The clients had to leave this market. Newcastle, Birmingham, London, Truro, Sheffield, Clydebank, Leeds, Perth, they all left Russia, and of course, left us.

25 years of work was gone in 90 minutes.

Then we had to let go of staff.

Eventually, we had just one person left in Moscow and one in Kyiv; both colleagues got along very well, by the way, even if this seems curious to the reader. War is not binary. There were so many, including our staff, who were Russo-Ukrainian, and still had relatives in Ukraine, whom they were now supposed to be fighting. It was surreal. Back in the UK, we retained one person part-time, and other than that, after the invasion, it was just Lorraine and I.

Then came phone calls from the media, the television and radio appearances, various stations and channels, all asking for views and prognosis.

My siblings reappeared, asking for transcripts. I dared hope, out of this madness might come a reconciliation, but no, just the transcripts.

Then came the odd sensation that we had no job. There was no coming back from this.

A career that had taken me to the USA, Australia, all over Russia, Europe, Asia, the Middle East, the Far East; all to end at the council tip.

I emptied drawers, the garage, deleted my career. I shredded documents, trying not to read them as I fed the machine. Occasionally I would see an invoice, a letter, a flyer for a seminar, an advert promoting Russia to exporters.

Russia Market Approaches a bestseller in its time

I had a sense of loss. That may sound odd, but the company had been with us more than 25 years; it was like family. There had been wins and losses, high fives and worries, travel, people, stories and jokes, contracts and meetings, threats and reconciliation. Articles, brochures, books, company stands, photos all went into the recycling bin. The projects, hopes and dreams.

The end of Albion?

This was what I think is known as "a hard stop", and it is difficult to describe. It had been my life, the thing I thought about as I went to sleep and in my waking moments – for years. I was not on the battlefield, the trees looked the same and the neighbours still had their newspaper deliveries.

For a few weeks, if I drove any distance, anything that involved a route south for example, it seemed that I was setting off on a business trip.

This was February into March, 2022. Only a few weeks earlier, this same car had driven all over the UK with my Moscow colleague, the two of us chatting to each other in Russian, visiting clients and talking about Russian projects.

I could not tell Lorraine how binning my career was making me feel. I kept it from her, just as I kept from her how I felt abandoned by my own brother and sister. I bottled it up.

We were not at war. It was tougher for others.

It was probably unsurprising that I had a health scare one morning. How did I feel at that point? A kind of dull inevitability. Not sadness, not fear, not regret, just inevitability. I recall thinking, after all that has happened, what a stupid ending.

At this point, more than ever, I wanted my siblings.

It marked the beginning of lots of tests. Something was not right, but whatever it was, it was to recede or vanish, and I would live another day.

For some years after these events, I would continue to have this sense of loss. I would hear a phrase, or see a building, I might see an advert for some product that we had been working on in Russia. Even just seeing my suits hanging up, unused, it all gave me this sense of something that had been real but now seemed to have been of a different time and place.

RESURGENCE

We did everything a company does to survive. We would worry about income later.

First, get rid of the dead wood, the things we can do without. Gone were the subscriptions, the speculative trips, the people who were not critical, the excess storage and the couriers.

We cut costs. We cut and cut and cut.

Weeks went by.

We dug into reserves.

The outgoings slowed down.

We paid off our tax, any outstanding debts, focussed on staying afloat and upright.

We had our China work.

I decided to resurrect some work that I had been doing for an American company, nothing to do with Russia. This was sales training. I had been doing this for some years; they would send me the client details, and I would run the training over a few days. I followed their programme but delivered in my style, with personal experience, anecdotes and so on. It had worked well.

What if, instead of just waiting for the training company to give me the details of the client, we were to find clients? I discussed this with them, they agreed, and off we went in search of clients. After three months trying to find companies interested in sales training, we admitted defeat. Perhaps there were too many courses available, perhaps our company name was too associated with Russia, or perhaps we just did not find the clients. Whatever happened, we dropped the idea. As my friend used to say, doing the same thing again and again, expecting a different outcome, is the definition of madness.

Crucially, one of our original Russia-related clients had also not walked away.

After a few weeks of unease, they suggested we help them in Turkey. A lifeline had been thrown, and I seized it with both hands. The person responsible for this decision was John Squire, businessman, philanthropist, CEO and thorough gentleman. His decision not simply to cut us loose and, instead, to give us an opportunity had the most profound effect not only on the business but on our mental health.

The possibility that everything had not just burned in a hellish, fast white heat, that something could grow, was powerful. I would give this client all I had.

25-YEAR COMPANY ANNIVERSARY

There was one thing that I could not really change because it had been in the calendar for over a year, and this was very odd in some ways. The previous year, 2021, November marked our 25th year of trading, and I had decided to "push the boat out" so to speak, by hiring a yacht on the Med, and inviting all staff from UK, Ukraine and Russia. We would float around Turkey eating mezze and enjoying the breeze, sailing from place to place. I was a qualified skipper, and we had done this many times with friends. November is not a great time to sail of course! So, the actual yacht had been chartered, paid for and was scheduled for a full week in the month of May, 2022.

Except that now there had been an invasion, I had not many staff left, and the business had been more or less sunk overnight.

The boat having been paid for anyway, I was determined not to lose it and, to be honest, a week away from this madness seemed like not a bad prospect. It would have been foolish to book a holiday under these circumstances, but this was already bought and paid for. Even rescheduling was not a possibility, because we had already done that once in the previous autumn and a second time was not permitted. No, this was "use it or lose it".

We still had staff, they had done nothing wrong, and then there was Lorraine and I.

We still had Sasha, based in Kyiv.

He is a young man, a qualified lawyer, and an asset to the company. He is the person to whom I would have handed the keys if I had had a company left.

He was well travelled, but the war had stopped all travel. An ailment with his foot stopped him from signing up to fight against the Russians.

Sasha wanted to join this yacht. We wanted him to be on board, so he decided to do a test border crossing.

Upon arrival at the border, he was met, not by immigration officers, but by men with automatic rifles slung over their shoulders.

It was an intimidating experience, perhaps unsurprisingly for a country at war.

They asked him if he was Ukrainian. He showed them a Moldovan passport.

They suggested that he also had a Ukrainian passport, and that they could check this easily on the PC a few metres away. All they would need would be his fingerprint.

He could leave now or do the fingerprint test.

Sasha is a smart guy, and with dual nationality, he knew his data would be on that PC.

They explained that if they found that he also possessed a Ukrainian passport, they would send him, today, to the front line. He went home.

We offered the remaining places to friends, and off we went. It would prove to be the oddest 25-year celebration ever.

Sailing out of Göcek, we enjoyed a week on the sea, and a good mixture of English, Russian, French, Irish and Scots. Day one was a bit rough, with the sea hitting us on the port beam hard for several hours, but we had buckets for the girls, all of which were used! It was unfortunate, but we knew it was a one-off, and indeed, the weather improved after that first day.

Pennants

We flew pennants up the halyard, displaying the nationalities on board. In Ekincek, a small group of Russian sailors noticed our Russian pennant and told us that they were too scared to fly theirs. Such was the world at the time.

It was good that I had Gary on board, who is a highly competent skipper, because my mood was not the mood to command this boat on my own.

My head was a scary place at that time, colourful and dark. Gary quietly had my back. Talking of which, one other close friend was on the boat that week, and so it was that we both sat on deck, under the stars, chatting, as everybody else slept below.

Author and Richard

The conversation turned to the unpleasant events and situations over the past few years, and he made a comment about life carrying on and about the need to stay strong.

I responded, and this was probably the only time I have expressed any such sentiment, "What if I don't want to be strong any more? What if I have had enough of this?"

He said nothing, but leant forward and gripped my hand, hard, but kind. It was not the gentle clasp of my daughters' hands at my mother's funeral, but the strong grip of a friend. And oh, my word, I gripped that hand back. There was a strength in that handgrip that I will never forget, understanding and a quiet undertaking to continue, and that is what I did.

Last night

After this sailing trip, some three months into the war, I routed into Istanbul before returning home. Following the invasion, I had various conversations with Kristina, and the main one was focussed upon her future and the future of the Russian part of the operation. I gave her a challenge, which she accepted: hold onto whatever the Russian business has in terms of finance, and even if it is impossible to grow the business now, at least don't lose it. One day this will all be over.

In that way, we were able to continue paying her from within Moscow, because there would be no more bank transfers between UK and Russia. Kristina had built up a small business for us, importing textiles. That was the reason I needed to visit Denizli and Istanbul. This tiny acorn might grow, and even although it had no immediate effect upon us in the UK, it might prove to be important later. It was certainly important to Kristina, who, despite all that was happening, continued to be our responsibility.

There may be readers wondering why we would continue any relationship with any Russians against the background of war. Well, here's the thing. Individual Russians did not send the tanks in any more than I did, and they absolutely cannot say anything publicly because they will be arrested. Think about that. We do not know how lucky we are here, where we can basically say what we like. I despair at the people here who bleat and carp about their rights. I wish I could send them to Russia or to Iran, just to give them a little perspective.

To put some more perspective on the Russian people (in other words, people not politics), many Russians I know have family in Ukraine and vice versa. Some Russians have Ukrainian relatives, wounded whilst fighting the Russians, and the Russian families are sending money to help with their medical care. This is a lot more complicated than it appears on TV.

In this post-invasion reality, where there were no calls to make, no clients to visit and no reports to write, I was able to do some more volunteering. This time, unlike during Covid, this was Ukraine-specific. It involved using my Russian language, helping with Ukrainians in the UK. Most of these guys speak Russian, and for those who do not, a Russian will understand a Ukrainian and vice versa. There were some tough calls on the phone. It sometimes felt intrusive, being a voice in a medical room hundreds of miles away. I felt so desperately sorry for these people who had been forced out of their country. How dignified they all were.

We met a Ukrainian family living not far from my sister's house, a delightful family, the son now attending school, the daughter and mother trying to find a job. Then there was the grandmother and the cat! Yes, they had returned to Ukraine to pick up the cat! I helped where I could. I took them out, gave them various items they did not have, drove them around and generally tried to be useful. I also found them a dentist. I had become something of a specialist. After my dentist retired, I discovered that my teeth were not in the condition I thought; it took four dental practices to sort it all out.

My wife and I decided to sell our home. We had no choice. In that regard, the decision was easy. Our siblings had not asked about it since we bought it out, though our parents had lived there for years and years, so it did not appear to hold sentimental value to the family after all.

I recall a strange call with my brother, when I mentioned that we had been trying to sell. His response?

"Well, that's what these assets are for, isn't it?"

I remember thinking, *You really don't get this, do you?* We lost our income, livelihood, career, home, car, everything, but that was his comment on the situation.

Nevertheless, I wanted another go at reconnecting with my siblings, and so it was that I met my brother again.

I was headed straight for the elephant trap I fell into when we met in 2020, hoping to chat, to get to an understanding, the start of reconciliation.

I was wrong – again. There was no kindness, little desire to talk.

He said one thing in particular, which made it clear. He and his wife were trying to work only four days a week, to enjoy more time together; they were looking forward to having their kitchen redone. Meantime, he said, my sister and her husband had bought a motorhome and they were enjoying that.

Whilst we were selling everything we had, they were talking lifestyle. It felt surreal.

Whilst we managed our financial decline, they offered no help. I could not ask.

Gopal and Dima did not ask for help when they were beaten up for skin tone or sexuality. I just helped. It seemed so obvious.

It seemed my siblings had moved on. There would not be the discussion that our own mother had wanted us to have, no reconciliation, no discussion of reconciliation. We had been asking for two years – mediation, meetings and reconciliation.

I needed to adopt a different approach, to sign up to their silence instead of seeking reconciliation – to cut loose, to stop caring.

I would write them a letter.

A CONVERSATION WITH THE ATLANTIC

At this time, I was planning a sail on the Atlantic with my very good friend, Gary. Gary is an amazing guy, self-effacing, but very talented, as well as being one of the funniest and most caring people I know. Gary had one other very interesting facet to his character. As well as being a husband, father, company owner and award-winning chess player, Gary was a very, very accomplished sailor. His boat had provided much pleasure to us all over many years. *Katy* was only 29 feet in length, with two small bilge keels underneath. These small, British-built yachts are hardy and tough. They sail well, but they are not generally designed with the Atlantic in mind, so that is exactly what Gary decided to do. I was to be on that sail, from Gran Canaria to St Lucia, but it was postponed because of Covid. With all that had come about, sadly, I could not join the sail across the ocean when it finally took place at the end of 2022.

What Gary did invite me to do, in early August 2022, was to sail *Katy* with him from Portugal to the Canary Islands, so that the boat would be in the correct position for the start of the race. This sail would be about a week on the ocean, non-stop, and not a bad test for the boat as well as for our sailing skills.

Gary likes to joke around, as do I, but when it comes to sailing, he has a sense of responsibility that puts the jokes on hold. On the Atlantic, we will be a dry boat. This makes sense because, at night, each person is alone on deck whilst the other sleeps. The last thing you need is a foggy mind.

When Gary sent me articles about killer whales and pirates off Africa, I wanted to think he was joking; but I knew he was not. The chances of attack by either were small, but the killer whales had become known to attack the keels and rudders of yachts, apparently as a game; a deadly game for those on board, of course. They chase the tuna, which come out of the Mediterranean and up the west coast of Portugal. Yachts provide light entertainment. This behaviour is apparently being transmitted from pod to pod and now extends as far north as the Orkney Islands. Most of the pirates, on the other hand, are further south, not off Morocco and the Sahara. I was less bothered about them.

There was one more thing, shipping lanes. I had raced through cruise liners on the Solent and encountered submarines on the Clyde, but this was a major shipping route west and east for all sorts of freight vessels.

Gary warned me about these dangers, as well as the danger of ripping your toenails off, cold, wet, all sorts. I was ready.

I recall speaking to the lawyer who had helped us with Mum's estate. He is also a sailor, and I happened to mention to him that I was about to sail on the Atlantic. He asked if I had a will, and when I said no, he said that now would be a good time to write one. He was not being dramatic or morbid, but practical. I took his advice, and scribbled a note to act as my last wishes, which I left with Lorraine. I would do a proper will when I returned.

There was one thing I needed to do before I left, to write the letter to my siblings.

Before the sail seemed like an appropriate time to make peace.

I apologised for any wrongs, thanked them for their help in the past. I explained to my brother that the will I had left for him to take care of had been replaced by the document I had left with my wife. I explained to my sister that it felt awkward to go to our niece's wedding, with all that had happened, but that we would love to go if we were welcome.

I felt I had to agree to their silent "non-engagement". What I was really hoping was that they would dig deep, reach out, tell us we were welcome at the wedding, everything could be fixed, we are family and there is blame on all sides.

The letter was sent the day before we sailed.

There is one thing to explain to you, before we set sail.

I have a certain fear of the sea. I admit this to very few people. To me it is logical, like heights, for example. If you are not scared of heights, surely you are an idiot? Falling kills. Drowning kills. I am proud of being scared, because I feel the fear and I do it anyway.

As children, my siblings learnt to swim on holiday with the help of a Frenchman by the name of Pierre. He was kind and patient, ahead of his time.

I was seven years old when my parents decided on holiday that I should learn to swim. Daniel gave me some lessons in a pool on the beach, and then took me out on a rubber dinghy into the sea.

Then he threw me over the side.

I remember not understanding and I remember going down. I climbed a pretend ladder to get to the bright surface. I floundered towards the rubber dinghy with ropes on the side. I clutched at one rope.

Daniel removed my hand and threw me back in the water. He kept doing this till I was full of sea water and fear.

That fear does not leave you. I love it too, but I learnt to respect it. You can never be complacent.

Fear keeps sailors alive, not just knowledge.

Ocean

Gary and I completed preparations for the sail. I checked with Lorraine that she had sent the letter (because there are no mobile phones on the Atlantic). We cast off from Lagos Marina, late afternoon; I had done what I could.

We sailed away from land, trimmed the boat. We had to keep the engine running. Sailing this through shipping lanes would be suicidal.

Night fell. My watch started at 21:00 as it became dark and Gary went below for three hours' sleep.

Then the noises began.

It is strange, because I had not really expected the noises. At that time, in the darkness, with only the noise of the steering gear, the engine, and the navigation screen and running lights, these noises took on a surreal character.

A surge from somewhere behind the boat in the dark; snapping and tearing from the mast and halyards; the thud of the engine; the crackle of the VHF radio as a ship spoke to the coastguard; the tug of sails on rope; the shackles and the mast all conspiring to create a dark concerto. It was more eerie than scary. I was on a good boat with a competent skipper and my sailing and navigation skills were up to this task (I hoped). I could see the large ships' routes. The screen told me their name, length, origin, cargo, their heading and the anticipated time of collision.

Gary had given me instructions to keep one mile off any tankers, and that was my intention.

Midnight came, and it was time to change watch. Gary could be seen below, donning his life jacket, his distress signal, his all-weather gear, his cut-loose knife. As he came on deck, we did a handover, with me pointing out any shipping vessels, collision times, while he checked the course and took over the watch. I went to my bunk at the front of the boat, a small, chilly sanctuary on the deep, blue dark, listening to the waves just the other side of the tiny hull.

Come 03:00, it's my turn to don my gear, my knife, my distress signal, my harness and I grab a packet of sweets. I come up on deck and the skipper greets me for the handover. In 90 minutes, we will hit a Chinese vessel heading west, 270 degrees. Gary suggests I use the VHF nearer the time to ask the ship to change course. With our settings, we have right of way.

I am sceptical.

I recall racing on *Katy* on the Solent, I am on starboard tack and we are under full sail. I have right of way over any engine, over any yacht not racing and over any yacht racing on port tack. Five long horn blasts from a P&O ocean liner signal "make your intentions clear". My intention is very clear. I want him to move a finger two microns to port to give me room, but no. The reality is the big guy wins. I write this rather tongue in cheek and did not really expect the liner to change course.

I suggested to Gary on the Atlantic that this Chinese vessel might not be interested in the rules of the sea. Long story short, he was sure they would stand down, and off he went to his bunk.

At 04:10, I don't recall the name of the ship except that it consisted of four words in Chinese. I call up on channel 16:

"Four long Chinese words, four long Chinese words, four long Chinese words. This is yacht *Katy*, yacht *Katy*, yacht *Katy*. Do you read? Over."

"*Katy*, this is four long Chinese words. What do you need?"

"Four long Chinese words, this is yacht *Katy*. We request that you change your course. Over."

"No. We are on 270. Out."

And that was that, the Solent all over again.

Gary came up at 06:00 and I turned in, having managed not to hit the Chinese cargo ship – so much for the rules of the sea.

Somehow, without a word of exaggeration, every time we changed shift at 03:00, I was on a collision course to hit something at 04:20, for an entire week.

The days were spent on deck together, trimming the sails, chatting, and gazing at the blue. This is not for everybody, and if you do it, you had better make sure you get along with the person on board, because there is nowhere to go on this enclosed space. Gary is such a good friend, and I have such an abundance of respect for him, that I cannot really imagine falling out with him. It surely must be difficult to fall out with somebody whom you respect. When I look back, anybody with whom I have fallen out is somebody whom I fundamentally do not respect, whether at the beginning of the process, or at its conclusion. I enjoyed this time on the ocean. My favourite time of day, as I look back, was as the sun was setting around 9 p.m., and Gary was going below. This was my time on the ocean, nothing to disturb my thoughts, and nobody to break the beautiful noise of being alone at sea.

I was glad I had written to my siblings. I hoped for a message from them when we made landfall. A comforting voice in my head predicted, as I gazed over the ocean, that there would be a message on arrival, when we got a signal.

I would later describe these days and nights on the ocean as a conversation with the Atlantic. There is nobody to talk to in the night, and the Atlantic was pretty good company. There was ample time to reflect. I was at peace. We might finally move forwards.

Self-steering gear

We made landfall at Rubicon one week later, throwing a rope and stepping onto a pontoon in the morning darkness. We were happy.

As dawn broke, we surveyed *Katy*'s deck, and for a small yacht that had just ridden through a storm, surfing 6-metre waves, she looked remarkably trim. Sometime later, we had a beer and Lorraine appeared, having flown in the day before. She had tracked our progress over the week.

Seeing her was a beautiful moment.

Sadly, it would not get more beautiful. There was no response to my letter. No Hollywood ending.

I learnt, a year after my letter from the Atlantic, that my sister had not even opened it. She said she felt too anxious. It's the oddest thing; she seems more or less oblivious to the anxiety of others, but her radar for her own anxiety seems second to none.

INTERROGATION AND THE LAST TRIP TO MOSCOW

Six months after the invasion, we were still here, despite the best efforts of world events. The Ukraine-Russian war is well documented, its atrocities and humanity. They made my little world seem trivial, but we have to deal with our little worlds too.

Having waited as long as possible, but with a visa shortly to expire, I knew I had to visit Moscow one more time. I did not relish this prospect. I did not know what to expect as a foreigner from an "unfriendly" state, but I had to finalise affairs, finances and say goodbye to people.

For those readers who think that Russia has a monopoly on controlling what people can see and do, I suddenly realised that a well-known web service, used by millions for searching travel options, had stopped showing any Russian-related flights. Russian flights were still operating, although not to all the previous destinations, but if you were to believe this travel service, Russia was not an option. There are plenty of business people and diplomats, people with family and so on, who needed to travel to Russia, but they would need to obtain the schedules from somewhere else. Russian flight apps were no longer supported, that web service was pretending Russia did not exist, and so to find a route through for example Dubai or Baku, Istanbul or Dalaman, I would not be able to rely upon Western resources to get my information, and I found that disquieting.

I learnt of the options from Russian colleagues, whose access to the internet had been affected, but who were at least not having flight information withheld.

With some trepidation, I headed out. Direct flights, London to Moscow, had been cancelled long ago, so I routed through Turkey and on to Moscow.

Upon arrival, I headed, as I had done for decades, for immigration.

As I stood waiting, I was removed from the queue and escorted to a room. A uniformed officer beckoned me to sit. He examined my passport, and asked me my purpose. I told him that I was here to wind up some business. He took my phone and demanded my passcode. He took the names of people whom I would be meeting. He takes notes, and goes right through my phone, pressing buttons very quickly. I do not know what he was looking for or looking at, but this reminded me of that time my phone had been taken by a Russian military officer back in May 2015, when I chaperoned Geoff. Being in this room, with no passport and no phone, and only a man in uniform for company, was very uncomfortable. These jurisdictions do not need a reason to take you away. They create one.

Finally, he told me I could go, and I made my way through to find my case, somewhat forlorn, beside the belt.

How that made me feel was quite surprising. It made me realise how vulnerable you are in a situation where you have zero control, and where things can just "happen" without your knowledge or participation, and of course, without them really having been true.

I have later, much later, learned that this is their new thing, the Russian officials. They are doing the same to everybody. This is unsurprising. I have seen it in Russian business and in Russian government, the bullying and intimidation, the falsehoods, and all the rest of it that helps keep them in power. This is a small example of it. It is from the school playground, but it seems to be their style.

For a country as sanctioned as Russia was at this point, my trip over the next few days would be remarkably uneventful. Shops were full, bars and restaurants were open, cars plentiful. On the face of it, nothing seemed to have changed. Probably some products had different names, some fast-food chains, but it was not remotely noticeable. I sat in the bar, where I had used to sit with Luke before he died. I could almost hear his voice, and I could remember conversations with him word for word. I pondered whether his death was really an accident and I recalled happier times. Grigory, Artem, Katya and I had sat here too, discussing business whilst having a drink. I had had a Christmas beer here when I was stuck in Moscow for a month, all alone. In short, I sat there, now with fewer people around whom I knew. I reflected upon events, life, and at this point my siblings, with their motorhome and their kitchen refurb, seemed so desperately irrelevant. Finally, I finished my food, drank up my beer and I left Paddy's Bar at

Belorusskaya, probably for the last time.

I conducted the rest of the meetings over three days, bade farewell to my remaining colleagues and a couple of other people whom I still knew.

There was nothing more to do. Most of the people I had known had left or died, possibly even been killed.

And that was my last visit to Moscow, somewhat different to my first visit, as a student, some 37 years earlier.

EPIPHANY

Whilst on this visit, I was talking in quite philosophical terms to Kristina. She was still my colleague, and perhaps unsurprisingly, given that we had been through quite an unpleasant journey together, she had become something of a friend. Knowing this may be my last trip to Russia ever, we started chatting. Kristina listened patiently as I told her, not in a melancholy way, but more just matter-of-fact, that my career had not been intended to end like this, that I had just wanted everybody to be happy and content, to make some money and for them to achieve their dreams. I suppose, I wanted to be like Michael. Over a meal, Kristina and I chatted and mused over past events, and what would happen next. Whatever happened, if we could keep the companies alive in the UK and in Russia, we had something to come back to one day, perhaps. We parted company, but again, not in a sad way, more as if to say "we shall chat soon".

Sometime after this, quite unexpectedly, I received a letter from Kristina, and this is what it said. It changed my view on my career:

Hi David,

It's important for me to tell you something. First of all, I thank you again for your trust. Thank you for believing me when I told the truth about how Elena treated her deputies. I found out that the girl who worked before me ended up in a neurosis clinic after being fired. She suffered from insults and bullying. The fact that you gave me the opportunity to raise this issue is very important for everyone. When I wrote to this girl that you fired Elena, she almost cried and asked to thank you for the fact that justice finally prevailed. Thank you for not being indifferent.

And one more thing. I know that right now you feel terrible about the fact that your business in Russia was destroyed. And I'm very, very sorry. If I could promise you that I would save Albion, I would. But we don't know what's next. Will we have the slightest chance to save what you have been creating for so many years? I know what you're thinking right now: it was all for nothing. That all the seeds that you threw onto the ground in Russia fell on stones. Believe me, this is not the case.

The way you treated people, how you ran your business, what kind of person you are, all this left a deep impression on people. I can talk about myself. You changed my outlook not only on business, but also on life. It's like opening your eyes after being in the dark. As if you finally see the world wider, to the very horizon. It's not easy to explain. But this is important for my consciousness and for the future of my family. Everything that you taught, I plan to pass on. To other people who want to work honestly and passionately, to create something useful for everyone. Believe me, there are many such people in Russia. I know you may not think so, but such people really exist.

I'm afraid I don't have enough words to explain why I'm grateful to you and proud to know you. Once you talked about your boss Michael, who actually created you as a businessman. And whom you respect very much and consider as your teacher.

So, David, you are my Michael.

Just thank you.

That letter was my pivotal moment. If the business, and everything it represented, had created positivity in the life of one person and her family, that was worth it.

My legacy.

Of the parade of people in my career, thieves, freeloaders, fraudsters, liars, hypocrites and bullies, one good person was enough, one life *actually changed*.

EPILOGUE

I had an interesting time with Russia – a learning experience, and a rapid and unexpected end, but we picked ourselves up from that.

I met some wonderful people from all over the world, made solid friendships.

I made peace with my career, my choices. And I understand better now.

My mentor, Michael, operated in the Soviet Union. He was good at what he did, and he had one other thing in his favour, the Soviet Union – grey, materially poor, with empty shops and little international travel, ten years to save enough for a badly assembled Lada, and no chance of shopping in the corrupt shops for the political elite. In Michael's Russia, gifts and gestures had enormous meaning. A fashion magazine, a new radio, these meant a lot to people back then.

By the mid-nineties, when I set up my company, Moscow was Sodom and Gomorrah, dog eat dog, every man for himself. Killings, theft, kidnapping, fraud, deception, it all became the norm. Half the people did not know what was going on, the other half had their hand in your pocket. A compliment or a bonus would be taken as a weakness to be exploited. I straddled two eras, one benign and poor, the next, crazy and murderous. I wanted to bring out the best in people, and I believe in treating people as you would want to be treated. Be honest, and expect honesty in return. That has not changed. But Russia had changed.

Putin appeared when people had grown tired of Sodom and Gomorrah, because not everybody could keep up. They wanted stability. In Russia, that means control. It has always been so. Weak government needs to control everything because they are incapable of handling democracy, and of course, control means corruption can flourish. The last time Russia tried democracy was under Yeltsin, and that ended in chaos. The previous time was under Czar Alexander II, and he was shot for his trouble. Russia does not want democracy; it is that simple.

And if Carlsberg, Volkswagen and many other giants could not keep things going, what chance did we have, a tiny company in a big, angry space?

I miss Russia and my business, miss having a company, colleagues, projects, dreams. Moscow was my patch. I knew it, I knew the streets and the places to go. I felt comfortable there. But what I believed in, was no longer there. That was difficult.

Russia then turned back into a Soviet Silo, control; shutting down challengers, hoisting the drawbridge, creating a narrative. Protecting those inside. Deny, fabricate, maintain position. Fortress under siege from those who disagree.

Sibling issues were more difficult than anything Russia threw at me. I moved on from their intervention at the start of Covid. They were trying to help, I get it. Clumsy, unplanned, illogical help of course, but paved with good intentions.

But what followed was different. The lack of interest in our feelings. The false narrative. The commentary. The *nonchalance*. The silence. The drawbridge.

My self-esteem evaporated. Slowly. We were collateral damage. That doesn't feel too good. I questioned why I was here. I felt abandoned by my own brother and sister, the people I grew up with.

I felt ashamed that I had no business and that I could not get back up again. I did not just not know *how* to get up; I *lost the will to get up*. I was exhausted.

I previously had vision, ambition, plans. Now my world was small and dark. I lost interest in everything. My "get up and go" had got up and gone. I could neither understand it nor change it.

Work kept me distracted during Covid. It was something to focus on, despite the problems. It was a support, a troublesome support, like a supermarket trolley with a wobbly wheel, but something to keep my mind off the hurt.

When that too vanished after the invasion, all that remained were my thoughts. It took good friendships, my wife and daughters and one businessman to help me to keep it together.

Some readers may feel uncomfortable with the themes in the latter part of this book. Well, this is what happened and how it felt. There is no easy way to say it, but there is a reason to say it now, finally, after several years.

I defend my right to make mistakes, to admit them, to ask for help, as I did. I defend my right to be honest, to challenge bad behaviour, and to refuse pretence.

Reconciliation is *always* the right thing. Whilst it was denied us, we tried. We are just not here long enough. Lance the boil, embrace, repeat.

I learnt to love other things. And I am proud of our achievements. Our little company treated people well, and more importantly, it *changed a person's life*.

I can distinguish right from wrong, honesty from deceit. Anxiety from self-absorption.

Years after the invasion, our company, which became so well known for doing business in Russia, still exists. Lorraine and I are proud of that and of the people who held out their hand to stop us going down. And if we go down, we can be proud we stayed upright so long.

I do things that I am scared of. I shall cross the Atlantic with my good friend Gary, switching off the electronics and crossing by sextant - stars, sun and horizon. I shall hear those noises again alone on deck at night, but this time, I shall understand them.

I hope this book might make some impact on how people look at mental health. My GP listened to me carefully. He saw that I was in a state of anguish, but did not believe it to be depression, more a relentless series of crushing events over years, which became oppressive at the end because they were created by people whom I might otherwise have relied upon.

I had not imagined it all.

I have much to be thankful for, and I discard the things that caused me the worry. I know exactly who the good players are and the bad.

And here's my understanding: To *feel anxious*, you do not have to have depression, nor be on medication. You may just feel exhausted, have a sense of loss, a sense of "why did this even have to happen?" I felt anxious. But that is not the same as clinical anxiety.

My wife, the kindest person I know, was treated poorly. I feel sorry that people can behave like that, and this is not a blip. This is learned behaviour, manifested over years. You see, my wife takes medication for *diagnosed anxiety*, part of the bipolar condition. One of the most heartbreaking things for me to witness was the effect of my siblings' unkindness upon her. It had a massive effect upon her, and even now, she has been left with a stammer. That is *anxiety*.

Then there is what my siblings have. They call it anxiety. I call it "we don't want to hear this," and that is not the same thing. I do not believe they understand what anxiety is. I do not believe they questioned their existence, felt worthless, lost their role in life, or had a deep sense of loss and abandonment.

That so-called "anxiety" seems very like their "Christianity". Christianity is about *how you treat people;* it is not about going to Church. My mother pointed this out many times, but in some cases, those seeds seem to have fallen upon stony ground, and the gong continues to clang.

I challenged my siblings over the years on incidents that took place. They would tell me how that made them feel; they gave their opinions, made out like I was the problem. Anything to keep the fortress intact. As their feelings are important to them, so I am making mine clear now.

We cannot have our feelings dismissed.

After the invasion, we lost our home, our car and many, many possessions, our career and a lot of our plans, hopes and dreams, I wondered at the time if my brother and sister might think it may be a good time to meet and talk. But no.

So, what is my conclusion? When all is said and done, these may just not be nice people. Was it that simple all along?

I know of families, which have been through far more trauma than our family, and they found a way back. My brother and sister have been so blatant in their indifference, that I have had the doubt and regret syphoned out of me. It pains me to write about certain people and their behaviour. But it seems wrong to let it slide into meaningless mutterings and hearsay without something coming out of it to give it all some purpose. Somebody had to stand up and say "enough, already."

I hope this book can help others who have felt abused. Don't tolerate it.

When you tire of the show, shine a light upon the actors, upon pretence and hypocrisy. Tell them the show is over.

As my wife says, "We can be unkind to ourselves all on our own; we do not need other people to do it for us."

So, for your own sake, shake them off. Focus on those who care and be sure to care for them.

My immediate family is now more together than it has ever been, and the love I have for my daughters will never be questioned again by an ignorant bystander.

My wife, despite what she had to tolerate, came out the other side still intact.

They all approved this manuscript; that was important to me.

Finally, I need to mention friends. Not props or distractions, the cycling club or the book club, not Facebook posts, definitely not the kitchen or the campervan, but actual friends. Friends who grip your hand, friends who take you onto the Atlantic, friends who pop back into the room to ask if you are OK, who help when they can see that you are not. Friends who talk *to* you, but not *about* you. Those are worth holding onto, and treat them well.

Make mistakes; they will forgive you. Let them make mistakes.

Be honest. That is friendship.

Why do I feel positive now? Because this all had to happen, so that I could get here. It is not sad; it is liberating.

I write this nearly three years after Russia invaded Ukraine, nearly five years after the fallout started with my siblings.

I dedicate this book to my beautiful, dignified wife, Lorraine, and to my two beautiful, smart, funny and sassy daughters.

And to my good friend, Luke, and to Andrew, who helped so much with this book but did not live to see it. God rest their souls.

I remain hopeful that my wider family can talk. Hopeful, too, that my sister's family will continue to talk to us, though I will fully understand if that is difficult for them. We have no argument with them.

I remain hopeful that I might one day go back to the Russia I knew before.

I also accept that all this may never happen.

Thank you for reading my story.

"Everyone whom you meet is fighting a battle you know nothing about.
Be kind. Always."
Robin Williams, 1951-2014

Nemo Me Impune Lacessit

ACKNOWLEDGEMENTS

To people who read the first rough manuscripts, made coffee, fed me with pakoras, gave me their views, checked the legal stuff, put up with me, and in some cases, were just there.

Eitan Grant
Daren Norris
Richard and Veronique Shaw
Patrick King
Andrew Child, who sadly passed away unexpectedly, and whom I miss every day.
Lorraine, Jessie and Natasha
Lodge Montefiore No. 753
Craig Hales
Bob Kosko
Derek and Dorinda Offord
Gary O'Grady
Izzy Allardice

Ken Read
Mark Selawry
John Squire
29 States
Michael Rae
Malcolm Hill
Boris Hadshi
Judith Robertson
Charles Winston
James Willis and team at Spiffing
Ben Barnard
Tom Anaya
Andrea Billen

And many more people who provided background and information, which I did not know, who prefer to keep their identities private, but whose input led me to believe that this book was the right thing to do.

Printed in Dunstable, United Kingdom